"Screenwriters pull hundreds of distinct ideas together in their heads as they write their screenplays. Linda Seger has taken three Oscar-winning screenplays, cleverly pulled their ideas apart, and laid them down in a highly readable book. There are lots of how-to-write screenplay books (and Seger has written several of them); this is more of a how-top-screenwriters-think-as-they-write sort of book, and it's valuable because that makes it so unique. A wonderful read for anybody trying to write a screenplay — first-timers, and perhaps some of those top professionals as well."

> — Marc Norman, Academy Award–winning screenwriter, *Shakespeare in Love*

"*And the Best Screenplay Award Goes To...* is so much more than a bread-and-butter deconstruction of three Oscar-winning films — it's a fascinating and detailed look at each script which combines Linda's incomparable knowledge and in-depth analysis with the wit and wisdom of the winning writers to boot! For all of us avid movie-goers and writers, this book proves to be both an invaluable reference resource as well as an informative and entertaining 'inside' look into how an Academy Award–winning screenplay comes to fruition."

> — Kathie Fong Yoneda, seminar leader, former studio exec, author of *The Script-Selling Game: An Insider's Guide to Getting Your Script Sold and Produced*

"We go to movies with friends so we can talk about them afterwards. Reading *And the Best Screenplay* is like going to the movies with your best friend, if your best friend was the smartest person you've ever met — you come out loving the movie even more after you've heard her tell you *why* you loved it in the first place."

> — Ellen Sandler, former Co-Executive Producer of *Everybody Loves Raymond* and author of *The TV Writer's Workbook*

"Everybody wins who reads Linda Seger's latest book, *And the Best Screenplay Award Goes To...*. And if you apply the insights and practical information in her book, your audiences will win, too, because you'll be using storytelling tools both profoundly basic and amazingly effective."

> — Pamela Jaye Smith, author of *Inner Drives* and *The Power of the Dark Side*

"I could write an entire essay on the merits of Dr. Seger's book, but it can be boiled down to this: forget film school and read this! It is a master course on how to analyze, write, rewrite, and make great movies. Just the insider experience of what it took to get these movies made is worth the read. The depth of wisdom, insight, and instruction in these pages is in a completely different class compared to the majority of books on the subject. Study it, absorb it, and take your craft and career to the next level!"

  — Derek Rydall, screenwriter and author, *I Could've Written a Better Movie than That!* and *There's No Business Like Soul Business: A Spiritual Path to Enlightened Screenwriting, Filmmaking, and Performing Arts*; founder, *ScriptwriterCentral.com*

"Informative, insightful and entertaining. A valuable tool for any screenwriter looking to improve and clarify their script."

  — Fern Field, Emmy Award–winning producer, *Monk*; Academy Award–nominated writer/producer/director, *A Different Approach*

"This profound, yet clearly understandable, exploration of what makes a screenplay truly great is an inspiration to writers who want to do their very best."

  — Pamela Wallace, Academy Award–winning screenwriter (*Witness*)

"Linda has done it again — written an enthralling and inspiring book which will prove invaluable to writers, filmmakers and movie lovers — and which has again made me very envious. With her rich, insightful analyses and wonderful interviews with their writers, she has examined three of my favorite films (which I already thought I knew well) and revealed layers of depth and artistry I hadn't recognized. A terrific book!"

  — Michael Hauge, story consultant and author of *Writing Screenplays That Sell* and *Selling Your Story in 60 Seconds: The Guaranteed Way to Get Your Screenplay or Novel Read*

"No study of the workings of a film script is better analyzed and better written than this. The work I am doing now as I read through this really valuable book has brought me to search deeper into my characters, their behavior, and the consequences of every progressing moment in the story. Seger is better at this than any books I've read about writing screenplays."

  —Alvin Sargent, Academy Award–winning screenwriter (*Ordinary People*)

"There is no screenwriting book in the crowded screenwriting market as unique and informative as Linda Seger's *And the Best Screenplay Goes To....* Using three Oscar-winning screenplays, she methodically illustrates what elements go into writing a great script and also provides wonderful examples throughout the book. By reading Linda's in-depth analysis and review of these scripts, I found myself getting fresh insights and novel information from one of the best script consultants in the business. This book isn't just theoretical but practical as well. Keep it next to your computer when you're starting a new script and you, too, will discover the elements that make an award-winning sceenplay."

> — Dr. Rachel Ballon, international script consultant, licensed psychotherapist, author of five writing books including *The Portable Writer's Therapist: 25 Sessions to a Creativity Cure*

"Here are three good reasons to buy Linda's book: to read it, to learn from it, and to get better at what you do. I haven't seen the cover yet, but if it has a cool one, that's reason #4."

> — Jeff Arch, Academy Award nominee (*Sleepless in Seattle*)

"Haggis and Moresco couldn't have said it any better and they have the Academy Award. Your dissection of every plot line blending into the other is so on the money. I even picked up some nuances from you, and I've seen the film 412 times. Thanks. Every upcoming screenwriter should read this. Come to think of it, almost every screenwriter should read this."

> — Mark Harris, Producer, *Crash* (Academy Award® for Best Picture)

And
THE BEST
SCREENPLAY
goes to...

Learning from the Winners:
SIDEWAYS · SHAKESPEARE IN LOVE · CRASH

DR. LINDA SEGER

MICHAEL WIESE PRODUCTIONS

Published by Michael Wiese Productions

3940 Laurel Canyon Blvd. – Suite 1111

Studio City, CA 91604

(818) 379-8799, (818) 986-3408 (FAX).

mw@mwp.com

www.mwp.com

Cover design by MWP
Interior design by William Morosi
Copyedited by Paul Norlen
Printed by McNaughton & Gunn

Manufactured in the United States of America
Copyright 2008 Linda Seger

Library of Congress Cataloging-in-Publication Data

Seger, Linda.
  And the best screenplay award goes to-- Sideways, Shakespeare in love, Crash : learning from the winners / Linda Seger.
     p. cm.
  ISBN 978-1-932907-38-4
  1. Motion picture authorship. 2. Sideways (Motion picture) 3. Shakespeare in love (Motion picture) 4. Crash (Motion picture : 2004) I. Title.
  PN1996.S3834 2008
  808.2'3--dc22
                                    2007036228

Printed on Recycled Stock

TABLE OF CONTENTS

ACKNOWLEDGMENTS

To the readers who have given me feedback, suggestions, constructive criticism, and additions, subtractions, corrections: Dr. Rachel Ballon, Pamela Jaye Smith, Devorah Cutler-Rubinstein, Kim Peterson, Cathleen Loeser, Pam Jones, Kathie Fong Yoneda, and Mara Purl.

To my assistant, Sarah Callbeck, who continually saves me from my mistakes.

To the writers and directors of these scripts, for their brilliance and their generosity: Rex Pickett (novelist), Alexander Payne, Jim Taylor, Marc Norman, Tom Stoppard, John Madden, Paul Haggis, Bobby Moresco.

To Elizabeth Stevens for breaking down the story beats of the films.

And always to my husband, Peter Hazen Le Var, who understands the life of a writer and is always there to support me, during the difficulties and the joys.

Thank you to Miramax Films for permission to quote from the 1992 draft of *Shakespeare in Love* by Marc Norman. Text from *Shakespeare in Love*, courtesy of Miramax Film Corp.

Thank you to Hyperion Books for permission to quote from the published screenplay *Shakespeare in Love: The Screenplay* by Marc Norman and Tom Stoppard. Copyright 1998 Miramax Film Corp and Universal Studios. Reprinted by permission of Miramax Books. All rights reserved.

Thank you to Lionsgate. Text taken from *Crash* provided through the courtesy of Lionsgate.

Thank you to Twentieth Century Fox Licensing & Merchandising for permission to extract quotes from the motion picture *Sideways*. Screenplay by Alexander Payne & Jim Taylor, based on the novel by Rex Pickett. *Sideways* ©™ 2004 Twentieth Century Fox Film Corporation. All rights reserved.

Note to the reader: All references to *Sideways* and *Shakespeare in Love* are from the published scripts. All references to *Crash* are from the script furnished to me by Lionsgate Films.

INTRODUCTION

I love a great script and a great film. It speaks to me on many levels: telling me something about my life, my loves, my yearnings, what I care about. Great films are worthy of watching and re-watching, studying, thinking about, and quoting from, which allows them to reach inside us and change us by their ideas, their characters, the power of their universal stories.

I hope this book will appeal to many readers: those of you who are studying to be screenwriters and want to learn from the great writers. Those of you who are already writers, perhaps even successful writers, but want to improve your craft and your art, finding new and more original stories and approaches. And I hope that some of you who simply love the movies will find this book helps you deepen your appreciation of what makes a great film. Just as you might read about music or art before going to a concert or art museum, perhaps you'll find this book helpful to better understand why some of these films win Academy Awards and are commercial successes — because they appeal to us on so many levels and because we are enriched by their insights and humor, their depth and their joy.

Choosing the Scripts

The three scripts in this book fulfill four criteria. First of all, to be included each script had to have won the Academy Award for Best Screenplay. Of the three scripts, *Shakespeare in Love* and *Crash* won for Best Original Screenplay, and *Sideways* won for Best Adaptation.

Secondly, I looked for scripts that were rich, complex, and original and that were worthy of study.

Thirdly, I personally had to love each of these films in order to be willing to spend several years writing this book and living with these scripts. It's one thing to spend two hours with a good film, but another to keep enthusiasm high about a film for several years. These films never let me down.

Finally, to be included, the writers and directors had to be willing to be interviewed for this book in order to use their script. Although there were a number of scripts that interested me, these were the three that I found the most intriguing for discussion, and, thankfully, all agreed to an interview.

With each script, I asked a specific question that guided me in analyzing the script. For *Sideways* I asked, "How can a writer take a simple subject — about two guys going to the wine country to taste some wine — and make it fascinating enough to hold our attention and deep enough to win an Academy Award?" Although we often think that an award-winning script has to be big and bold, with big stars and special effects, *Sideways* proved otherwise. I also particularly enjoyed *Sideways* because I learned more about wines and wine tasting, had an enjoyable few days taking the *Sideways* wine tour in the Santa Ynez Valley in California, and loved watching a film that paired a specific location with a story.

Sideways was nominated for five Academy Awards: Best Supporting Actor (Thomas Haden Church), Best Supporting Actress (Virginia Madsen), Best Directing (Alexander Payne), Best Picture; it won for Best Adapted Screenplay (Jim Taylor, Alexander Payne).

Shakespeare in Love was an obvious choice for me. As an English and theatre major in college and graduate school, I always loved Shakespeare. I have read most of his plays and sonnets, yes, even those considered not up to his usual genius, such as *Titus Andronicus*. I have seen many performed, and took at least three Shakespeare classes in college and graduate school, approaching the plays from the viewpoint of English literature, dramatic literature, and the theological and philosophical themes. One summer when I was in college, my sister and I did our own private study of Shakespeare. We read a play a week, rented audiotapes (no videotapes in the 1960s!), discussed them, and then attended several of the plays during the summer.

It was natural for me to love *Shakespeare in Love*. I am charmed by it, and intrigued by its ability to make a period piece so contemporary. I am emotionally involved with the yearning of Viola, the passion of Will, and what the film has to tell us about the creative process, about writer's block, about love, and even about Hollywood. The insider jokes are delightful. The insights are profound.

The film was nominated for thirteen Academy Awards in 1998, including Actor in a Supporting Role (Geoffrey Rush), Cinematography (Richard Greatrex), Film Editing (David Gamble), Directing (John Madden), Makeup (Lisa Westcott, Veronica Brebner), Sound (Robin O'Donoghue, Dominic Lester, Peter Glossop) and in addition, won six Academy Awards in the following categories: Best Actress (Gwyneth Paltrow), Actress in a Supporting Role (Judi Dench), Art Direction and Set Decoration (Martin Childs, Jill Quertier), Costume Design (Sandy Powell), Music (Stephen Warbeck), Best Picture (David Parfitt, Donna Gigliotti, Harvey Weinstein, Edward Zwick and Marc Norman), and Best Original Screenplay (Marc Norman, Tom Stoppard).

While analyzing *Shakespeare in Love*, I asked the question, "How does a writer make a period piece contemporary?"

Crash was of great interest to me because of my background in theology and sociology. I enjoy films that carry a strong theme and tell us something about the society we live in. Although many of them get too preachy and too talky, *Crash* is an exception. I found the structure unusual and workable, the intersection of the various plotlines extremely well crafted, and the theme insightful, even profound. Having lived in Los Angeles for twenty-five years, through the film I was able to see this world through a different perspective. The movie led me to examine some of my own attitudes, and try to understand more about how we learn these attitudes and why these attitudes are so deeply ingrained in us. Yet, it also offers the hope of transformation.

Crash was nominated for six Academy Awards, including for Best Song ("In the Deep" by Kathleen York/Michael Becker), Best Director (Paul Haggis), and Best Supporting Actor (Matt Dillon), and won the Academy Award for Best Editing (Hughes Winborne), Best Picture, and Best Original Screenplay (Paul Haggis, Robert Moresco).

With *Crash,* I asked the question, "How does a writer explore a theme through action, story and character, rather than talking about the theme through long speeches?"

Although there were many other issues to explore in these scripts, I allowed the central question to lead me, hoping it would also help writers resolve challenging script problems.

In each case, I wanted to present some challenges that every writer who writes more than a few scripts may encounter. Then, my goal was also to analyze the basic script elements of Structure and Story Development, Theme, and Character to see how these other elements achieved their brilliance as well.

What Makes a Great Film?

As I analyzed these scripts, and considered other possible scripts for this book, I also asked myself another question, "Is there anything most of these award-nominated films seem to have in common? Would it be possible for a writer to analyze the patterns we see in Academy Award–nominated films, in order to learn to write up to the level of a great script?" As I looked at the many films nominated over the past twenty years, I began to see some patterns that had not been quite so obvious at the beginning.

Most great films have reached a high level of both art and craft. The art of the film could be defined by its originality. Is it different from most of what we've seen before, or is it derivative, predictable, superficial, and unoriginal? The run-of-the-mill derivative film doesn't make it to the finals, and often doesn't even make it commercially at the box office.

Originality comes, partly, through the writer's ability to express his or her specific artistic voice. The artistic voice can be defined as the specific point-of-view and style that distinguishes one writer from another. We would never mistake a Woody Allen film for one written and directed by the Coen Brothers. A Robert Altman film would never be mistaken for a film by James L. Brooks. Sometimes the artistic voice is expressed through the types of stories or characters in the films. Altman's characters are quirky and often strange. The Coen Brothers use black humor and satiric humor in their stories. Woody Allen has a psychological, New York slant to his stories, and James L. Brooks looks deeply, with humor, into human situations and human problems.

Most great writers peer deeply into their own lives to find rich material and insights. Akiva Goldsman won the Academy Award for *A Beautiful Mind*, although he has been known as a screenwriter of action films such as *Batman and Robin, Lost in Space, The Client,* and more recently *Poseidon* and *The Da Vinci Code*. What made him capable of writing this difficult and complex story? His mother was one of the foremost authorities on childhood autism and Akiva grew up in a group home for emotionally disturbed children. As a result, he gained insights into how mental illness worked from an early age. Tom Schulman won the Academy Award for *Dead Poets Society* after writing a number of derivative scripts. He looked deeply into his own experiences with great teachers, and with poetry, to write a script about creativity versus conformity.

Most great films are also well-crafted. Writers have studied and learned how to work with structure, sometimes working with the principles of the three-act structure in unusual ways, as Quentin Tarantino did with *Pulp Fiction*, a film with a beginning-middle-end, but which presents the story by changing the order of the telling to a beginning-end-middle. *Memento* tells its story backwards, while preserving a three-act structure chronologically and in reverse. *Crash* shows how many stories can be interwoven together, creating a film based on subplots, rather than any one plotline. *Traffic, Syriana,* and *Babel* also play with structure in original and unusual ways to convey their stories.

Award-winning writers know their art and their craft. But there are other elements that seem to be true for Academy Award–nominated films.

On the surface, it often seems that the big, expensive, elaborate films with scope and big panoramas win the Academy Award, such as *Gone with the Wind, Titanic, Out of Africa, Lord of the Rings, The English Patient.* Yet, for every big expensive film that won, we can see a number of others that weren't even nominated, in spite of great marketing campaigns: *Pearl Harbor, Troy, Alexander the Great.*

Sometimes it seems that all that is needed is a best-selling book or a popular play as the basis for a great film. Yet, for every *Driving Miss Daisy* or *Chicago*, there's a *Chorus Line*, and for every *Million Dollar Baby*, there's a *Bonfire of the Vanities.*

To find what makes a great film, we have to look more deeply. Most Academy Award–nominated films are significant. They have something meaningful to say. They give us insights into humanity, shed light on the human condition, help us understand the problems and struggles that are common to all of us, and, in most cases, show hope and possibilities for resolution.

Some of these films deal with important social issues, looking at an issue that is destructive to our society and causes human suffering. *Norman Rae* looked at life in a factory and the desire to unionize. *Erin Brockovich* examined water pollution and how it affected the health of a community. *Mississippi Burning, A Soldier's Story,* and *Crash* examined racism. *Good Night, and Good Luck* told the story about the integrity of one reporter who confronted the witch hunt of Joseph McCarthy. *The Insider* took a deep look at the deceptions of the tobacco industry, and *The Cider House Rules* and *Vera Drake* took on the difficult subject of abortion.

Some films looked at political issues, usually where one of the players in the story was a corrupt or oppressive or unjust government. Many of these films are set against a war, which presents the greatest conflict and the highest life-and-death stakes. These include World War I (*Joyeux Noel*), World War II, (*Schindler's List, The Pianist, Saving Private Ryan, Hope and Glory, Life Is Beautiful, The Thin Red Line, Letters from Iwo Jima*), the Vietnam War (*Platoon, Born on the Fourth of July, The Killing Fields*).

Some deal with other wars, other political problems, other corrupt governmental policies, such as *Dances with Wolves, The Official Story, Gladiator, Missing, A Few Good Men, Hotel Rwanda, Munich.*

In all these cases, these films are not just about the corrupt policy, but put a human face on the problem. While the film is examining, in depth, the problem itself, it also examines the courage and commitment needed by the protagonist to overcome the problem. We care about the protagonists who are caught up in a difficult moral or ethical dilemma which may seem that it's better left alone. We are brought into their struggles, their decisions, and the consequences. The films bring up important questions about the human cost of war (*Joyeux Noel*), about power and the misuse of power (*Born on the Fourth of July*), about the worth of one human life (*Saving Private Ryan*), about the effects of war (*Letters from Iwo Jima*), about the ambiguity of goodness (*Schindler's List*).

Some films are significant because they explore psychological problems such as the wounds, battles, and inner problems that many people face and have to overcome. These might include a tragic event in childhood (*Mystic River*), the cycle of violence and how it affects those who participate in it (*A History of Violence*), obsession and egotism (*Capote*), the problems the creative person confronts (*Dead Poets Society, Shakespeare in Love, Amadeus*), psychological conditions that threaten to debilitate a person (*As Good as it Gets, A Beautiful Mind, Good Will Hunting*), or simply a crisis of meaning (*Jerry Maguire, American Beauty*).

Some films look at historical events and find a new approach to them. *JFK* looked more deeply into the conspiracy theory about his assassination. *Titanic* explored issues of classism on a ship where the poor were trapped below and the arrogant wealthy were above. *The Mission, The Last Emperor, Gangs of New York,* and *The Queen* looked at historical events while adding human insights to the big picture.

Besides being about important events, which forms a pattern for most Academy Award–nominated films, some stand out because of their originality of style. The satiric slant of *O Brother Where Art Thou?* The humorous and tender look at the Holocaust in *Life Is Beautiful.* The dark, film noir style of *L.A. Confidential.* The fantasy overtones of *Chocolat* and *Amelie.* The clever sweetness of the talking animals in *Babe.*

Most Academy Award–nominated films are realistic. Most are dramas and epics. Occasionally a film is nominated in a genre that rarely gets critical recognition. *Fatal Attraction* is a psychological thriller. *Witness, The Fugitive*, and *The Departed* are detective stories. *Beauty and the Beast, Finding Nemo*, and *Shrek* are animated children's films. *Silence of the Lambs* contains horror elements.

Moonstruck, Tootsie, and *As Good as it Gets* are comedies — although with deeper meanings than many comedies. *Lord of the Rings* and *E.T.* are fantasy/sci-fi. *The Sixth Sense* deals with the supernatural.

What do we find true about all of these?

✦ In each case, the genre is raised to a higher level through deep and dimensional characterizations, unusual stories, and sometimes a new spin on an idea that we've seen before.

✦ Each film puts a human face on the story, no matter whether the events are big (*Schindler's List*) or small (*In the Bedroom*).

✦ The films humanize and dimensionalize the main character. There are no perfect people here.

✦ Many of the writers already knew a great deal about the subject matter and loved the subject matter before writing about it, yet the scripts still needed vast amounts of research to make them ring true (*Out of Africa, Sideways, Shakespeare in Love, A Beautiful Mind*).

✦ Most of these help us understand, more deeply, the human condition, so the film helps us reflect on our own lives.

✦ Many of the films are transformational stories, showing hope and the possibility of overcoming problems and moving toward resolution.

And now, for a closer look at three great scripts: *Sideways, Shakespeare in Love,* and *Crash.*

I hope you will enjoy reading this book as much as I enjoyed writing it. I hope these films will enrich your lives with insights and will continue to delight you. I hope the questions about each film and the analysis will ignite your own creativity by being in the presence of great art.

SIDEWAYS

NEW APPROACHES, NEW DESTINATIONS

Every once in a great while, a film comes out that changes the way we think, or act, or react to the world around us. It opens up our perceptions, and ushers us into new worlds that we would ordinarily never inhabit.

Annie Hall changed our views of fashion and style. How many of us actually bought a vest and tie after seeing that film, and wore it once or twice?

Remember how *Fatal Attraction* raised our fear level about the danger of stalkers, as we began to recognize how prevalent they were? The film raised consciousness about the dangers of extramarital affairs about the same time that AIDS was becoming prevalent. Sex could equal death, whether through STDs or through a crazy, rebuffed lover.

After the classic film *Psycho* came out, people admitted they were afraid to take showers for months, because of the horror of the shower scene.

Talk to many Baby Boomers and they'll tell you how *Easy Rider* and *The Graduate* defined the great divide between the establishment and the counter-culture.

Lawyers changed the way they approach their profession because of the integrity of Atticus Finch in *To Kill a Mockingbird*.

Dead Poets Society taught us about "carpe diem", to "seize the day." I've talked to several people who changed their jobs after their film, looking for more meaning in their lives.

These films led to changes in style and habits and attitudes.

Sometimes a film adds another level of change by creating ancillary markets that create interest in the movie, while the movie also creates a new tourist destination.

Thousands of tourists have taken the tour of Savannah, Georgia, based on the book and the film of *Midnight in the Garden of Good and Evil*. Tourists went to Florence to stay at the same *pensione* as the one in *Room with a View*. Tourists sipped coffee on the Via Venito in Rome to get in the mood of Fellini's *La Strada*. Tourists kissed beneath the Bridge of Sighs in Venice, after watching *A Little Romance*. In Salzburg, tourists take the *Sound of Music* tour. (Although we were told that Salzburg was the only city where *Sound of Music* did not do well, since the real Maria von Trapp was no Julie Andrews!) Some tourists, such as myself, went to the Louvre in Paris to see exactly where the murder took place in *The Da Vinci Code*, and then spent two hours in Rosalind Chapel in Scotland, looking for that elusive sign on the stone floor that was supposed to be one more clue. (It wasn't there!)

Sideways brought us into the world of wine, and led to a spike in the wine industry for pinot noirs, and a decline in buyers who learned that cabernet sauvignon was prosaic. The film opened up a new tourist industry as thousands of tourists descended on the small towns that make up the Santa Ynez Valley, to visit the locations from the film, to drive drunk on the back roads, and in some unfortunate cases where reality follows a bit too close to a film, tourists have gone to the Fess Parker winery to re-enact the scene where Miles overturns the spit bucket. This, of course, doesn't sit well with the wineries, and has led some of them to advertise "We were not in the film *Sideways!*"

When I took the *Sideways* tour in June 2006 with my friend, Mara Purl (actress and author of the Milford Haven novels set near that area), Mara and I stayed in the same room used for the film, Room 234 at the Days Inn (sometimes called the Windmill Inn) in Buellton, although the film expanded the size of the room and added steps right outside the room which are no longer there.

The idea of setting a movie in what might become a tourist attraction adds another level of appeal to a film. Many times the location is well known by the writer, and the film is a way of sharing a special world with the audience. Sometimes this special world lends richness to the script, or might even be the difference between simply another story, and a commercial and critical success. However, in creating a special world in a specific location, one must be careful that the location is accurate, or at least looks similar. I heard more than one person say they wanted to go to Wyoming to see the views used in *Brokeback Mountain,* but they aren't there. They'll have to go to the Rockies of British Columbia.

Creating the Context

Sideways, much like a number of other films, also found an audience by introducing us to the world of wine — how to swirl it, smell it, taste it, and, perhaps, even drink too much of it.

Other films have created fascinating contexts and new worlds, often worlds which we never knew about before the film. The writer takes a journey to research a new window to a new world, and the audience benefits by its exposure to a new and special place.

The Color of Money introduced us to the world of pool, placing the exposition we needed to understand pool at the very beginning of the film, under the credits. *Raiders of the Lost Ark* built its story based on a line or two from the Bible, about Tanis, in Egypt, and introduced us to the world of the Lost Ark. From *Titanic,* we learned about how the class system reigned even aboard luxury liners and how pride can lead to tragedy. From *Apollo 13*, we learned about the problems of finding the right trajectory for a rocket to return to earth; from *Days of Thunder* and *Heart Like a Wheel* we learned about race car driving; and from *The Red Violin* we learned about those special elements that create the sound of a priceless violin. *Lonesome Dove* taught us about cowboy life in our recent past, and *A Beautiful Mind* revealed the mystery and wonder of mathematics. *Full Metal Jacket, Thin Red Line, Platoon,* and *Apocalypse Now* uncovered the grim realities and ridiculousness of some parts of war, as did the long-running TV series *M.A.S.H.* and *China Beach*.

But we learned far more from *Sideways* than rediscovering the beautiful wine country in southern California and learning to be snobbish about pinot noir.

Sideways proved that a small film, with a low budget ($16 million), with no stars, no special effects, no explosions, and only one car crash, (and a minor one at that) could lead to an Academy Award for Best Writing (Adaptation). The film revitalized the careers of all its four major actors. Since *Sideways*, Paul Giamatti has been in *Cinderella Man, The Hawk Is Dying, The Illusionist, Lady in the Water,* and has four movies in pre-production which should be coming out about the time this book is published. Virginia Madsen has been in *A Prairie Home Companion* and *Firewall,* as well as done several television episodes and has several films in post-production. Thomas Haden Church has been in the mini-series of *Broken Trail,* plus done voice-over work and is in *Spider-Man 3.* And Sandra Oh has been nominated twice for Emmy awards for *Grey's Anatomy,* as well as appearing in other television episodes and the movie *The Night Listener.*

The film showed how one could take the simplest of stories — two guys who are best friends go up to the wine country to drink some wine — and turn it into a rich story where a wedding is in jeopardy, love and sex can be threatening and wonderful, and transformation is possible, although not always probable.

SIDEWAYS AS A VARIATION OF THE ROAD MOVIE

Sideways is a variation of what is often called the road movie, or the journey story, or the trek film. These are difficult stories to pull off, because they are so simple, because the destination can be vague, and because most road movies have much too much road in them to sustain interest. Road movies can be repetitive and episodic. Characters go to one city, meet someone, have a little adventure, go to another city, meet someone, have a little adventure, and just keep traveling on, repeating the same pattern. If a writer isn't careful, road movies can become talky, and can seem more like a documentary or travelogue than a fascinating story. They get bogged down with repetition, chat, lots of deadening, non-dramatic scenes in cars, restaurants, and motel rooms.

Yet, the history of films is filled with stories of people who hit the road, for one reason or another, and whose lives were enriched as a result of the adventure.

In some road films, the character leaves a place to get away. Sometimes it's to escape danger (*Two Mules for Sister Sarah*). Sometimes it's a road trip to get somewhere, as in *Midnight Run*, when a bounty hunter brings a small-time criminal to justice, or in *Planes, Trains, and Automobiles*, when two men simply want to get home. Sometimes it's to escape boredom in order to find one's identity — *Leaving Normal,* or to relive their past, as in *Trip to Bountiful, Two for the Road,* or *The Way We Were.*

Sometimes the reason for leaving or the goal at the end of the road is not important, and may be barely mentioned, in order to put the focus on the events that happen along the way. In *Breakdown,* the focus moves to the dangers that can occur, simply by being on the road where men in semi-trucks may not be what they seem, and are out to steal and kidnap and kill. In *Thelma and Louise*, a simple desire to get away for a weekend turns into a dangerous getaway.

Sometimes the character hits the road to go after a specific goal, which might be a treasure (*The Treasure of the Sierra Madre, Romancing the Stone*) or a dead body (*Stand by Me*), or trying to figure out a way to get money out of his soon-to-be-rich brother (*Rainman*) or ventures out to fulfill a dream (*Little Miss Sunshine*).

Sometimes the adventures are done for comedy, as in *It Happened One Night*, where the road held out sexual and romantic possibilities, or in the famous Bing Crosby and Bob Hope road films of the 1940s: *Road to Rio, Road to Zanzibar, Road to Singapore, Road to Morocco, Road to Utopia, Road to Bali, Road to Mandalay.*

And sometimes, in the great films, the focus is on all three elements. In *The African Queen,* there is a strong motivation for leaving: the village has been destroyed and Allnut and Rose have no place to go. When Mr. Allnut offers to take Rose on his boat, away from the village, she agrees, intending simply to leave her old life behind. The beginning of the film puts the focus almost exclusively on the motivation for leaving. Quickly, her focus moves toward a goal: to blow up the German ship, the *Luisa.* As soon as they start on the journey, the focus moves to the many adventures they have along the way: going over the rapids, falling in love, getting stuck in the reeds, being captured, and finally achieving the goal.

Sideways is a simpler variation on this same idea: of getting away to enjoy freedom one more time. Miles decides to take Jack, his friend of many years, on a wine-tasting tour of the Santa Ynez Valley, located north of Santa Barbara. Jack has a reason to go — his wedding is on Saturday, and it's his last bachelor days to enjoy freedom. Miles has a reason to go — to introduce Jack to one of his favorite places, to drink some good wine, eat some good food, and spend time with his friend. The basic storyline suggests a rather boring film with episodes of them driving, eating, drinking, and sleeping. In the hands of lesser writers, this might be what the film would be.

But writers Alexander Payne and Jim Taylor had a history of creating simple films that were, nevertheless, rich in character and theme. They had been nominated for an Academy Award for *About Schmidt* for Best Actor (Jack Nicholson) and Best Actress (Kathy Bates), and for *Election* for Best Writing for an Adaptation. They saw the potential in Rex Pickett's novel, *Sideways,* which was given to them in manuscript form before it even had a publisher. Taylor and Payne were already great writers, ready for the challenges that seemingly simple material had to offer.

Strong Characters Make Good Journey Stories

Almost all journey stories are character-driven. Although there needs to be events to make the trip interesting, without strong characters the film can easily become boring, too talky and dialogue-heavy. The longer the characters spend in the car, the more they eat and drink, the more apt they are to have to chat about things that don't advance the story and become repetitive.

While focusing on character, the writers have to keep the journey active with strong plot elements. As in most films, these plot elements contain conflict, tension, and action. Some, like *Thelma and Louise*, add a chase, as police come after the two women. Some, like *Deliverance* and *The River Wild,* focus on the dangers of the wilderness which come, not just from the danger of rapids, but from the wildness of the human inhabitants of the woods.

Some contain a secret, and strong subtext. In *Rainman*, Raymond doesn't know that this journey is just a way to get his money, and Charlie doesn't know that Raymond is the loving brother, who was one of the best parts of his life.

Most, although not all, journey films present transformational stories. In *Thelma and Louise,* Thelma discovers her adventurous spirit which has been repressed by her husband. In *Stand by Me,* the four boys encounter mortality for the first time, and learn about the difficulties between sons and fathers, and learn that sometimes friends are the ones who best know who you are. In *The African Queen,* Rose learns about the physical pleasures of fast-moving rapids and a kiss, and two people who don't seem to have the qualities to make a couple, come together in a true partnership.

The journey gives the characters time to find out about themselves as they interact with events that are out of the normal course of living. Sometimes they come to some realization about themselves — what's important to them, who they are, as in the journey to a strange land in *The Lion, The Witch and the Wardrobe.* Sometimes characters come to realizations and make new decisions (*The Lion King*), fall in love (*Romancing the Stone*), have great adventures in far away places (*Hidalgo*), and try out new behaviors (*Bonnie and Clyde*).

However the journey story is told, it still needs to work with the basic dramatic elements of motivation, action, goal, conflict, story structure, story development, and character dimensionality.

Establishing the Timeline

Most journey stories take place over a short period of time — a few days, a week, perhaps a month or so. A shorter timeline is more realistic, since most journeys don't last very long, and they tend to get repetitious and boring if they go on for months or years.

A shorter timeline also increases the drama, since short timelines are more dramatic. Sometimes they apply pressure on the characters to get something done quickly as in treasure films, such as *National*

Treasure, Pirates of the Caribbean, Maltese Falcon, or *Romancing the Stone,* where the bad guys want the treasure quickly — or else.

The timeline acts as a pressure cooker, or incubator, where the combustion can lead to a boiling point that forces changes. It presents an urgency and sometimes an absolute need — the character must stay in the pressure cooker until some new human understanding or realization or behavior has occurred. Sometimes the timeline is a ticking clock, where some action has to be taken immediately — or else. Many James Bond and *Die Hard* films set up a very short timeline to create extra pressure on the protagonist to save the world — quickly. It heats up the action, and creates tension in the audience as they anticipate, and hope for, the best possible outcome, against all odds.

Sideways sets up a timeline of a week. Miles and Jack leave for the wine country on Saturday, return for the rehearsal dinner on Friday (an off-screen scene), and both show up for the wedding on Saturday. Some period of time then passes during the resolution, giving Maya enough time to read Miles' novel, to think about him, and then to contact him and suggest he stop by next time he's in the area.

The shortened timeline of *Sideways* brings heightened drama and urgency to a deceptively simple story.

Establishing the Goal

Every great story has to have direction, sometimes called the Goal or the Objective or the Intention of the trip. Although some goals are not world shattering in any way, nevertheless, they provide a road map and a destination for the story so it doesn't become just a series of repetitive episodes with no strong narrative drive. In some road movies, the goal is strong enough so every scene, in one way or another, advances the story toward achieving the goal. In *The Treasure of the Sierra Madre* the goal is there from the beginning of the story — the men are after gold — and the gold pulls them through all the events of the film to the end. Everything in the story is connected to the goal.

But how does a writer establish a goal when the story is based on a motivation — the desire to get away for a few days? Since a good film needs a goal, *Sideways* begins by clarifying the end of the film — Jack is going to get married on Saturday. Already at the beginning, *Sideways* is creating a variation on the use of the goal in journey films. Whereas most journey films are about a character going on a journey in order to achieve the goal, Jack and Miles are not going to the wine country in order to get home for the wedding. The wedding is simply the end point of their journey. Any events leading up to the wedding don't intrinsically seem to have any connection to the goal. In fact, most of what Miles and Jack intend to do while wine tasting is totally unrelated to the goal. But if the events and the goal are not connected, the story would be simply arbitrary events, rather than integrated scenes that relate, in one way or another, to the end of the story. The writers had a challenge — they had to figure out how to connect the events in the story with a goal that seems, at first glance, to have little to do with their trip.

How did the writers create a strong goal? The goal of the wedding isn't the reason Miles and Jack went to the wine country, although it was Jack's goal for the end of the week. They went to the wine country so Miles could share his knowledge and love of wine with Jack while Jack was still unmarried. But at the 1st Turning Point, Jack's goal of getting to the church on time and marrying Christine on Saturday becomes Miles' goal. Miles wants Jack to get married, even though Jack suddenly does not seem committed to this goal. At the 1st Turning Point, Jack makes an announcement that doesn't bode well for his wedding day — he announces to Miles that he has an intention for this trip — to get laid before returning to his fiancé and to an appropriately monogamous marital relationship.

Miles knows Jack could be sacrificing his wedding and his future happiness by his crazy behavior. At this point in the story, when Jack seems to be in danger of jeopardizing his marriage, Miles takes on Jack's initial goal to get married. Miles wants Jack to go forward with his wedding and not jeopardize his future. By the 2nd Turning Point, when the wedding is again in jeopardy, the wedding becomes Jack's goal as well.

This specific goal, which is in jeopardy throughout, creates other elements along the way which are necessary to create great drama: conflict, tension, and obstacles. It also creates adventures that the two will have along the way: adventures in romance, sex, getting drunk, Jack breaking his nose, and Miles having to rescue Jack's wallet from a crazy husband.

Creating Conflict Through the Clash of Intentions

The goal is connected to the conflict. *Sideways* doesn't begin with conflict — it begins with two guys going off to have a good time, who have no intrinsic conflict between them, and who we wouldn't expect to have conflict, considering the simplicity of their journey. Since Miles and Jack have been friends for a long time, have known each other well, and know each other's flaws, we might expect that they'd just accept what the other one is doing, and live and let live. But this wouldn't create drama. Drama occurs when one character doesn't let the other character do what he (or she) desires, but wants to influence another. Conflict occurs because of contradictory intentions.

Miles' intention begins the story, and Miles presumes it's the same intention for both of them. At first, the intention is general, "I'm really glad we're finally getting this time together… I've been begging to take you on the wine tour" (p. 8).

Then, the intention becomes more specific as they drive up the coast. Miles' plan is to have some laid-back friendship time, go wine tasting, eat good food, and simply be together. Nothing more than that. Miles presumed that Jack had the same intention. But he didn't.

Jack has a goal for himself, but he also has a goal for Miles, which comes as a surprise to him: "I'm going to get you laid this week. That's going to be my best man gift to you" (p. 21). For Jack, sex is better than wine. This is the catalyst for the film, and begins to set up the events of the story that will flow out of this intention. As the story proceeds, complications pile up because of the different expectations and goals. This clash of intentions is the engine that keeps driving the story and escalates the conflict between these two friends.

During Act One Development of the script, Jack sees Maya, and believes he has found a way to achieve his goal for Miles.

<pre>
                    JACK
        Miles. Check it out.

                    MILES
        Oh, yea. That's Maya.

                    JACK
        You know her?

                    MILES
        Sure I know Maya.

                    JACK
        You know that chick?

                    MILES
        Jack, this is where I eat when I come up here.
        It's practically my office. And
        sometimes I have a drink with the
        employees. Maya's great. She's worked
        here about a year, maybe a year and a half.

                    JACK
        She is very hot.
</pre>

According to Jack, his intention for Miles will lead to greater happiness for Miles, so Miles can get the sex that Jack has had, and wants more of. And Maya looks like a very likely prospect.

Miles immediately negates this idea. Maya is nice, but she's married, and Miles has too much respect for marriage, and for Maya, to pursue this.

But that doesn't stop Jack. Drama is created by strong intentions, and Jack is determined. He's a strong dramatic character, capable of creating a story where none existed. Jack doesn't let up, and, as a result, he pulls Maya and Stephanie and Miles into the circle of his intentions. If Miles were on his own, he would have seen Maya, said "hello," had a little chat, and that would have been the end of it. Miles' intention was not strong enough to create a story; Jack's was. Conflict was then created, because Jack's intention ran counter to Miles' intention in order to create enough problems to make a story.

A story is created through characters with a strong will. If characters have no will and no intention and just go along with everyone else, there's no story. Stories are created when events don't go according to plan. One character thinks everything will go one way, but it takes another turn. Another character wants to do something to get the nice, smooth, normal world back. But the normal is not a story. Drama is hyper-real and larger than life. Dramatic stories exist in the world of the unexpected, the extraordinary, the abnormal, the world of dashed hopes and ruined expectations.

It is exactly this clash of intentions that creates a story out of a simple journey. This clash creates every event, reveals character, and sets up the theme, making something that could have been prosaic into a dramatic film.

The story, then, continues to get complicated at each structural point. At the 1st Turning Point, Jack announces his own intention which has been kept secret from Miles — Jack intends, not only to make sure Miles get laid, but Jack also wants some good sex to celebrate his last week of freedom. Neither of these intentions sit well with Miles. He realizes there won't be as much friendly togetherness as he had hoped for, which means his expectations for how the week would go will be dashed. He also knows it's not a good thing to sleep with someone else right before getting married. This sets up another intention for Miles — to talk Jack out of this crazy idea, which is a futile endeavor, as Miles soon learns.

These competing intentions give energy to the story and to the characters, because the actors are playing the conflicting intentions *between* each other, but also the competing intentions *within* each of them. Miles didn't come to the wine country for sex, and yet, he truly likes Maya and, on some level, is clearly interested in this idea. Jack doesn't want to destroy his wedding, and yet, on some level, he does.

Each of these intentions has its opposite, and each shows that the character wants it, and doesn't want it, sometimes all at the same time and sometimes consecutively. As the characters bounce back and forth with their contradictory intentions, this becomes the fuel that drives the forward progression of the story.

If Jack did not have a strong enough intention, or didn't have the determination to go after it, Miles and Maya would not have gotten together and created their own subplot. Jack and the obliging Stephanie would not have gotten together to create another subplot. Because Jack wants the best for his friend, and the best for himself, there's a story.

The story was created because of the collision of intentions, and the conflict that resulted from this collision. And the story happens because this conflict results in new action which advances the story from the beginning, through the middle, to the end.

Creating the Journey's Sequence of Events

Conflicts and goals, even action, in itself, is not enough to make a story move. Events have to develop, progress, advance, so the journey truly takes the characters closer to a goal.

In our normal world, we go through our activities usually without conflict, with little momentum, and with a certain degree of repetition. One event doesn't intrinsically lead to another. We live our lives through episodes and small events that are not connected to each other. We don't live in the world of story, but in the real-life world of errands, eating breakfast, going to work, coming home and doing any number of arbitrary events. Although at the end of our life, someone may be able to select out and choose events to create a narrative out of them, most of the time, unless there are events that create a sequence of events with conflict, we aren't living a story, although we may be living meaningful lives.

In a story, however, one event needs to flow into another event in order to create momentum. The second event is a consequence of the first. One action results in a reaction which results in another action which results in another reaction. For instance, a crime is committed. As a result, a detective is told to try to solve the crime. As a result of this assignment, the detective goes to investigate — whether it's through talking to witnesses, or searching a house, or doing some research. Perhaps he hears that the criminal is hiding out at a farm. As a result of hearing this, he goes to the farm, hopefully with back-up (unless, of course, he's Clint Eastwood or Bruce Willis or James Bond, who never seem to need back-up). Then, as a result of arriving at the hide-out of the criminal, there's a shoot-out. As a result of the shoot-out, either the person dies or is captured.

Notice how each event leads to the other. Look at how there's a beginning (the crime), a middle (the investigation), and an end (the capture), and how all of these events are related.

In a story about two people going to the wine country, we might expect that they would taste wine, maybe they decide to then go out to eat, maybe they decide to golf, or swim, or take a drive. Or perhaps they change the order of what they do, eating first, then playing golf, then drinking. It wouldn't matter what the order of the events would be, because each event does not grow organically out of the previous event. These are all arbitrary decisions. They are just individual events with no intrinsic connection to previous events.

To create a story, the writer has to find a way to create scene sequences that are connected to each other, so the story flows, and has energy and direction. How did the writers do this? They already had an ending to the story — the wedding. But going to the wine country and then going to a wedding have no intrinsic connection to each other. There are thousands of people who go to the wine country to taste wine that don't get married at the end of the week. There are thousands of people who go to the wine country and don't golf, and don't swim, and don't go to sit in a Jacuzzi or get lost on the back roads. Individual events, by themselves, don't make up a story. There needs to be an organic connection between the events to make the story work.

In *Sideways,* connections are created throughout. If Jack wants to get Miles laid, then he'll have to find someone for Miles to lay with. He sees Maya, and starts the ball rolling with her. They'll have a date the next night. The date goes well, and that leads them to decide to go back to Stephanie's place, since that allows Jack to get the sex he wants, and hopefully to give Miles a bit of sex as well. But the evening doesn't go according to Jack's plan — Miles doesn't get laid. In fact, Miles doesn't even set up another date with Maya. So the initial intention set up a scene sequence that lasted for about twelve minutes. That's not long enough for a film. Now Jack's intention has to come back into play. He tries to push Miles into seeing Maya again, hoping things will work out better the second time. The second time, they do. At this point, it seems that the mission is accomplished and the film should now be over. But at this point, we're only eighty-three minutes into the film. We still need more action. So the writers play a reversal — Maya gets angry at Miles and leaves him. So what was all working well, has now reversed itself and everything is going wrong.

This reversal that affects Miles also affects Stephanie, since Maya tells her friend about Jack's wedding plans — with someone else. This sets in motion another sequence of events. Stephanie hits Jack and leaves, and Jack's nose is broken, thus ending this subplot, but creating another possible obstacle to the wedding. Now comes the next series of events — Jack has to be taken to the hospital and has to figure out what to tell Christine about his bandaged nose. Now his wedding is in jeopardy, not because of Stephanie, who is now out of the picture, but because of the visual results that prove Jack was probably up to no good, in one way or another. How can Jack explain the broken nose? If he doesn't explain it well, Christine could still reject him.

That sets up another sequence of events — creating an auto accident as an explanation for the broken nose.

Meanwhile, Maya's departure sets up another series of events for Miles which will pay off at the end. Miles never wanted to hurt Maya, and realizes how much he likes her. So he wants to make things right, which adds to some other actions. He says he's sorry, calls her, and eventually drives to see her.

The writers are constantly setting up catalysts to create action-reaction scene sequences which keep the story moving.

THE STORY STRUCTURE AND ITS DEVELOPMENT

The Story of *Sideways* works because it has a clear, three-act structure, with a plot and subplots. Although the book begins with several incidents before Miles and Jack leave on their journey, the film begins with the journey. The dialogue tells us what they are doing and why they're doing it:

MILES

```
        Jack. This week is not about me. It's
        about you. I'm going to show you a good
        time. We're going to drink a lot of good
        wine, play some golf, eat some great
        food, enjoy the scenery and send you off
        in style. (p. 22)
```

In the *set-up*, Miles and Jack leave, and head for the Wine Country. At the end of the set-up, at fifteen minutes into the film, Jack announces his intention — for Miles to get laid, and the question is raised, "Will Miles find love, romance, and sex in the wine country?" It's a small catalyst, but it's a good way to begin the story.

Act One Development focuses on the journey to the wine country. They stop to see Miles' mother, who has her birthday that day. They celebrate over champagne and dinner, Miles steals some of his mother's money, and they leave. The 1st Turning Point occurs at thirty minutes into the film, when Jack announces his intention — he also wants sex on this journey.

During Act Two, the story begins to develop and become more than just about wine tasting and two guys shooting the breeze, drinking, chatting. It looks as if both intentions will easily be met. Miles sees Maya at twenty-four minutes into the film. Jack meets Stephanie who shows interest and accessibility, thirty-two minutes into the film. These two subplots begin to develop during Act Two. The jeopardy of the wedding, the uncertainties between

Maya and Miles, the deception between Jack and Stephanie all begin the emotional roller-coaster ride of Act Two.

By the 2nd Turning Point, at ninety minutes into the film, both Jack and Miles have lost their new loves, and now the focus turns to the wedding in Act Three, and what has to be done to make sure Jack doesn't lose his fiancé. This brings up a new set of obstacles. When he has sex with the married waitress, he has to get his wallet back, since the special wedding rings are in the wallet. He has to find a way to justify his broken nose, so he drives his car into a tree and claims that they've had an accident. He has to make sure that Christine sees the wrecked car, so that she won't find out what he's really been up to. Act Three is a time of tying up loose ends and getting Jack to the church on time.

Within this basic structure, the story achieves variety by creating a journey for both Miles and Jack. The film works with subplots to further deepen their journey.

Miles has several plotlines. His major subplot is the story of his relationship with Maya. He sees her, and discovers that she is no longer married. At the 1st Turning Point, they double date with Jack and Stephanie. During Act Two, they develop their relationship, eventually sleeping together at the 2nd Turning Point. At the Climax, she finds out that Jack has betrayed Stephanie and that Miles hasn't been honest with her, so she leaves. During the Resolution, she writes to Miles and he decides to go to see her.

Miles also has a subplot about his novel which he hopes to get published. It's discussed in Act One, and Jack presumes it will be published, although there is not yet a publishing deal. At the 1st Turning Point, Maya asks to read it. At the 2nd Turning Point, Miles learns that it's been turned down — again, and that his agent has no idea where else to send it. At the Climax, Maya tells him that she's read it, and was very touched by it.

Miles has a throughline about his relationship with Victoria. There are no turning points on this throughline, but there is development. With the Victoria throughline, we understand why Miles is depressed. It begins when Jack mentions her during the drive up the coast and tells Miles to get over her. At the mother's home, we see the photograph of Victoria and Miles' wedding when he was happier and life was better. On his first date with Maya, after drinking far too much wine, he "drinks and dials" and calls Victoria. He learns from Jack that she's coming to the wedding, and then learns the additional information — that she's coming with her new husband. At the wedding, he finds out that she's pregnant.

The photograph of Victoria at the mother's home serves another important story function. Although the stop at the mother's home is not essential, and could easily have been lifted out of the film without any negative consequences, the photograph helps connect it to the rest of the story. Although Victoria could have been set up in other ways — by showing that Miles always carries a photograph of her, by having him talk incessantly about her, by showing that Miles still carries or wears his wedding ring — the photograph at the mother's home creates a connection with the ongoing storyline so the mother scene is threaded together with the rest of the story. It implies that something is still unresolved, and it foreshadows the resolution that will come at the end of the story.

Jack's journey can be divided into three separate storylines. The one storyline can be seen as his overall emotional journey. This story begins by establishing his relationship with his fiancé and her family and establishing the upcoming wedding. At the 1st Turning Point, he meets Stephanie and spends the second act getting to know her — in as many intimate ways as possible which puts the wedding in jeopardy. Toward the end of Act Two, he breaks up with her, but isn't ready to give up on women — yet.

By the 2nd Turning Point, he realizes his behavior is jeopardizing the wedding, breaks down and cries, and pleads with Miles to help him. At the Climax, he gets married.

He also has a subplot line with Stephanie. They meet. At the 1st Turning Point, she agrees to have dinner with him and Miles and Maya, which begins the development of their relationship. In Act Two, he spends more time with her than with Miles. At the 2nd Turning Point of their relationship, we discover he's made all sorts of promises to her, and that she believed them. The actual 2nd Turning Point is off-screen, which would be the moment that Maya tells her that Jack is getting married. Her reaction occurs at the Climax of their storyline — when she breaks up with him right before Act Three begins.

Jack also has a small throughline with his fiancé. He leaves for the trip in Act One. During Act Two he balances his relationship with her and with Stephanie through a series of phone calls and through his dates with Stephanie. At the Climax, he chooses the marriage.

WHAT IS THE MOVIE REALLY ABOUT?

No matter how simple the film, or what genre it is, the story needs to be about something. Drama tells us about the human condition: What are the problems most of us encounter? What are the issues that are important to us? Where is the meaning or the depth in life? Who are we and who are we becoming through the course of the journey of the story? What do we have the potential to become?

Finding the theme can be a process, since many films seem to be about a number of different ideas. But a good film has one over-riding theme, one idea that is being explored throughout the course of the story. Sometimes you can find the theme of the movie by asking yourself, "If I were to sit down and talk about *Sideways*, but wasn't talking about the story, what would I talk about?" You might talk about how important it is to get out of the morass that we sometimes get into, and to get on with life. You might talk about starting over, or seeking resolution, or about transforming as a result of a journey. You might discuss infidelity, or talk about the problems that even adults can have in growing up and settling down.

In the case of *Sideways*, we can find some understanding of the theme by exploring the idea of the title. "Sideways" means to be drunk, two sheets to the wind, a wobbling and unfocused crab-like creature who can't walk head-on, who can't see clearly where he's going, who walks to the side, even though he might think he's going forward. The title implies characters who aren't moving on with life, who aren't standing straight up, but who are moving sideways, sometimes even backwards, instead of moving directly forward. The metaphor also tells us something about the nature of wine. Wine can be about joy and camaraderie and fun and laughter, but it can also be about intoxication, when one can't talk straight or think straight. With too much wine, one escapes into a kind of oblivion, rather than living life fully.

We can then look at this idea and apply it to each character, to see how each character represents some aspect of the theme.

Miles is a character who's stuck. He's in a morass, still thinking of the past. He can't get Victoria out of his mind, even though she has gone on with life, is married, pregnant, and facing the future with happiness. Miles needs to grow up, to let go of the past, to get away from his dead-end life, and to have the courage to move on from the attitudes and emotions that are killing his spirit. Miles is halfway looking back to Victoria, other times, living a static life, which is repetitive, doing the same things over and over again. He teaches middle school, tries to sell his novel, drinks wine, goes up to the wine country every once in a while, spends some time with his friend, Jack, and drinks and dials — calling

Victoria — when he gets too stuck in his depression. Miles is not moving forward, and without Jack's prodding, would not even move forward enough to ask Maya out.

Jack, who should be moving forward to the wedding, is not looking forward to getting married. To him, the wedding is the loss of freedom, and he'd rather look backward to his days when he was a rake, going after every woman who interested him.

Stephanie can't see beyond her nose. If someone like Jack is in front of her nose she follows it, even though she knows nothing about him. She's unable to discern the subtleties, the difficulties and complexities. Although she might be discerning about wine, she's not discerning about people. When she discovers Jack's deception, she takes no responsibility for her own part in it, but goes into a violent rage. Although we might say that Jack deserved her anger, her rage is out of control. And although Jack is certainly to blame for the deception, her reaction shows that she believed every word from someone she had known for a few days. Although we don't know where Stephanie's life heads after this incident, there is little reason to believe that she will go forward or make any changes. One might expect that the next man who comes along and romances her will receive the same response from Stephanie — flirtation, acceptance of whatever he says, wild sex, and rage when she discovers she is once more deceived.

Maya is the contrasting character and the stable center of the film. If we want to know what it means to stop going sideways, and to meet life directly, we can look to Maya. She shows the possibilities of recreating a life after a divorce. She proves that it's possible to face the problems directly, and to get on with life. Obstacles, set-backs, and dashed dreams and hopes are part of life's journey, and rather than wallowing in them, or refusing to face them directly, Maya has learned how to take another road. Whereas Miles is stuck, incredibly stuck, Maya represents what it means to get on with your life.

After her divorce, Maya went back to school for a master's degree in horticulture. She has clear and realistic dreams. She's learned from her first marriage. She learned that not only does she love wine, but she has a good sense of taste. She uses this self-knowlege and now has decided she wants to work in a vineyard or winery. She's dating again, she's clear about her interest in Miles, she's clear about her integrity. As a result of her marriage, she's learned that she won't put up with deception. She has clear boundaries, a clear direction. She's not afraid to meet life head-on, and to move forward toward her own goals.

By the end of the film, three out of the four major characters have taken some steps forward. Although there's no reason to believe that Jack's marriage will be a success, he goes forward with the wedding, by no means unhappily, at least not on his wedding day. Maya continues with her studies, moving toward her goal. Miles shows direct movement at the end. By the end, he's no longer just meandering. He drives directly to Maya's, and with the knock on her door, we can see that he is moving toward what he really wants.

A good, rich, universal theme relates to the lives of the movie characters, but also resonates with our own lives as audience members. With a good theme, in one way or another, we also share the same experience and the same problems. Like the characters in *Sideways*, we also get stuck, we also despair, and look back to another time that is gone and irretrievable. We also need forgiveness for our mistakes. We also need to be willing to start over, to go forward, to have something new and wonderful happen to us that will allow us to find something good in life again.

A theme needs to relate to the story and at least to the main character. In many of the best films, the theme broadens and expands because each character shows us another aspect of the theme, as if we were turning a crystal to catch more light with each turn.

The film continually shows us characters who are stuck, get unstuck, and get stuck again. The movement of the characters toward getting unstuck resonates with the question we might ask of Miles: "Will Miles get unstuck enough to be honest with himself and to learn to love someone more than he loves his despair?"

Making Choices

Many movies are about choice — about the decisions that characters make to say "yes" or "no" to choices that confront them. The theme can often be found within the choices that characters make. Someone sets one choice into motion, someone else makes another choice. The choice can be determined by an antagonist or the protagonist. Movies can be about choices that make their life worse, or choices that make their lives better.

In *Sideways*, the choices become even more important than the action. Without the action coming from choices, there wouldn't be a very interesting movie because the story is driven by the characters, not vice versa. All the action flows out of the character choices. Choices define character, they create conflict, they change the intention and direction of the story, and they tell us what the movie is really about.

All the major characters in *Sideways* make choices about their lives. Stephanie says "no" to Jack in order to reject this kind of betrayal, although we don't know if she'll continue her same behavior, or make new decisions.

Jack says "yes" to many situations that he should be saying "no" to. He says "yes" to Stephanie's flirtation moment, because he doesn't want to get on with life. He doesn't want to go forward with a wedding, with marriage and children and adulthood and maturity. When that doesn't work, he says "yes" to the starry-eyed waitress. And when that doesn't work out, he goes to the wedding, not like a lamb to slaughter, but with a sense that he still has left some options open.

When Miles says "yes," he is choosing to move forward. He says "yes" to dating Maya, "yes" to giving Maya his manuscript, "yes" to opening up his special bottle of wine and finally "yes" to going to see Maya.

Maya says "no" to deception, "no" to Jack and Miles and their behavior. But she leaves the door open to a "yes," by writing to Miles, having seen the depth and the pain and the humanity that is beneath his story about today, in hopes of a tomorrow.

CREATING THE CHARACTERS

Creating the Protagonist and Antagonist

This conflict between the different choices one can make helps define the protagonist, who has a certain desire, and the antagonist who opposes that desire.

In most films, the antagonist is the negative, evil character who opposes the heroic protagonist. Sometimes the antagonist begins the story, such as in most James Bond films, where the antagonist does something, or threatens to do something, that must be stopped. The protagonist enters into the story to solve the problem because the government of England, or someone else, has an opposite intention — to stop the evil from happening.

In *Sideways,* there's not the good guy (the protagonist) and the bad guy (the antagonist). Instead, although Miles is the central figure, and the protagonist of the story, both Miles and Jack are antagonists to each other's goals.

The Question of Integrity

Many films are about integrity — showing the hero standing up to The Bad and working for The Good. It might be *High Noon,* or *The Gladiator,* or *To Kill a Mockingbird,* or the many *Batman* and *Spiderman* films that show a heroic character, larger than life, true blue throughout, who manages through courage and will and strength to achieve big but seemingly impossible goals, without compromise. We almost expect to see protagonists with integrity in most films. Yet in *Sideways,* most characters can be defined by their lack of integrity. Although this is not a story about characters losing integrity or finding integrity, each character, except for Maya, is dishonest and lacks integrity. In that sense, most of the main characters have negative traits, rather than being presented as heroic or positive model characters.

Sideways is by no means a morality story, since nobody has their life together. Nor is it a story about people seeking a moral high ground. But it's possible to look at each character in terms of who's dishonest and who isn't, and how their dishonesty affects their relationships.

In my interview with novelist Rex Pickett, he said that he believed most men are dishonest. The script clearly sets up this idea fairly quickly. Miles has overslept, and is late for his drive up the coast to pick up Jack. But he takes no responsibility for sleeping late. He first lie occurs when he tells Jack, "I had a bunch of stuff to deal with this morning" (p. 2). Not true; he overslept. He then tells him, "I'm on my way. I'm out the door right this second" (p. 2). Not true. He sits on the toilet, reads, showers, flosses his teeth, and stops for a triple espresso (p. 3). We see him driving on a fairly easily flowing freeway, but when he arrives, he lies to Jack: "The freeway was unbelievable today. Unbelievable. Bumper to bumper the whole way" (p. 5).

But just as Miles seems to have been set up as a negative character, he shows twinges of honesty. His negative characteristics are shaded. He nuances his lie to Jack by adding: "Granted I got a late start, but still" (p. 5).

When he stops at his mother's to celebrate her birthday, he steals from her dresser drawer — even though she would gladly give

27

him money. When she asks, "Do you need some money?" he replies "I'm fine" but then, immediately takes another drink of wine (p. 19). Looking at the film, perhaps you see a flicker of conscience in his answer and his action.

Upon arrival at the hotel, Miles does what most would consider another negative action — he tosses the Gideon Bible in the trash, "apparently his hotel routine" (p. 29).

Just as we might wonder about this guy, he again shows some sense of decency and moral standards, telling Jack to "shut up" when he goes on too long about trying to set Miles up to have sex with Maya.

When Jack lets him know that he's going to get laid on this trip, Miles lets Jack know that he doesn't approve of his behavior and he's angry at the change in intentions.

> JACK
> I am going to get my nut on this trip,
> Miles. And you are not going to fuck it
> up for me with all your depression and
> anxiety and neg-head downer shit.

> MILES
> Ooooh, now the cards are on the table.

> JACK
> Yes they are. And I'm serious. Do not
> fuck with me. I *am* going to get laid
> before I settle down on Saturday. Do you
> read me?

> MILES
> Sure, big guy. Whatever you say. It's your
> party. I'm sorry I'm in the way and
> dragging you down. Maybe you'd have a
> better time on your own. You take the car.
> I'll catch the train back.

His dialogue conveys that he's not happy about this development, since it interferes with his expectations for the trip. But the dialogue also implies some sense of morals, of boundaries, of appropriate behavior. If we weren't sure about his moral scruples here, we can more clearly see that his integrity shows through as the story progresses. He doesn't consider dating Maya because she's married. He's very torn by Jack's behavior toward Stephanie, knowing that Jack is leading her on and jeopardizing his wedding. He doesn't know how to tell Maya about Jack's wedding, and yet is sorry and realizes that he is partly to blame when she blames him for not telling her.

Jack clearly lacks integrity. He's self-involved, insensitive to the feelings of others, won't take responsibility for his own actions, and is generally unconscious about his negative character traits. He lives by his own rules and his major concern is himself. Even when he expresses regret about his fling with the waitress, his regret does not come because she's married, but because her husband showed up which caused him a problem — losing the wedding rings.

But Jack is by no means a totally negative character. He is complex and multi-dimensional, containing positive characteristics as well. He sincerely likes Miles, and wants to help him get over his depression. His intention for Miles is positive — he wants him to have a good time and get happily on with his life.

Although Stephanie is not a woman who has much integrity, nevertheless, she has a sense of how a woman should be treated and what she considers abusive treatment. What Jack has done to her is a great wrong, and she lets him know it. Although she takes no responsibility for her own behavior, she's honest enough not to stick around for a little more sex with a man who has betrayed her and lied to her.

Sometimes a script can be analyzed in terms of where the moral center is. In the old Western films, there was the good guy, usually without flaws, who clearly stood for integrity. And there was the bad guy, who compromised the moral code.

Maya's presence helps ground the script with some morality, so we don't come away from the film thinking that everyone is negative, or believing that the characters have no moral code and they can do what they want, without consequences. What starts out as looking like a film with negative, although interesting, characters, ends up as a film that has something to say about love and life and the decisions we make and the way characters handle situations.

Defining the Characters

A character can be defined in a script through many different methods. In some acting classes, the actor is taught to look at the character and ask: "What does the character say about him or herself?" "What do others say about the character?" "What do the decisions and events say about the character?" "What is not said about the character but implied, or expressed through subtext?" Many writers will search for the definition of a character by asking, "What does a character want and what is the character willing to do to get it?"

The character of Miles

Since Miles is not a pro-active character, nor is he particularly introspective, much of what we learn about Miles comes from the comments others make about him.

Miles would be considered, by many, to be similar to the nice guy that lives down the block but that many people don't know well. He's reasonably polite when asked to move his car. He's reasonably friendly. He's not tremendously disciplined since he overslept, and he's not a model of integrity, since he lies about it. But at first glance, he seems like an okay, but not very exciting, fellow.

Jack tells us the most about Miles' character. He clarifies that Miles is depressed. He mentions that Miles is in a morass and has been there since Victoria divorced him two years ago. He's trying to get a book published, but isn't having any luck. As the story moves along, we begin to sense that he's quite a smart guy. He has a rich vocabulary which comes partly from being an English teacher, even if it's in middle school. He has become an expert on wine, and is defined partly by his love of pinot noir, a rich and multi-layered varietal.

But with Miles, as with most real-life people, things are not quite as they seem. He is a bundle of complexities, uncertainties, insecurities, and seeming contradictions. He has the positives and the negatives, and for every negative, there is shading to his character that shows he's not quite so black. For every positive, there is shading that shows his character is not quite so white.

Miles is filled with dashed hopes. He is full of regrets and "if onlys." If only I had treated her better. If only my book was published. If only I hadn't had an affair when married to Victoria. His life has come to a standstill as a result of living in the past. He thought he could go back to Victoria, but soon realizes that she's married, so he realizes that any hope of getting back together will never be fulfilled. He had hoped that his novel would get published, but his agent calls to tell him that just doesn't seem to be happening. He had hoped to spend the week with his best friend, but Jack changes the expectation and instead Miles spends more time alone than he wished for.

We know that he teaches English and writing, loves books, and has his middle school students read from *A Separate Peace,* a book that's respected by readers and scholars. The student reads a section from the book that could also describe Miles. "'The marrow of his bone' …Phineas had died from the marrow of his bone flowing down his blood stream to his heart." (p. 134). *A Separate*

Peace focuses on two contrasting characters, and explores themes of friendship, betrayal, jealousy, irresponsibility, and denial. These lines could almost describe, in this beautifully written prose, what Miles' problem is, and will continue to be, if he doesn't begin to move out of his morass.

His creativity and sensitivity is defined partly by the book that he has written. It has an original title — *The Day After Yesterday* which is, of course, Today.

We know that he's worked hard on that book for a period of time, so he's a disciplined writer. He's managed to complete a novel (no small feat, for anyone who has ever written!). From the dialogue, we know something about the book and the journey of the book over quite a long time.

We suspect that the novel has merit and that it's probably quite good because he was able to get an agent with the book. The agent believes in him and his work, and has really tried to sell it. His relationship with her is not just in name only, but they have a good relationship. She's sent the material out and is now running out of ideas about where to send it.

For those of us who know publishing, we know that ordinarily an agent would send a book to the larger publishing houses, in hopes of a large advance. If they aren't interested, the agent would then try smaller and smaller publishing houses, until it was clear that the work wasn't saleable. We know that the agent is very supportive of Miles. She has tried many times to sell this book, but is now at the end of her ideas.

We learn more about the book, and thereby of Miles, from the agent's dialogue.

```
                    EVELYN
        I'm not sure how much more mileage I can
        get out of continuing to submit it. I
```

```
think it's one of those unfortunate cases
in the business right now - a fabulous
book with no home. The whole industry's
gotten gutless. It's not about the
quality of the books. It's only about
the marketing. (p. 107)
```

From Evelyn, we learn that the book is quite brilliant but it doesn't fit neatly into a genre. Like Miles, the book is not so easily categorized.

The title of the book also tells us something about Miles. Miles is defined by the past, by yesterday. If he could get past the day after yesterday, he would be able to go forward to today and the day after today which is, of course, tomorrow.

We also know that Miles is talented, because of Maya's response to his book and because we trust Maya. Maya says, "I think it's really lovely, Miles. You're so good with words.... There are so many beautiful and painful things about it. Did you really go through all that? It must have been awfully hard" (p. 136).

Maya is not giving an analytical, intellectual response to the book, but an emotional one. Maya helps reveal Miles' character because of her reaction to the book. Not only do we find out about the book through Maya, that it's a touching, well-written book, but the book did what a book is supposed to do —make the reader respond emotionally and touch the reader in a deep and profound way. Through her response, we learn that there's an emotional richness and sensitivity to Miles.

We learn about Miles' backstory and his life through small implications that are shown in the film. We know that he seldom comes to see his mother, and it seems that he often comes unannounced. We know that he doesn't have a close relationship with his sister, since he makes no effort to join her family for his mother's birthday.

We know that Miles knows the bartender, so we understand that he has come to the wine country often in the past, although it seems that he usually has come alone. From his casual conversations with the bartender, we get a sense of Miles' life. He goes wine tasting, teaching, working on the book.

Miles is defined by the pinot noir that he drinks. The grapes used to produce Merlot and cabernet are easy to cultivate. But the pinot grape is difficult to grow. Pinot noir becomes a metaphor for someone who wants to be seen as special. For those readers who have tried pinot noir, you might notice that it has rich flavors and that the flavors are more complex than with cabernet or merlot. Although I'm not a wine connoisseur, I enjoy it, and have developed a finer sense of taste as a result of the wine tour, and as a result of tuning in to some of the descriptions of wine in the film. I find pinot noir a multi-layered wine. Sometimes I compare wine to music, and I find that pinot noir has more of a harmony to it, rather than one clear tone. Pinot noir is a good metaphor for Miles, a multi-dimensional character, a layered person, a deep person. The choice by the writers of the particular grape and the choice of the particular wine becomes an overall metaphor for what kind of person Miles is.

What Miles knows about wine, he knows well. He knows the vocabulary, he knows the subtleties. Although Miles is not able to afford the kind of cellar he would like, he has a few wonderful bottles that he treasures.

At the same time, Miles is a snob when it comes to wines. He doesn't want the ordinary, and prides himself on his understanding of wine. The joke in the movie, however, happens at the very end when Miles tastes that most special of wines, a '61 Cheval Franc. After spending the entire movie talking about how cabernet and merlot are prosaic and pinot noir is for connoisseurs, the wine he drinks at the end is not pinot noir at all, but a blend of merlot and cabernet sauvignon.

The Character of Jack

Jack is a contrasting character to Miles. Just as Miles has a rich vocabulary, Jack fits the stereotype of actors, which says that actors don't know what to say if they're not given lines to read. Although this is a stereotype, and an untrue one in most circumstances, it adds humor to his character. Jack is the kind of actor who has managed to get by on his good looks. He has tried to make it as an actor but he's not going to ever be a great one. His career had one big part in it — on a soap opera, as the doctor — which in itself is humorous, since in real life Jack wouldn't be smart enough to be a doctor. His career has now been reduced to commercials advertising Spray and Wash, low 5.8% APR financing, and pills with dangerous side effects. His future will probably include working in a boring job in property management for his wealthy father-in-law.

Jack is also a me-me-me character. He's somewhat clueless about the real reason for people's behavior. He's insensitive to the feelings and sensibilities of others. He doesn't understand why Stephanie is angry at him. He doesn't understand why Miles might feel he's crossing a line. When he's with the waitress, Cammi, his problem is not that she's married, but that his wallet is left behind which could ruin everything. When Miles suggest he get the wallet, Jack makes it clear that he expects Miles to help him out. He made the mess, but he doesn't want to fix it.

Maya centers the story as the warm, clear, moral center. Miles and Stephanie like and respect her. Although it's not said clearly, even Jack seems to respect her. He encourages Miles to go after her. Jack defines most women by whether or not they're a hot chick, but he seems to genuinely like Maya and sees something worthwhile in her. Eventually Maya takes a stand for what she believes is right, and leaves Miles. Since Stephanie is her friend, according to Maya's moral code, friends don't wrong friends. She knows what Jack is doing to Stephanie is wrong, and that Miles is wrong for not having told her or Stephanie about his impending marriage. She is ready to walk away from a relationship with someone she likes if he's dishonest. She has learned from her past, and makes it clear that she has had enough of deception. Neither does she deceive, or collude with anyone who deceives. Her action of leaving Miles then leads to Stephanie leaving Jack.

The character of Stephanie

Stephanie is flirtatious, and, like Jack, still clings to seeing herself as defined by her sexuality, even though she's a mother, and seems to have a reasonably close relationship with her daughter, Siena. There's an implication throughout the script that Stephanie screws around a bit, and her daughter stays with her mother to give Stephanie the freedom that she wants.

Stephanie and Maya are good friends and look out for each other. Stephanie wants Maya to be happy. She encourages Miles to call Maya, because she notices that Maya seems to like Miles more than anyone else she's dated since her divorce.

The Minor Characters

Siena and Caryl

Stephanie has a daughter, Siena, who often stays with Stephanie's mother, Caryl. Siena softens Stephanie's character, and implies that Stephanie takes her responsibility seriously enough because there is a loving relationship with her daughter. She helps Siena with her seat belt, introduces her to Jack, and is clearly enthralled by their rapidly developing happy relationship. However, Siena is conspicuously absent when Stephanie wants to have fun.

The child often stays with the mother, Caryl, who's described as a "fifty-something, two-pack-a-day Mother Caryl" (p. 84). Caryl also has some regrets about her past, although her past doesn't relate to love lost, but to blowing the chance to buy "in Santa

Maria when I had the chance, I would have made a fortune when they put in that outlet center and that Home Depot" (p. 85).

Phyllis

Miles' mother, Phyllis, is also a minor, although fascinating, character, who is surprised and pleased by the attention from such a famous actor as Miles' friend, Jack. She's got plenty of advice for Miles — about letting her know in the future when he's coming, about getting back together with Victoria, about staying to see his sister — but Phyllis is never overbearing. "Well, you boys do what you want" (p. 17), and they do.

Phyllis is a character that could have been cut, and the writers mentioned to me that this scene of stealing the money is often discussed as being an unnecessary scene. It does serve some purpose, since it brings Victoria to our attention, and shows the photograph of Miles and Victoria on their happy wedding day. The scene also gives Miles a context — showing he's in relationship with his mother and, to a minor extent, with his sister and her family.

The scene shows Miles' lack of integrity, when he steals the money, but this is a thread that is not paid off during the film, since we never clearly see him using the money and since he never repays it. It is, however, a thread that could have connected to the rest of the story if Miles had used that money during the trip, perhaps unrolling his wad of bills at various times to pay for expensive wines or expensive dinners. He could have tucked it away with some sense of guilt. He must have had a reason to take the money, but this is not shown, nor does he bring it back to his mother on the way home. This short scene stands out as one of the few that has a set-up without a pay-off. Just as it's said that one doesn't set up a knife in Act One without paying it off in Act Two or Act Three, it's the same with setting up the stealing of the money in Act One without paying it off somewhere during the rest of the film. Generally, one doesn't want any dangling set-ups that have no consequences later in the script. Although Phyllis adds more shading and gives more backstory information to the character of Miles, and adds some variety to the road trip, like Caryl, the character of Phyllis might have also been cut with few repercussions for the film. As you watch the film, you may want to decide just how much these two characters are adding to the film, and whether you feel it would have worked better if they had been cut.

Do the Characters Transform?

Transformational stories, in one way or another, are journey stories. A character goes on a journey — whether a real journey in trains, planes, or automobiles, or a journey into an adventure or a relationship or a new world. Sometimes, by getting away, getting a new lease on life, the character sees life differently. During the journey, the events and people the character meets along the way impact the character. Sometimes this impact is sufficient to make a change in behavior, or attitudes, or new decisions. These changes can be small, or they can be profound. This depends partly on the strength of the relationships, on the dramatic punch of the events, on the character's resistance to change and willingness to change.

At first glance, it does seem that *Sideways* is a transformational story. Miles finds love at the end, and seems to come out of his two-year funk from his divorce, gains a measure of confidence in order to go after what he wants, and accepts his former wife's new marriage and family. Jack finally breaks down, crying over his behavior, pleading with Miles to help him so that his fiancé won't break up with him. He seems to have come to a realization that he wants this marriage, and a realization about his bad behavior.

When I first saw *Sideways*, I saw it as a transformational story, even though the transformations were in a beginning stage. At the 2nd Turning Point, Jack breaks down and cries, and is willing to do almost anything to save his wedding. (Actually, he's willing to have Miles do almost anything to save his wedding, including sneaking into a house and stealing back his wallet which contains the wedding rings.) Although the crying scene was strong and implied change, after more thinking about Jack, and after interviewing the writers, I came to the conclusion that Jack's transformation would be short-lived. Although Jack may have, for the moment, realized how much he wanted to marry Christine, his weak moral character and weak self-discipline would probably lead him, eventually, to have other affairs and to get tired of monogamy. Whether Christine would stay with him, in spite of his "bad boy" behavior, could be questionable, but from the little that we know about Christine and her family, we might expect her marriage to fit into appropriate standards of behavior, which eventually Jack would not fulfill.

In spite of the small transformations that Jack makes, we can still map out the movement forward and how events and other characters influence that movement. A transformation can be mapped out by looking at where the character begins in Act One, how the character moves forward in Act Two, and what the character achieves in Act Three.

Jack has a transformational arc, although it leaves the audience with questions about whether his transformation can stand the test of time.

In Act One, he seems fine with his upcoming marriage, making phone calls to his fiancée throughout the story, insisting on his love for her. Act One defines the character as we expect him to be — a man ready to get married to a very pretty woman, from a very rich family. By the 1st Turning Point, we can see that everything is not like it seems. Jack states his intention to betray Christine and allows his roving eye to respond to Stephanie's flirtations, and start a relationship with her. When she finds him out, he still doesn't give up, but responds to the admiring hero worship of a waitress, and sees his chance for another last fling. When that doesn't work out, he decides to make his various injuries look like a car accident, in order to maintain the wedding which gives him the hope of a rich, although not entirely satisfying life. Although these events are strong enough to create a transformation, the audience can interpret whether or not he's truly transformed. We don't know the end result, except for the wedding. We have no idea how the marriage will turn out, although we may have our doubts. Although the crying scene was a Turning Point, it's a turning point that may not truly "take." A case could be made that there was at least a transformation of understanding and attitude, as Jack realized what was at stake for him if he blew this marriage opportunity. This could make his lack of transformation more tragic, since he now has a firmer grasp of what the consequences of his behavior might be.

Miles shows the beginning steps of transformation, even though we just see the beginning baby steps of moving forward with his life. But the seeds have been planted for him to be a better, and more pro-active person — if he so chooses.

By the end of Act Three, with the combined influences of a warm and caring Maya who read his book and showed her understanding of him, and the prodding of Jack, Miles is able to make a rather dramatic decision — to drive to the wine country and knock on her door. For Miles, this requires great effort and new behavior, and as a result it shows his willingness, and ability, to change.

Maya doesn't need to transform since she transformed between the time of her divorce and the time of the beginning of the film. Stephanie gives no indication whether or not she'll transform in her behavior, or attitudes toward men, or through any decisions she might make in the future about her life.

The Dialogue

The dialogue in *Sideways* serves the same function as most dialogue: It advances the action, it reveals character, it suggests subtext, and it implies the theme. *Sideways* adds another addition to dialogue which is quite unusual — it creates metaphors.

Dialogue Sets Up the Context

Some of the dialogue sets up the context that we need, in order to understand the movie. What does one look for in a good wine? We need some exposition to clarify the world of wine tasting — how to sip wine, what to look for, and how to analyze what we're noticing. The words are specific, and for many of us, the dialogue opens up a whole new special world.

Miles explains:

```
Color in red wines comes from the skins.
This juice is free run, so there's no
skin contact in the fermentation, ergo no
color." (p. 9)

I like all varietals. I just don't
generally like the way they manipulate
chardonnay in California — too much oak
and secondary malolactic fermentation." (p. 23)
```

Miles uses words like "good concentration," "nice fruit" (p. 32), whereas other wines are "flabby, overripe" (p. 48).

Upon arrival at the Sanford tasting room, Miles tells Jack about the art of wine tasting:

```
                    MILES
First, take your glass and examine the wine
against the light. You're looking at color
and clarity…
… Just get a sense of it. Thick? Thin? Watery?
Syrupy? Inky? Amber, whatever…
```

...Now tip it. What you're doing here is
checking for color density as it thins
toward the rim.
Tells you how old it is, among other
things, usually more important with reds.
... Now stick your nose in it....
What do you smell?

> JACK

I don't know. Wine? Fermented grapes?

> MILES

... you can still find...
a little citrus... maybe some
strawberry... passion fruit... and
there's even a hint of like asparagus...
or like a nutty Edam cheese.

> JACK

Huh. Maybe a little strawberry. Yeah,
strawberry. I'm not so sure about the
cheese.

> MILES

Now set your glass down and get some
air into it...
Oxygenating it opens it up, unlocks the
aroma and the flavors. Very important...
(p. 27-29)

> JACK

When do we get to drink it?

The dialogue adds humor and characterization so it doesn't become a lecture. By contrasting the characters of Miles and Jack, we understand more about each character. We may identify with Jack, who knows little about wine. We laugh at the very specific, even snobbish, Miles while also learning something about wine tasting.

In *Sideways,* we need to know certain information about where we are, and the world of the story. Some of this information comes across through images — the images of the freeway that runs between San Diego and the wine country, the images of the vineyards and the tasting rooms and the spit bucket and the wine labels.

Some of this comes through the dialogue. When Miles is late to pick up Jack, Jack says "We were supposed to be a hundred miles away by now." The distance, from Paso Robles to the Santa Ynez Valley is then defined as about a hundred miles away (p. 6). As they travel north, Miles informs Jack, "the ocean's just right over that ridge" (p. 23).

He then gives more contextual information about why this region is known for pinot noir.

```
                  MILES
    See, the reason this region's
    great for Pinot is that the cold air off
    the Pacific flows in at night through
    these transverse valleys and cools down
    the berries. Pinot's a very thin-skinned grape
    and doesn't like heat or humidity."
```

The various places that provide the context for the Santa Ynez Valley are defined, shown, and sometimes discussed. The Hitching Post is less than a mile from the motel. They're near Solvang, the golf course, the Los Olivos Café, and the ostrich farm.

Dialogue Can Be Comedic

Most of the humor from *Sideways* comes from the various character traits, particularly from the characters of Miles, Jack, and Stephanie. Miles, a bit of a wine snob, won't date anyone who drinks merlot. As he arrives for their date with Maya and Stephanie, Miles announces, "If anyone orders Merlot, I'm leaving" (p. 52).

Jack tries to taste wine and chew gum at the same time. When Miles asks if he's chewing gum, the generally clueless Jack answers, "Want some?" (p. 28).

Stephanie's flirtatious ways adds humor. She over-fills their glasses of wine, which is against the rules of the tasting rooms, but she doesn't care. When Jack says, "You're a bad, bad girl, Stephanie," she lets him know just how bad she can be, "I know. I might need to be spanked" (p. 48).

We get more humorous character details when the husband comes home, to find his waitress wife has also been a naughty girl. In the dialogue, we get the impression that this is a game they play to enliven their sex life.

```
                      CAMMI
        I'm a bad girl. I'm a bad girl….
        I liked it when you caught me fucking
        him. (p. 124)
```

Much of the humor comes from the contrast between Miles and Jack. While Miles can wax eloquent about the properties of wine — "And how long in oak?" — Jack replies, "Yeah, oak. That's a good wood" (p. 42-43). When Miles criticizes a glass of wine for being "quaffable but far from transcendent" (p. 47), the most that Jack can say is, "I like it. Tastes great. Oaky" (p. 47).

Humor is also used to soften the moments of compromise. We see Jack juggling his relationship with Christine and Stephanie and Miles with an amusing, frenetic energy. He moves from his relationship with Stephanie, who he says is "nasty" (p. 74) and "jammin'" (p. 51), but later decides she's become "clingy" (p. 88). He tells Christine, often, that he loves her, even though he's happy when she's not in and he "lucked out — got voice mail. Everything's cool" (p. 77).

There's humor and comedy from almost every character, except for Maya. She remains the warm, straight, non-humorous although light-hearted character that deepens the film.

The Dialogue of One Character
Can Represent Audience Members

Some dialogue is used to connect the audience with certain characters in the film. If the audience doesn't know about wine, they can identify with Jack, who's in the same situation they are. By moving with Jack through his journey of finding out about wine, they also learn about wine. If they know a great deal about wine, they can identify with Miles, perhaps even reflecting on how they, too, can become a bit too snobbish and erudite about wine. Through these two characters, we too can move from being an outsider to an insider.

We too can learn to swirl and oxygenate and check the color and smell. And for many of us, who had been drinking the more prosaic wines, we too can learn the vocabulary of wine tasting, and begin to drive the market for pinot noir.

Dialogue Advances the Story

Dialogue moves the story along by setting up action and then paying it off, thereby creating momentum through scene sequences. Jack suggests they get together with Stephanie and Maya for dinner, which they do. Later, Jack tells Miles that they'll have some fun and they do. Jack tells Miles not to drive away until everyone sees the crashed car, and he doesn't, and the family does see the car, mortified at the damage.

Dialogue Expresses Motivation

With this situation about the background, we also understand the motivation of the characters — why are these two guys going to the wine country? Because Miles had been wanting to take Jack to the wine country for some time: "You know how long I've been begging to take you on the wine tour. I was beginning to think it was never going to happen." says Miles (p. 8). Why does Jack want to get laid? Because it's his last week of freedom and

"I am going to get laid before I settle down on Saturday" (p. 41). Why does Maya walk away from Miles when she finds out that he lied to her? "I just spent three years trying to extricate myself from a relationship that turned out to be full of deception. And I've been doing just fine" (p. 100).

Dialogue Reveals Character Backstory and Biographical Information

Dialogue reveals character, telling us what we need to know in order to understand each character. Throughout, various people fawn over Jack for his acting achievements (even though minimal.) Phyllis says: "A famous actor bringing me flowers on my birthday. Don't I feel special? You were wonderful on that show. I never understood why they had to give you that brain tumor so soon. Why that didn't make you the biggest movie star in the world is a sin" (p. 14).

Cammi is impressed when she hears this attractive man in her restaurant is "Doctor Derek Sommersby? You mean from "One Life to Live?"... "No way!" (p. 117).

Even Maya is impressed when she discovers he's an actor who can do voice overs about low APR financing. "That's hilarious. You sound just like one of those guys" (p. 37). And Jack responds, "I am one of those guys."

Many of the characters are also impressed with Miles and his novel, cheering him on and applauding him. Jack says he knows "it's going to happen this time. I can feel it. This is the one. I'm proud of you, man. You're the smartest guy I know" (p. 7). Maya says "That's fantastic. Congratulations" (p. 36), believing Jack's lie that Miles novel will finally be published. Even the bartender knows about the novel, saying "we all want to read it" (p. 31).

Dialogue Reveals What the Character Knows, and Doesn't Know

Dialogue reveals character through the character's vocabulary, and through its originality. Miles is smart. He has a very rich vocabulary, undoubtedly formed by his love of books, his love of writing, his love of teaching. This vocabulary is also very specific about how he talks about wine.

Jack is not knowledgeable about this world so he has dialogue that shows his lack of knowledge of the intricacies and nuances and shading of wine-talk. His dialogue reveals his character by contrasting his knowledge with Miles' knowledge. When Miles explains about wine, Jack is at a loss. He knows little about wine, so his dialogue is vague and generalized, ranging from "I like it. Tastes great" (p. 47) to "Tastes good to me" (p. 48), although after a day with Stephanie, he's learned to say, "still a little sour but already showing potential for great structure" (p. 81).

But when Jack talks about golf, we see he knows something about the game and his dialogue is specific. He tells Miles, "Don't whiff it" (p. 89) and "Don't come over the top. Stay still... It's all about stillness, Miles" (p. 90-91).

Since Jack is driven by his sexual desire, much of his vocabulary shows this orientation. Women are "chicks." The best ones are "hot." Jack tells Miles that Maya "digs" him. Jack's vocabulary rarely goes beyond the vague, such as "she likes you," but is shaded through the metaphors, the implications.

Jack also is someone who knows, or has read, New Age books and is able to talk basic New Age philosophy (provided it doesn't get too complex). Here, we can also get a sense about the point-of-view of the writers about New Age stuff. They use it to define Jack's character, while also subtly making fun of it.

```
                    JACK
Look, Miles. I know you're my friend and
you care about me. And I know you
disapprove. I respect that. But there
are some things I have to do that you
don't understand. You understand wine and
literature and movies, but you don't
understand my plight. And that's okay. (p. 118)
```

Dialogue Reveals Subtext

Subtext is dialogue that tells us what people are really talking about, as opposed to the text which may be quite the opposite. If you ask your spouse what's wrong, and s/he says "nothing," even though the frown on the face says that something is terribly wrong, the "nothing" implies the truth under the text, or the subtext.

In *Sideways*, there is little subtext because everyone is very direct with each other. Miles lets Jack know what he thinks about his plans. Jack lets Miles know what he thinks about his depression. Stephanie and Maya let both men know what they think about their deception. Everyone is straight with each other. They generally say what they mean. Even when Jack says he loves Christine, it's not subtext. Jack does love Christine, in his own way.

The true subtext in *Sideways* exists as metaphor.

Dialogue Can Be Metaphoric

Some of the dialogue is metaphoric. It evokes images and expresses the theme that tell us more than just the text, but implies underlying feelings and perceptions. This is best seen in a type of aria between Miles and Maya, as they sit on the back porch and talk about wine.

Maya asks, "Why are you so into Pinot?"

And Miles responds with a monologue about pinot noir.

```
                         MILES
I don't know. It's a hard grape to grow. As
you know, It's thin-skinned, temperamental,
ripens early. It's not a survivor like
cabernet that can grow anywhere and thrive even
when neglected. Pinot needs constant
care and attention and in fact can only grow
in specific little tucked-away corners of the
world. And only the most patient and
nurturing growers can do it really, can tap
into Pinot's most fragile, delicate qualities.
Only when someone has taken the time to truly
understand its potential can Pinot be coaxed
into its fullest expression. And when that
happens, its flavors are the most haunting and
brilliant and subtle and thrilling and ancient
on the planet. (p. 69)
```

Miles sets up a simile between himself and pinot noir. Miles thinks he's just talking about the pinot noir grape, but he's telling the audience a great deal about himself. He's revealing something about the essence of his character. He's not prosaic like a cabernet. Like pinot, he's sensitive. It's a delicate wine and needs to be nurtured, much like Miles needs to be nurtured. There's depth to it, much like Miles would like to think he, too, has a depth that takes a special person to tap into his special qualities.

Maya then responds with her own aria, her own metaphor of wine, and of herself.

```
                         MAYA
I do like to think about the life
of wine, how it's a living thing.
I like to think about what was going on
the year that grapes were growing, how the
sun was shining that summer or if it
rained… what the weather was like. I
think about all those people who tended
and picked the grapes, and if it's an old
wine, how many of them must be dead by
```

```
now. I love how wine continues to evolve,
how every time I open a bottle it's going
to taste different than if I had opened it
on any other day. Because a bottle of
wine is actually alive — it's constantly
evolving and gaining complexity. That
is, until it peaks — like your '61 — and
begins its steady, inevitable decline.
And it tastes so fucking good. (p. 70)
```

Maya is like the life of wine — with passion and life and beauty. When Maya talks about her love of wine, it seems as if she's talking about wine, but she's really talking about her love of life, her sense of people, her desire for Miles. Like wine, Maya is constantly evolving and growing and gaining complexity. And like her speech about wine, Maya thinks about other people, and their complexity, and how things can be good, if only one reaches for the good things in life.

Metaphors reveal character by implying how a character is similar to the subject of the conversation, which in this case is about the qualities of wine. Before *Sideways*, I had never noticed this kind of dialogue in film, although I had noticed it in Shakespeare's plays, when he sets up a raging storm, as in *King Lear*, to show that there is a storm inside of Lear as well. The *Sideways* writers are particularly skilled at this type of dialogue. When Miles and Maya sit on the patio and discuss wine, their text is clear as they describe the qualities of wine. But underneath the text, is a reinforcing subtext that is also a metaphor about who they are.

It's very possible that neither of them realizes they're talking about themselves, and yet the dialogue reveals much more about them than if they had simply said, "I'm a complex guy. There's a lot there, if you care to dig for it!" Or, if Maya had said, "I really like life and that's why I like wine." By using the metaphor, the scene becomes a kind of duet, with each of them singing their piece in counterpoint. Although we expect that the aria could end with a romantic kiss and bed, it moves to an awkward kiss and a good-bye because of Miles' insecurity and uncertainties.

A TOAST TO *SIDEWAYS*

Perhaps others imbibed, as we did for the Academy Awards of 2005, drinking pinot noir while watching the awards show and giving a special toast to *Sideways* —a character-driven film with less than heroic characters, who nevertheless entertained us, taught us something about wines and getting on with life, increased the number of tourists traveling to the beautiful Santa Ynez Valley, and taught us that a script needn't have a big budget, with stars, with much action and complexity, in order to be recognized and awarded and embraced.

CREATIVE THINKING AND STUDY GUIDE TO *SIDEWAYS*

(1) In your writing, have you ever had to research a location? If so, how did you do it? Did you use it specifically in your story, referring to specific streets, or buildings, or monuments? Or did you use it to inform your imagination? What are the advantages, and disadvantages, of both approaches? What do you learn about the Santa Ynez Valley as a result of watching the film *Sideways?*

(2) Why do you think the Santa Ynez Valley became a tourist location? What were the elements in the film that made people want to visit this area? Is there a location you would like to write about, that you would hope would become a tourist destination? If so, why? What kind of story would you write that would naturally take place in that location?

(3) Why do you think that Jack and Miles are friends? Do you have a friend who has contrasting qualities to you, in the same way that Miles and Jack are contrasts? What holds your friendship together? What threatens to tear it apart? What kind of story would you write about you and your friend?

(4) How was wine used as a prop in *Sideways*? Can you think of a prop that you could use in your stories that would be similar to the use of wine in *Sideways*? Write a piece of metaphoric dialogue, similar to Miles' speech about pinot noir, that would both describe your "prop," and also describe a character.

(5) What did you think about the scene where Miles steals money from his mother? Did you think it belonged? Or could be cut? Or needed further integration? Did the scene pay off in the script? Why, or why not? If not, how would you pay it off? Write the scene.

(6) Look at any of the conflict scenes in *Sideways,* such as the scene where Maya is angry at Miles and leaves, or the scene where Jack asks Miles to get his wallet from the waitress' home, or the scene when Stephanie is enraged about Jack's actions. What did these conflicts reveal about these characters? Are there other times in the story where there could have been conflict? If so, what kind of scene could there be? Write it.

(7) What was the particular dialogue that Miles used to introduce Jack to the world of wine? Look at some of those scenes again. Notice the words that Jack uses (that were obviously learned from Stephanie) when he began to learn the vocabulary. What words did Jack use to show his lack of knowledge? Is there a certain subject matter that you know a great deal about, and that a friend or acquaintance of yours knows little about it? Write a scene where you would be using the specific dialogue that is common to that subject, and where another character would be grasping at words because of a lack of knowledge.

(8) Look at the structure of *Sideways.* Study the structure of catalyst, turning points, and climax. How did this structure keep the story from simply being about two guys hanging out? How did it serve to add momentum, advance the story, and give direction to

such a simple story? Can you think of other structures that would have worked for this story, either by making up a new story about two guys in the wine country, or by looking for implied turning points that could be strengthened and placed in a different location of the story to create different Acts One, Two, or Three? (e.g., if Jack broke his nose at the 1st Turning Point, how would that change the story? If Miles slept with Maya on the first date, how would that change the story and structure?)

(9) What words would you use to describe Stephanie, Maya, Miles, and Jack? Are there implied characteristics that you expect to be true, knowing what you already know about them? For instance, what kind of relationship do you think Miles has with his sister? How do you think that Jack met Christine? What kind of relationship do you think Stephanie has with most of the men in her life? What do you think Maya's first marriage was like, and how difficult do you think it was for her to get her life together?

(10) What did you learn about wine from this film? What did you learn about the Santa Ynez Valley from this film? What did you learn about life from this film?

CONVERSATION
WITH NOVELIST REX PICKETT,
CO-WRITER AND DIRECTOR ALEXANDER
PAYNE, AND CO-WRITER JIM TAYLOR

A CONVERSATION WITH REX PICKET,
AUTHOR OF THE NOVEL *SIDEWAYS*

The Beginning of the Idea

I got the idea for *Sideways* during a trip I took up to the Santa
Ynez Valley wine country with my friend, Roy Gittens. We
caroused and shambled from tasting room to tasting room
and I guess I was cracking him up with stories about two guys
who go wine tasting and get into increasingly more mischief.
He then said that I should write it as a screenplay. I did, but
it didn't work. It so didn't work I didn't even show it to my
agent. Then I was writing a short story centered around my
experiences at wine tastings at a small wine shop here in Santa
Monica called Epicurus. When I got to the end of the story
I suddenly had an epiphany and thought: This could be the
opening to *Sideways*. Not only was it prose, but it was also
written in the first person singular and there was something
about the voice of Miles — that had no place in the screenplay,
of course, because all screenplays are by their very nature,
third person — that pulled me in and jump-started the novel.

But the idea really got its unwitting inception around 1990 when
I started sojourning to the Santa Ynez Valley to play golf. At
the time I was going through an amicable divorce, my writing career — what it was — was spiraling downward into
oblivion and I needed to get away. I would stay at the budget

Windmill Inn in Buellton, amble over to the then-blissfully uncrowded Hitching Post, sit at the bar, sip Pinots, stagger back to the motel, play golf in the morning, and head home to my dreary life as a washed-up indie filmmaker and screenwriter. It was a cheap, and wonderful, vacation locale, and I always wondered why more people didn't come up, why it was so relatively unknown.

Before *Sideways,* I had written another novel, a mystery called *La Purisima,* that got me a literary agent. We tried, but we couldn't sell it. So, in desperation, I wrote *Sideways,* which has blatantly personal echoes of that guy who couldn't sell his novel. My literary agent, Jess Taylor, decided to come out to L.A. to be a book-to-film agent at the Endeavor Agency. That turned out to be a lucky stroke for me. He loved *Sideways* and we decided to go out to both the publishing world and the film world in a kind of unprecedented two-pronged attack. Initially, the book was titled *Two Guys on Wine,* but Jess thought that that sounded too much like a nonfiction travelogue and he got me to change it. *Sideways* came quickly, as I love one word titles when they're appropriate.

Most people think of me as a novelist because of *Sideways,* but in truth I was an independent filmmaker — with two features to my credit — and a screenwriter. I'd written spec scripts, written for hire — was one of the last, uncredited writers on *Alien III* (although what I wrote was never used) — and wrote a short film that won the Academy Award for best live action short in 2000. I turned to novels as a way to distinguish myself from the hordes writing screenplays and because I also found it eminently more satisfying as a form, compared to screenplays which, by their nature, are adumbrations of novels and precursors to movies, but rarely literature in their own right. That said, a great screenplay is just as hard to write as a great novel.

The publishing world loathed *Sideways* and my new publishing agent pulled it and asked me to rewrite it. The Hollywood world also turned up their noses at it. That was in the winter of 1999.

Submitting the Story

One of the many film submissions involved my agent Jess Taylor walking it down the hall to Alexander Payne's agent, David Lonner, and pitching it to him. This was just before the release of *Election* and there was some mounting heat on Payne as a writer/director of note to be reckoned with, but he was by no means a big fish, as it were. Lonner told Jess that they were looking for bigger things for Alexander but that he would pass it along to him as a courtesy. Well, it took Payne nine months to read the manuscript of *Sideways* and in that very, very long interim, Jess grew disenchanted with the business and one day just up and walked away from it. That day was a veritable nadir in my life.

Actually, Alexander, to clarify things a bit, read *Sideways* on the recommendation of his young assistant, a guy named Brian Beery. Beery's one of the names, along with Jess's, that has sadly gotten lost in the avaricious clamor for credit on who did what since the film has grown so ridiculously successful. Beery loved it and gave it a ringing endorsement to Payne, and without that endorsement, and given all the material Payne was inundated with, I really wondered if he would have ever read it.

Meanwhile, I was agent-less, destitute, and about ready to walk away from the business. I didn't have the desire or energy to rewrite *Sideways* for another ostensibly humiliating round of rejections from the publishing industry, and for all practical purposes, now that Jess had left the business, it was dead in Hollywood.

So, nine months after all the submissions had failed to yield anything I got two back-to-back calls out of the blue from my new agent at Endeavor, Brian Lipson, and Michael London, who had been shopping the book around for "no fee" to no avail. The next morning Alexander Payne called and said a lot of exultant things about the book. After a meeting in which Alexander expressed his desire to make it below the radar screen in Super-16 for a no-budget, he eventually optioned the material.

The Film Rights Are Sold

After Payne optioned the material in 1999/2000, Artisan Entertainment greenlit it as a $10 million dollar movie. Galvanized by that excitement, my publishing agent went out with the manuscript a second time and, despite the front page news about Artisan and Payne in both *Variety* and *Hollywood Reporter*, the publishing industry still turned a cold shoulder. The consensus of their pejorative was that the manuscript was basically nothing more than an over-sexed screenplay. The manuscript was pulled again, and again I was implored to rewrite it.

Sometime in the spring of 2000, Payne decided that *About Schmidt* would be his next film, owing to a concatenation of circumstances: finished script, Jack Nicholson's interest in playing Schmidt, and some other factors. Payne continued to renew the option on *Sideways*, which was always a nail-biting moment because you never know when your project's been put on the back burner if the bloom is going to be off the rose. But the novel now was in a purgatorial state of being both unpublished and one of several projects a now very hot writer/director had on his plate. Although, in all fairness, I think Alexander always had a weak spot in his heart for *Sideways* because of his initial excitement when he read it — and the wine angle.

Writing and Rewriting

After Alexander finished *About Schmidt* he returned his attention to *Sideways*. This was around the winter of 2003. I had already decided to rewrite the novel per my agent's request. As I neared the end of the rewrite, I decided to switch publishing agents, and this turned out to be a good move. So, prior to there being a film deal — Alexander had gotten out of the contract with Artisan — St. Martin's Press stepped up and purchased *Sideways* for an advance of $5,000. I was disappointed at the time to learn that it would be coming out as a trade paperback and not a hardback, but I was relieved that it had finally been sold in advance of there being a movie and that the publishing date would be six months before the release of the movie. It's not true, as has often been misreported, that the novel was published because it was going to be a movie. When St. Martin's bought it they only had the knowledge that Payne held an option on the book and not that it was a *fait accompli* that it was going to be a movie someday.

When Alexander and Jim started working on the script in the winter of '03 they had access to all the drafts of the novel. They generously gave the first draft — and all the subsequent drafts — of the script to a select few people, including me. I annotated the script, offered suggestions, even dared to throw in some new dialogue. They didn't use any of my dialogue suggestions, but they did pay attention to some of the small factual corrections. For example, Maya's (Virginia Madsen) speech on wine was not in the first two drafts and my notes indicate that I thought it might be a good idea to give her a complementary speech to Miles's expatiation on the Pinot Noir grape. The speech that came was all Payne/Taylor, but it was a beautiful, lyrical addition to a script that changed very little from the first draft.

I did make some suggestions about the wineries represented in the movie, as some of them were out-of-date, or were in the process of being updated, in the novel. Alexander, unlike Jim, is very knowledgeable about wine, but he wasn't up to speed on the wines of the Santa Ynez Valley. I made a number of suggestions. He ran with them in pre-production, got to know the winemakers, became their friend, and really took on a course in Santa Ynez enology that ultimately far exceeded what I know. I made some dialogue suggestions, especially in terms of how people rhapsodize about wine, but in the end I had very little, if anything, to do with the final script, other than the salient fact that I wrote a novel which both of them have generously and self-effacingly admitted was one of their easiest adaptations as they plundered it liberally and faithfully and voraciously.

Changes for the Adaptation

In the novel, Miles lives in Santa Monica and is a failed screen-writer-cum-novelist whose first novel has garnered 39 rejection letters. Payne/Taylor relocated him to San Diego to get him away from the film industry — Alexander isn't fond of movies about Hollywood, viewing them as tautological or too close to what he does for a living — and by giving him a real job as an eighth-grade schoolteacher he mired him in a white-collar existence. In the book, Miles is more of a bohe-mian, dancing on the precipice, borrowing from anyone and everyone. I think Alexander relates more to regular guys in his movies and wanted to submerge Miles in the quicksand of a rather ordinary existence.

In the book, I had Maya show up unexpectedly at the wedding at the end, and she and Miles leave in a kind of mutual dis-dain for the whole wedding ritual. Payne/Taylor thought that ending "too Hollywood," and changed it to what it is in the movie. I like his change and wish I had had the courage to end my novel on a more despairing note, as my editor at St. Martin's exhorted me to do. In the end, sentimentality won out over bleak realism.

In the movie, the original ending did not have Miles return-ing to Buellton to knock on Maya's door. Maybe it was the fourth or fifth draft when they finally tacked that on. There was something unfinished about Miles just getting a message from Maya on his answering machine and listening to it — the original ending in the script — that was unsatisfying, that was neither fish nor fowl. So, in the end, they came a little closer — but not all the way — to that Hollywood ending of mine that they originally disparaged.

And in the book, Jack went to the hospital three times which was changed to one time.

It's funny. I took out a couple of scenes in the rewriting of the novel that then appeared in the early drafts of the script — remember, they had access to every draft of the novel — and I quickly overhauled the novel to reinstate them. Whew! I didn't want readers of the book to think that they weren't my source material.

Some of the major changes from book to screen include the omission of a big scene where Jack and Miles go out boar hunting with a psychotic young boar hunter who tries to scare them by firing shots at them. Alexander thought it was too big of a set-piece to shoot and didn't include it. Other changes were minimal: some abridgement, some moving around of the chronology, e.g. But it's amazingly faithful. For instance, a great deal of the dialogue in the movie is pulled straight from the book, which kind of floored me and flat-tered me at the same time. Additionally, the novel is written in first person, which means that I couldn't go where Jack goes without Miles. In the adaptation, Payne/Taylor had the license to do so, but they chose not to, remaining in the first person, as it were, without employing voice over. Furthermore, the chapter structure of the novel — "Saturday," "Sunday," etc. — is used in the movie with each day of the week before the wedding initiated by a title card with that day of the week. I thought that was pretty cool when I first read it; it was almost an homage to the novel as it were.

It's often said about adaptations that the screenwriters should read the source material three times and then throw it away and ignore it. There's both truth and utter stupidity in that adage. I do think that one has to be freed from the source material in order to adapt it, if only because an adaptation, by its own nature, willy-nilly must be an abridgement of the novel. In abridging it the screenwriters must have the liberty to not only truncate and lose scenes, but they must possess the freedom to write new scenes, hopefully in the tone of the author's voice, to bridge moments, amplify character and narrative motifs that may come across too subtly in the source material. Payne and Taylor really respected the source material in this instance, and with the exception of giving Sandra Oh's tertiary character an overloaded backstory — of which she was principally involved in creating — I have nothing but exultant things to say about their adaptation.

About the Characters

Miles is kind of a Hollywood lumpenproletariat, the lowest of the low subsisting on the penumbra of this moths-to-the-flame world. One of the first things that Alexander said to me when we met was that what he liked about the book so much was that the characters were so pathetic. (Later he would get me to change this recollection for an article I was writing, fearing perhaps that some might falsely misinterpret that he was unsympathetic to the characters.) For some reason I never saw them as pathetic, but then it was the life I was living circa 1998/1999 when the book was written and one never likes to see their own life as pathetic, which mine had probably unwittingly become.

Some people had a problem with how Jack and Miles could be friends, and the easy rebuttal to that is that opposites attract. The real Jack and I have very little in common, but I like his extroversion, his wanton ability to throw himself with abandon into any situation. There are a lot of men who would like to have this facility at times, especially when it comes to meeting women. Jack is an unreflective life force. He lives totally in the Now. Miles lives in the past (regret) and the future (the imagined bleak outcome of his life). Jack knows neither regret nor despair — for him the future is endlessly hopeful and the past is just that, the past. Despite analyses to the contrary, Jack is drawn to Miles' predilection for introspection and Miles is drawn to Jack's ability to function in the world and get what he thinks he wants. If the two could merge and take all of their best qualities in the merging the splicing would result in possibly a great man.

When I was 19 years old I took two quarters off from the university and read the entire Collected Works of C. G. Jung. Volume Six is titled *Psychological Types* and that one book has had a huge influence on me when it comes to creating character. I don't actively refer to it or even consciously think about it, but after the fact it strikes me how formative reading that, and all his books about mythology, alchemy, religion, etc. were for me in becoming a writer.

When Jack cries in the scene where he returns at dawn after having been chased out of the house with the married woman I really thought for one moment he was genuinely worried that he had totally lost control and that he was in fear of losing his fiancée and that this prospect struck him to some primal core of his being. Others see it as a pathetic, actorish attempt to enlist Miles in his sordid mission to retrieve his wallet and the lost wedding bands and they howl in the theatre at that moment, but the brilliance of the film is how that scene is such a two-sided moment, both this and that.

They definitely romanticized Maya in the film. In the book she's a terrific woman, but not so idealized as a romantic love interest. Although personally, maybe she was like the woman I dreamt about after my divorce. Someone simple, ostensibly uncomplicated, with whom I could fashion a more grounded life. But then that's not what I really want in the long run.

The Writing Process

For me character drives the story and the plot is incidental. When I write it's in my head, and when it's there and when I feel it, then I just go. And when I go, I go fast.

I work in the morning, break for lunch, then write in the afternoon. I like to leave the late afternoons for exercise and the evenings for other activities where my unconscious can work on whatever I'm writing without any pressure that I have to go into my little office and get it down on paper. Although when I get into rewrites I'll often wake in the middle of the night and have ideas I don't want to lose and I'll jot them down on a legal pad, then deal with it in the morning. I like Raymond Chandler's advice to an aspiring writer — I'm paraphrasing — "Take four hours every day and do nothing but write or think about what you're writing or going to write, but do nothing else in that four hours."

I don't care about plot. As a result I've never done outlines and when I hear the word "treatment" a fuse starts burning in

my head. I refuse to write treatments. A treatment or outline is imagining a movie and synopsizing it without having
ever written it. What kind of writing is that? A story doesn't
come alive and start to take shape until the characters actually speak, and in treatments and outlines they never speak.
Also, I want to be open to every moment along the journey
to detour, invent, go off the beaten path and see where that
will take me. I don't want a road map of where I'm going. If
I had one I wouldn't follow it anyway. Vivid, fully realized,
three-dimensional characters are the pillars of any good film
story, dialogue is the glue, and the story is only the body of
the vehicle, not the engine.

Some writers write every day, day in and day out. I don't. I like
to let characters and stories build up in me until I feel like
there's enough there to begin because I don't like to start
on a journey without some sense of where I'm headed and
whether I think it'll work or not. I once said to Alexander
— or maybe it was some interviewer somewhere — that I
write from the inside out and he writes from the outside in.
I don't think Alexander is interested in putting his personal
life on the screen as I did. Part of that stems from the fact
that he has a writing partner and it would be difficult to be
really personal in writing with someone else in the room. But
I think — at least in the case of *Sideways* — they're drawn
to the personal. But had it not had the comic thrust and
breakneck forward movement that I created I don't think
they would have been so drawn to the material. The truth
is, I start with what's going on inside me and I'm absolutely
fearless when it comes to self-effacement and self-depreca-
tion and the revealing of myself. I didn't always write like
this, but once I found this vein I mined it like for a forty-
niner with nothing but half a loaf of stale bread and dreams
of riches.

I usually begin with an ending. I like having an ending so that I know what my destination is. I have no idea how I'm going to get there — and I don't want to know! — but I like knowing when I'm going to stop. It's comforting. But I want the journey to be full of surprises to me, the writer. I want to enter into a story with a sense of childlike excitement and anticipation. And, of course, along the way, there'll be highs and lows and hopefully the lows will be excised and only the highs will remain. I want the journey to be about discovery, because writing fiction, whether as a novel or a film, is a miniature of life: birth, discovery, self-realization and development of ego-consciousness to its highest degree, and death.

Payne/Taylor have been called satirists and I guess they technically are. In their first two films they were satirists of the withering kind, brilliantly and mordantly skewering the *dramatis personae* with no prisoners taken. In *About Schmidt* they started to soften a little at the end of the movie and instead of Schmidt being just a totally hollow shell of a man, there is a moment where we sense that at least he's not unself-aware of this fact. And in that awareness there's a glimmer, however fractional, of hope. In *Sideways*, there's a major leap in their attitude toward their characters: they actually like all of them and though at times they may make them look foolish and bumbling, they find an inexorable emotional resonance in them, and that's what makes this film their most critically acclaimed: the ability to cross over into the emotional.

Drawing on Experience

Miles is clearly me circa 1993–1999 when I lived, and then wrote, the novel. The failed novelist, the guy rueful over a failed marriage, the wannabe writer who knew he was running on fumes. Jack is based — only character-wise — on a friend of mine. I drew from his speech patterns and his outsized approach to the world, but I changed all the bio-graphical details of his life. We're nearly total opposites, but we're friends. Maya was loosely based on a waitress who used to work at the Hitching Post. I didn't really know her except as that statuesque woman who served oak-grilled ostrich steaks in the dining room and occasionally would hang out at the bar after work to pound a couple of glasses of Pinot. I wanted to know her better, but it was never meant to be, so I got to know her in writing the novel, had my own literary affair as it were. Terra — Stephanie in the movie — was more a composite of some women I knew from New York, but no one in particular. Because she's with Jack almost all of the time and because the first person narrator couldn't go where Jack goes, she's a tertiary character and I didn't really spend a whole lot of time getting to know her.

When Miles steals from his mother in the novel there is a justi-fication — in Miles' mind — for the act: He's late on his rent. Period. A lot of people had problems with that moment in the script. Some wags even suggested that it's classic alcoholic behavior. It's funny, when you have a success you have to hear it all, even the idiotic prattling of para-critics. Anyway, I like the moment in the movie, even if it comes across as more pathetic in the novel — in the book, Mile's mother is affluent and he's stone broke whereas in the movie his mother is living a middle class existence and Miles has a job — because there's a music cue that starts, right after he takes the money and then looks longingly at some pictures of his past, for the first time that becomes a haunting and melancholy leitmotif throughout. At that moment I was drawn into the soul of Miles and the first time I saw the movie it was that moment when I realized that Alexander totally got what I was going for.

I knew all along that I was writing a very personal, vulnerable novel, about failure and despair and low self-esteem, but I thought to myself that if I write an introspective whiny novel no one is going to publish it and certainly no one is going to make a solipsistic film rendering of my life. I *had* to make it funny. I *had* to spice it up with comic set pieces. But, more to the point, my life was so miserable at the time, I was really writing the book to not only reflect what I was feeling, but also to entertain myself. I used to write and laugh out loud, write and laugh out loud some more, until my roommate probably thought I was a madman getting ready to go on a shooting spree. I got so lost inside the book because I so wanted to escape the quotidian destitution of my life. And, while I was writing, it worked. Unfortunately, all great escapes must come to an end and I suddenly had to go out to the world with my own little private world that I had created. And that's when things get tough. The pure joy of creation is usually vitiated by the skein of people you have to go through in order for it to become a published or filmed reality. It's a long, tortuous — and torturous — process and by the end there's often little joy when the battle has ended and the dust has finally settled. Only in my case I was left alone on the battlefield, victorious, expiated, vindicated for the life I had led and the people I had burdened to achieve what I tried to achieve. It was more than a Pyrrhic victory, I guess, but just rewards, I thought, for all the suffering I endured during that time.

Finding Success

The success of *Sideways* was a huge, satisfying vindication for me for all my years plying my trade as a writer and meeting with only minimal success. And I think the critical success of *Sideways* was way more important to me than its commercial success. Someone pointed out to me that we won over 350 critics' and other organizations' awards. To this day, it gets the highest score of new releases on one of my favorite websites, *Metacritic.com*. That means a lot to me, to be recognized by people who take film seriously as an art form.

Ultimately it's better to write and create in anonymity, when there are no expectations on you, no watching eyes, no pressure to repeat a success. It's crippling in some ways. Not to compare myself with J. D. Salinger in any way, shape or form, but I totally understand why the guy walked away from it and disappeared from the public eye. The adulation can be intoxicating and it's fun and rewarding to be recognized and to be revealed as the guy who wrote all this funny stuff that entertained people but at the end of the day success does not the next novel or screenplay write.

ALEXANDER PAYNE/JIM TAYLOR INTERVIEW

The First Response

ALEXANDER: I remember I was on a flight from London to Los Angeles after showing *Election* at the Edinburgh Film Festival in August of 1999. *Sideways* was one of the manuscripts I brought with me to read on the trip, although I didn't get to it until my flight home. Just halfway through the book during that flight I knew that I would make it into a film. It's rare that I get excited about something, or at least know immediately that I want to do it. Often with books or scripts that you maybe want to do, you are hooked by the beginning, but usually let down in the second half when it becomes formulaic. I like it when things remain human and not contrived. So often American films seem to begin with an interesting human set-up, but it's just a set-up to bring in the contrivance. *Sideways* remained human all the way through. I disagreed with some of the choices the writer had made, but in general, I thought it was something really worth doing. If

I were to describe the story it would be just those pathetic guys and those girls and the wine.

JIM: Alexander gave me the novel and I agreed with him. But we had to do *About Schmidt* first, so this was a real nail biter for Rex Pickett. It meant a lot to Rex, the progress of this to production and it got put off a long time. But Alexander lived up to his promise. He said this would be his next film, and it was.

ALEXANDER: We optioned the book from Rex because it didn't yet have a publisher. So the publishing deal and the movie deal were in conjunction. We've had that experience on two movies. Both *Election* and *Sideways* reached us when they were unpublished. And by unpublished I mean they didn't even have a publisher interested.

Those two books probably would have found publishers anyway, but I think the momentum of a concurrent film helped tip the scales a bit. And then the publishing house dovetailed the release of the book with the release of the film, so they could benefit from the publicity of the film for their book sales.

JIM: Rex was still working on the book when we were writing the screenplay. He edited it down a bit after Alexander optioned it and revised the ending. So it was interesting to be discussing the ending of the screenplay with Rex while he was still thinking through his ending for the novel. We definitely influenced each other.

The Writing Process

JIM: We start by reading the book, making notes, and talking about it. Eventually we put the book away and start writing. Once in a while, we'll say, "There's some good dialogue here, let's use it." With *Sideways* we did that more than on other adaptations we've worked on. We relied on the book more because Rex had such great dialogue we could use.

ALEXANDER: When we write together, Jim and I work in the same room. We go back and forth. We might both be on a computer, or one of us might be on it and the other thinking.

JIM: Sometimes we say, "Who's driving?" One of us will tackle a section while the other person is off thinking about something else or working on another problem in the script. And then we'll get together and rewrite. But we always work together so if one of us is getting frustrated they can turn to the other and say, "Can you help me out?"

ALEXANDER: Our creative urge in making the films is to capture life. Your duty in a way is to wrack your brain to tell a new story. And not just in terms of content, but equally important in terms of form. I'm thinking constantly about form. The challenge is to make every film in a form which I've never quite seen before. And that again speaks to my point of not planning because, in a way you can't plan. You stumble. You have to be open. Your number one duty is to be open. And disciplined enough to capture that. And then little by little you're seeing with your headlights, twelve feet in front of you, and eventually a film comes. And if you're lucky the film will be watchable. But at certain moments, when deciding a piece of content or a structural move to make, we'll ask, "What's more like life?" And our whole sense of what a story is, is not the movie version of what would happen, but what would really happen. How would this really happen in real life? And then you fashion a movie version of that. Little by little, day by day, the new film comes.

JIM: The ending, though, was a challenge. In the book, Maya comes to the wedding but that was hard for us to swallow. So we thought, "He's had this gut-wrenching time and there was this woman that he really was getting close to, and then it blew up in his face. What happens? Does he just sit there depressed, or does he maybe try one more time?"

Pre-Planning and Writing the Script

JIM: It usually takes about nine months for us to complete a first draft. Our partnership has been going on now for fifteen years. For the first two years we shared an apartment, but mostly I've been in New York so I'll have to go to L.A. or Alexander will have to come here since we always work in the same room together.

ALEXANDER: We don't work with an outline or treatment. We see no value in outlining at all. Because you're just filling in the blanks. I think that the whole emphasis on outline is one of the large reasons that American films are so bad. Because they're all about that plot. And you can sometimes plug in different people to fulfill that plot. So it's not really about the people any more. I mean I'm exaggerating to make a certain point about this, and it would be comforting to Jim and me if we could outline. If we knew what was going to happen next, it would be so delightful. But we experience no such comfort.

JIM: Different people work in different ways. We tend to try and be more intuitive, rather than doing a lot of pre-planning, which can be dangerous since we're writing without a net. If we do create an outline, it's very sketchy and without much detail. I've tried outlining in the past, but I found that it kills a lot of the inspiration that you would have in the moment. Sometimes we think we know what the ending is going to be when we start writing, but every time it's turned out differently than we thought it would. We try and just let the story grow.

Over the years, we've learned to write a little faster. Part of the reason for that has been because we've been hired on rewrite jobs where we have to work very quickly. In one case we wrote a complete draft of a script in four weeks. When we're doing a rewrite, we work six or seven days a week, usually starting about ten in the morning. We'll work for a few hours, have some lunch, usually a working lunch, and then keep working until we have a late dinner. So pretty much all we do is sleep and eat and work. Sometimes we'll do a "night shift", until three or four in the morning, and then start later the following day.

ALEXANDER: I think the day of writing should be as spontaneous and as exciting an act, or depressing, as a day of painting, or doing anything else you love. You just go and see how you feel and what's my idea for today.

Re the Characters

ALEXANDER: If you're dealing with the old debate between character and plot, it seems to be fifty-fifty, but really it's not fifty-fifty. It's more character, because the characters determine what the plot will be. It's what those specific people would do given those circumstances up to that point. By definition we would not know how to anticipate in advance what our characters would do as situations change. We have to get to that moment.

JIM: What I liked about the book was the voice, the flavor, a kind of comic humanism. We are drawn to people who are flawed, and sometimes border on pathetic. We feel affection for these people as opposed to looking down on them. Their flaws make them human, and can also make them funny. The comedy grows organically out of these kinds of characters in a way that makes our job easier.

ALEXANDER: Maybe looking back over our films one can see very real, flawed protagonists with vague yearnings for a better life, and maybe without the wherewithal to really achieve or understand what that better life would entail. I guess we find that very human and very funny. People who live somewhat with delusion, as all people do. Human beings live off delusion. In fact that's the thing they most fight for. People live off artificial constructs. Joseph Campbell said that we all live for myths.

JIM: In the book Miles lived in L.A. and we moved him to San Diego. We were a little tired of seeing the film world in movies so we wanted to get away from that. We also felt we needed to give Miles a job and he seemed like the kind of guy who might be a teacher. Somebody who doesn't have a job in L.A. could be seen as pathetic, but it might also seem romantic. We gave him a job that has become a grind that he wants to escape from. Working as a middle school English teacher gave Miles another dimension.

Many people were really bothered by the fact that Miles steals money from his mother. It would have been easy to cut that, but we felt as though it's the first place where you see this truly pathetic side to Miles. He's stealing the money and at the same time he's looking at pictures of himself in happier times. It's an important moment to me, seeing his desperation. In the novel and in some drafts of the script, that thread of the story continues and he tries to return the money. If we had included the attempt to return the money, I think it would have made it easier for people to tolerate the earlier scene since I think what disturbs them is that there's no consequence to his actions.

Do the Characters Transform?

ALEXANDER: It isn't clear whether Miles transformed, but Jack doesn't change at all. Jack cries out of fear, not out of transformation. But I don't really know about change. Does anyone really change? Do I change? I don't know. Do I expect more from a literary character than I expect from myself? I don't know. But you do see toward the end of the film Miles growing a bit out of his paralysis and inertia from the mourning over his lost marriage. And beginning to have this sense that he could be open to the idea of loving again. There's a small thing that happens with him. But for him, it's a big thing. That for me is a transition. I don't know about a transformation. Who the hell is transformed?

JIM: I don't think they transform. I don't think that Jack wakes up. There's this tremendous sense of melancholy at the end of that movie that sort of sneaks up on you. These two close friends take different paths.

ALEXANDER: A lot of the movie is about lying. Everyone lies. And it's introduced at the beginning. Miles says there was bumper to bumper traffic the whole way. Jack is always lying. Jack calls up his wife to say, "I love you" before he goes out to fuck someone else. And Miles lies about not telling Maya about Jack's impending wedding. Well, Maya doesn't lie, but everyone else does.

JIM: Maya is a horticulture major so maybe the idea is that she's honest in the same way that nature is honest. I think that Virginia Madsen captured the character beautifully with the honesty and warmth and openness she brought to the role. But the movie is not really about moral issues. I think it's just inherent in people that they have some sense of guilt when they misbehave, or treat other people badly. But Jack is always going to be Jack and he's probably going to cheat on his wife and then not really understand the consequence of that. He's like a child. He needs Christine in an infantile way.

But I do think that Miles grows. Maybe not transforms, but grows. In the end, he drinks the wine that he was saving to share with his wife on their anniversary. He moves on, becomes unstuck, puts his past behind and takes some risks. And I think it's kind of beautiful that his rejected manuscript winds up being his bridge to Maya. She's got his manuscript sitting around her house and for some reason she doesn't want to throw it out. Miles decides to give it one more try and he writes her a letter. Then, because he wrote the letter she decides to read the book. And during the process of reading it, she forgives him a little bit.

As we were writing, we talked a lot about wine. Wine is integral to human history and there's something inherently profound about it. It seemed like we'd really be remiss if we didn't seriously explore it as a metaphor. We beefed up Miles' speech in the book, where he talks about pinot noir and then we thought, well, he has an aria so maybe Maya should have her own aria. It's interesting that many people comment on those two speeches and say "What beautiful writing!" Although I'm proud of those speeches, I also think it draws attention to the writing. And you don't really want people to be thinking about the beautiful writing when they're watching the film, you want them to be involved in the story.

The Directing Process

ALEXANDER: We both think like directors. A screenplay is nothing more than the written record of the conception of a film. We have to be thinking: "What is this film going to be? What is a film in general? And then what is this film in particular?" And again I'm exaggerating to make a point, but I think all screenwriters should think like directors. A film is a combination of the visual and the aural. It's an advantage to being both writer and director, although sometimes a writer/director can fall in love with his writing and has to make a nine-hour film out of it. Sometimes the director's side becomes self-indulgent, or the writer's side becomes self-indulgent and there's nobody to censure. It starts getting out of control. I do think that having a co-writer keeps each of us disciplined in terms of the screenplay. We are in constant search of economy. Economy of expression on the page, and later of course as I do my work as a director, and with Kevin Tent, my editor, economy of expression on the screen.

The last thing you should ever want is for people to say the film is too long, or the film is boring. Some people think *About Schmidt* is really boring. Or some people think *Sideways* takes too long to get started. I wanted *Sideways* to feel looser than my other films. That's the direction I've been trying to grow as a director. I think the first three that Jim and I wrote, I did a competent job of directing them. But in *Sideways* I wanted it really to feel lifelike. The script was 140 pages. But I didn't want a 140-page movie. So they all had to talk fast and over one another. Also, you had to believe the friendship between these two disparate guys. Even the two guys cast are very different guys. Yet you had to believe that they've been friends for over twenty years. So that to me was the main challenge. It was keeping the pace going, having the kind of fast naturalism. And selling their friendship.

Making the Film

ALEXANDER: We did a lot of research. I spent a lot of time in the wine country. We started shooting in September of 2003 and Jane Stewart, the production designer and I had moved up there since June to begin preproduction which was basically figuring out where to shoot. That meant visiting all the wineries up there, and of course you have to taste everything, and choose which wines to put in the film.

For my wine education it wasn't just a matter of reading the wine magazines, going to wine stores, and going to tastings.

Now it was meeting winemakers, going out into the vineyards and into the barrel rooms, and seeing how it was made. That was my great education.

Editing the Film

ALEXANDER: You feel it in the editing whether you're going on too long. You just feel it. I show my work constantly. I love the preview process. Not that I want to respond to anyone's card, or what a studio exec has to say, but especially when you're making comedy you must constantly pay attention to that discourse between film and audience. That's how you learn what the film is.

The Rewards

JIM: We wrote the script on spec and Alexander and Michael London controlled the rights to the book so it was possible to stipulate that whoever financed the film would allow Alexander to cast it however he wanted. I don't think we would have been able to make this movie with the actors he cast otherwise. It had a radical impact on the careers of Thomas Haden Church and Virginia Madsen. And Paul Giamatti definitely became better known. I thought this story was very funny and that people would enjoy it, but I didn't think it would be the kind of film that would garner awards. So that was a very nice surprise. Did we think we'd win the Oscar? When we were nominated for *Election* we knew we wouldn't win, but this time, there was a lot of momentum and we thought we had a good shot at it, but you can never be sure. Choosing "the best" in each category is really to create drama so the show will be exciting to watch. For me (and I'm certainly not the first to say this) the nominations are the most meaningful part of the process. But winning sure is fun!

What's Next?

ALEXANDER: We are currently beginning our tenth screenplay. And we have a basic concept for it, but we don't know what the story is about at all. We have an idea, but we don't know the story. And yet we just decided to begin writing. This is an original screenplay. Of the four scripts I've directed, *Citizen Ruth* was original, *About Schmidt* was largely original even though it contains elements taken from the book. *Election* and *Sideways* were our only true adaptations. We rewrote, uncredited, *Meet the Parents* and received credit on *Jurassic Park 3,* and then we've done two other rewrite jobs, one of which is the upcoming Adam Sandler film, *I Now Pronounce You Chuck and Larry.* We also just finished working together on *The Lost Cause* which will be Jim's first directing job.

Story Beats for *Sideways*/The Film

The following are minute-by-minute beats that make up the story of *Sideways*. When analyzing a film, you may find it helpful to go to the movie theatre with a notebook and a small flashlight or a light-up pen. Of course, sit far away from others or they'll be annoyed by the sounds of pen scratching and little lights in the dark.

Act One/Set-Up

00 —   Knock on the door in the dark/CREDITS BEGIN – UNDER CREDITS

Door opens/WORKER asks MILES to move his car/Miles moves his car. Miles realizes he overslept.

SATURDAY: San Diego, CA

Miles slept till 10:50 am — packing — Calls JACK to tell him, "On my way" and says he's out the door "right this second."

Then takes a shower, flosses his teeth, goes to a café, gets an espresso, a *New York Times*, a spinach croissant, works on a crossword puzzle while driving. Goes through L.A.

3 min.   Miles arrives at Jack's place. CREDITS END — Miles says the freeway traffic was unbelievable (freeway traffic was moving well)

Set-Up (Jack & Fiancée Story)

Fiancée CHRISTINE asks Miles to check the cakes.

MRS. ERGANIAN asks Miles about his book.

Miles says nothing finalized — some interest.

6 min.   Miles says likes both cakes but prefers the "dark."

Set-Up (The Trip)

They leave, Jack says Miles is hung over. Miles asks Jack why he told his folks his book was being published/Miles says he stopped caring/they discuss book and how smart Miles is.

They open a bottle of a 1992 Byron champagne.

8 min.   They toast to a great week — 100% Pinot champagne — Miles explains about color in wine. They discuss the new ending — but there isn't a new ending.

They stop to say hello to Miles' mother.

10 min   At Oxnard, go for Mother's birthday, give her flowers and champagne and card. PHYLLIS (the mother) talks about Jack's acting career.

Establish (Jack's Background)

She mentions he was Derek Somersby on TV 11 years ago. They eat. She mentions about their brunch with Wendy, Ron and the twins. Miles goes to his mother's bedroom. Takes money from Ajax can.

Set-Up (Miles & Victoria)

14 min   Miles sees family photos and also of him and Victoria.

They discuss Jack's commercial for Spray n' Wash.

Phyllis asks when Miles will get married again and she suggests he get back together with Victoria.

Phyllis asks if Miles needs some money.

15 min   In the morning, *Sunday*, they sneak out, past the TV that's on, past Phyllis sleeping on sofa. At breakfast, Jack notices waitress.

Set-Up (Jack's Intention/Catalyst)

He states his intention — that Miles should get laid. Says Miles has been officially depressed for two years, mentions he's wasting away teaching eighth graders. Miles mentions he takes Xanax and Lexapro. Miles states his Intention — this week is about Jack. They'll drink wine, play golf, eat, enjoy the scenery.

Act One Development

17 min   Miles suggests they hit Sanford first, he talks about "varietals" — Miles comments on the scenery and on the Pinot grape.

Jack says he hopes Miles' novel sells.

20 min.   They go to Sanford. Miles explains about drinking wine and what to look for.

They head for Solvang, to Buellton to motel Windmill Inn.

Jack asks whether a mistake marrying Christine. Jack mentions his doubts about entering the property business. Still wants to act.

22 min.   Go to the Hitching Post. Sees GARY. Gary asks about his novel.

Introduces Jack, mentions he's getting married.

Set-Up (Miles & Maya)

They toast to Jack's last week of freedom. Jack notices MAYA.

Miles says she's married. Maya comes over to them.

Miles introduces Jack. Jack says, "She's into you, Miles."

Maya comes to the bar, orders a Highliner.

Miles asks her to join them. She asks about the book.

Miles says it's finished and Jack adds, it's getting published.

Jack criticizes Miles for not responding to Maya.

They return to the motel. Jack says "Chick digs you."

Jack clarifies she's not married. Miles goes to the bathroom again.

28 min.   On *Monday*, go to Solvang for breakfast, discuss the plan — they'll do the grape tour.

1st Turning Point

30 min.   Jack declares his Intent, he's going to get laid.

Miles is angry at Jack, he says it's "last chance/our week."

Montage, they drive past vineyards, showing sampling:

Use of two screens, then three screens, then three screens, then one screen, then two, three, four screens of harvest.

31 min. Miles discusses wine with POURER at Foxen Winery.

Set-Up (Jack & Stephanie)

They meet Stephanie; Miles says doesn't like Cab. Jack asks if she lives around here. Jack is interested. She knows Maya. They then move on to Syrah. She pours them a whole glass and he says she's a bad girl. She responds, "I need to be spanked" — Jack buys two cases, says they're all going out.

33 min. Jack tells Miles that Maya has been divorced for a year. They drive. Mention view and how he had a picnic here with Victoria. Says she had the best palette.

1st Turning Point (Miles & Victoria)

Jack tells Miles that Victoria is coming to wedding with her new husband. Miles is upset.

Miles angry, he wants to go home. Miles says he'll feel like a pariah at the wedding. Miles takes wine bottle to hill, he drinks by vineyard and by grapes.

37 min. They drive to the motel. There's a golf competition on TV. Jack to swim, Miles sleeps. Jack sprays feet. They get dressed/ wonder what to wear. Jack calls Christine.

To *Los Olivos*, to dinner. Jack mentions he's to say his novel is coming out in the fall. He tells Miles, "Don't sabotage me." Miles says if they drink Merlot he'll leave. Jack asks where's his Xanax.

1st Turning Point (Miles & Maya, Jack & Stephanie)

40 min. They go to the table. Women are drinking Sauvignon blanc with a hint of clove. They laugh. MONTAGE: They talk of wines, of Miles' book deal, they have more wine, more food, more wine and more wine.

Miles imagines himself on the phone. He leaves, goes to phone, the phone rings, he waits, Victoria answers, they talk about marriage, he's sarcastic and drunk, says decided not going to come to the wedding, she agrees. She hangs up.

47 min. Steph nods at Maya/they leave for bathroom. Jack complains about Miles and his ten-minute lecture on Vouvray, Miles is uncomfortable. Jack mentions his affairs with Brenda.

50 min. They go back to Stephanie's place. Jack gives Miles condom ("one for you, three for me"). Jack kisses Steph. Maya is in the back with the wines.

They look at Pinots and Syrahs, says they can open anything but a Richebord. They decide on an Andrew Murray. Miles says he doesn't have a collection but has a '61. Maya thinks it might have peaked. She says, "The day you open a '61, that's special." They open an '88. He likes it, she thinks a bit over and has no real resolution. She mentions Steph's kid, Siena, is at grandmother's. Neither Maya nor Miles have kids. They sit on sofa, Maya asks about his novel.

55 min.   He says it's called, "The Day After Yesterday" and Maya says "Today." Talks about his novel and the parallel narratives. She congratulates him, says she has a paper due, she's going for her M.A. in horticulture at the college in San Luis Obispo, maybe she'll work in winery. She wants to read his manuscript, and he mentions it's in the car. They hear Jack and Steph in background.

58 min.   They go out on porch. She asks why he's so into Pinot Noirs. He asks her why she's so into wine. She talks about the life and peak and decline of wine. She puts his hand on his.

Midpoint

60 min.   He changes the subject, asks where the bathroom is, he goes to bathroom, washes face, calls himself a "loser."

62 min.   He kisses her, she hugs him, they drive away in two cars. She says she had a nice time, says still wants to read his novel. He gives it her, it's in two boxes.

63 min.   *Tuesday*: Christine calls, Miles ignores it.

66 min.   Jack returns, says Steph is unbelievable, nasty. Steph is there on bike. Jack announces a change of plans, not golf, but says that Miles can use his clubs.

Miles tells him to check his messages and call Christine. Steph tells Miles to. They leave on Steph's bike. Miles is at loose ends. At hotel, has coffee, grades papers in pool, check messages — no messages, eats alone (2:25 pm). Plays golf, he's alone. He returns to the motel and finds Jack and Steph on bed. He goes to bar, and Jack comes to join him for a drink. Steph is upstairs.

70 min.   Miles asks what Jack is doing. He says he's putting the wedding on hold, Steph has opened his eyes.

71 min.   He says he's in love with Steph. He'll give up everything, they'll move, buy a vineyard. He plays video game with Siena, and Steph's mother is there with them at the bowling alley.

Miles buys a copy of *Barely Legal*, he sleeps, gets up/showers.

75 min.   He walks to the Hitching Post. He orders a bottle. He learns that Maya is not working today. He leaves, drunk.

76 min.   *Wednesday*: He and Jack play golf. Jack says that Maya really likes him. Jack coaches him at golf. Asks if he's heard anything from his agent. Suggests that he self-publish. Also says he can choose to be less hostile. Some other golfers hit into them, they hit back and chase them. Jack talks about Maya and uses metaphors about her.

80 min.   Steph calls — to Los Olivos garage with Maya, she had class last night — They all drive together and listen to speech on Pinot and leave. They have a picnic at sunset.

83 min.   At Steph's house, they call Jack, "Uncle Jack." He helps put Siena to bed. Miles and Maya leave and go to her house. They kiss.

Thursday morning: Maya drinks coffee. Miles in bed.

Maya mentions a Bordeaux tasting over the weekend and Miles mentions the rehearsal.

2nd Turning Point (Miles & Maya)

87 min.   Maya is angry and tells Miles what Jack is saying to Stephanie. She says she hates deception. He tells her there's been no one since his divorce and that he really likes her. She leaves.

2nd Turning Point (Off Screen/Jack & Stephanie)

Act Three

Miles comes back, Jack says he's proud of him. He asks for details but Miles won't give him details.

90 min.   Christine calls. Miles lies down in a fetal position — wants to go home. They go to Frass Canyon, a tourist winery. Miles doesn't like the wine.

2nd Turning Point (Novel Story)

> He asks to use Jack's phone, calls his agent, and learns that he's been turned down again.

93 min.   He returns, starts drinking, wants to fill his glass. When they won't, he drinks from spittoon. Jack takes him out of there and says his mother died.

96 min.   They talk of famous suicides. Miles uses metaphors that Jack thinks are very good.

Climax (Jack & Stephanie)

> They return to motel and Steph is waiting. She hits him and breaks his nose. She leaves.

> He calls Maya, apologizes, says he thinks she's great.

100 min. Miles takes Jack to the hospital. He calls Maya and tells her the truth about his book. Jack returns with a bandage, says he'll have to have an operation, but won't sue Steph to protect Christine. He keeps asking Miles how Stephanie knew.

> They return to motel and watch *Grapes of Wrath* on TV. Miles says his nose looks like a car accident.

101 min. Jack is hungry. He sees a waitress. Explains that he was Derek Somersby. She says "no way!"

103 min. He flirts with her, and Miles goes to the bathroom. Jack says he'll hang around until she gets out of work. Says Miles doesn't understand.

> Jack returns in the morning, freezing and naked. He says he needs a Vicodin. Says waitress is married and husband came home. He ran from Solvang. Jacks says they gotta go back, he left his wallet.

2nd Turning Point (Jack & Fiancée Story)

106 min. Jack says the wedding rings in wallet. They were a special order with dolphins and Sanskrit. Asks Miles to go back. Jack is desperate. He starts to cry. Pleads that Miles must help him. He can't lose Christine. He says he fucked up bad. They drive back to house, see the tow truck.

109 min. Jack says to Miles, "You go," says his ankle hurts.

Miles goes into house. The waitress is having sex with her husband and screaming, he calls her a "bad girl." Bush is on TV — Miles sees wallet, grabs it, he runs, man chases him, Miles drives, says got it.

They leave. Jack says he should invite Maya to the wedding. Jack wants to drive. Tells Miles to put on his seat belt. He drives the car into a tree, but damage isn't sufficient. They take out wine, use stone to accelerate car but it misses the tree. They drive home.

Climax (The Trip)

115 min.   At home, says goodbye to Jack. Explains that Miles was not hurt because wearing a seat belt.

Climax (Jack & Fiancée)

Saturday: The wedding ceremony/they exchange wedding rings.

Climax (Miles & Victoria Story)

119 min.   Miles watches, he sees Vicki and Ken, Victoria asks about book. He sees she's happy and also that she's pregnant.

120 min.   He drives away/goes upstairs to his apartment.

121 min.   Miles eats alone at a fast food place, has the bottle of '61 (in a Styrofoam cup) in diner.

At school, kids are reading from *A Separate Peace*.

Climax (Miles & Maya Story)

124 min.   Miles reads letter from Maya, she's finished the book and liked it.

125 min.   Miles goes upstairs/to see Maya.

part

2

SHAKESPEARE IN LOVE

FINDING THE CONNECTIONS

The genesis for *Shakespeare in Love* began with a phone call that Marc Norman received from his college-age son, Zack. Growing up, Marc's sons had learned to pitch ideas to their father, if for no other reason than to keep him writing and to keep food on the table. Zack pitched a one-liner: "Shakespeare just starting out in the Elizabethan theatre." Marc recognized the brilliance of the idea, but didn't know where to go with it for some time, until he began to look at the one thing that he and Shakespeare had in common: "We don't have genius in common, we don't have poetry in common, but we were professional writers... I mean, I know all about that" (Writers Guild of America *Journal*, p. 20).

Where to Begin/Find the Connections Within Yourself

In many cases, great writers begin with themselves. Something has to grab them. Something in their own experience has to resonate with the material. They need to feel as if the material is speaking to them, not just to some vague audience out there.

Writing teachers often say to writing students, "write what you know about." If one doesn't write out of experience, or at least out of a great deal of research that makes the material personal, the story and characters can seem inauthentic, contradictory, and superficial.

It wasn't obvious that a script about Shakespeare would be based on personal experience, but that's where Norman began — with his own personal connections with the material. He recognized that, like him, Will Shakespeare must have known the struggles of writing, the searching for the muse, the creative leaps that come suddenly, the writer's ability to hear a phrase in real life and build on it. Norman built into the script his own personal understandings of his own creative process, peppering his early drafts with moments of Will struggling with the process and giving all the excuses, justifications, and procrastinations that writers give for not getting to work. Writer Tom Stoppard further built on the ideas already in the script, and added many of his own. Together they were able to make Will's struggles, the struggle of every artist.

Connecting with the Audience through Creativity

Once writers find the connections within themselves, they can presume that at least some audience members will share those common ideas. The question becomes: "How universal is my idea? How many audience members will understand, even identify with, what matters to me?"

Shakespeare in Love is multi-layered. If an audience doesn't find a connection with one layer, chances are that another layer will connect with them. One of the first layers is the exploration of the writer's process, which is really an exploration of the creative process. All of us, at some time or another, have made something, drawn something, written something, or created something original. We've struggled to write the novel or maybe the annual Christmas letter. We've gone through the angst of making a painting, a sculpture, or, perhaps, a piece of pottery in our beginning pottery class. We might have tried our hand at composing some simple little piece of music, or been a professional musician composing the great symphony. We've decorated our houses, or designed the costumes for the school play. Life forces us to be creative. And writers, like Shakespeare, find that nothing seems to go smoothly when trying to complete the play, film, or novel.

By shading in the struggle with the creative process throughout the entire film, Norman and Stoppard created connections that could, on some level, touch almost every audience member.

The film moves back and forth between the creative process, and more specifically, the writer's process. And it makes Will more human, because he is just like us. Like Will, what we want to accomplish creatively doesn't come easily. Like Will, we need a Muse. We meet objections from those who want to make us ordinary. We try to inspire through our writing, but sometimes we lack our own inspiration. By tuning in to those universal struggles with creativity, the writers of *Shakespeare in Love* were able to make a film about somebody long ago, who seems so much greater than us, relevant to our own creative struggles.

Exploring the Creative Process

Creative ideas come to us, often half-baked, in little snippets, an idea here, a chance remark, a thought there, an idea in one context that makes us think of something else in another context, some little possibility to grab onto that comes seemingly out of nowhere.

The creative process constantly draws upon ideas from what the writer sees in real life or through discussions with others. Sometimes ideas come by brainstorming, stretching ourselves to think of unique solutions. Sometimes we get ideas by looking at other art and thinking how we might have done it. Sometimes an idea simmers for a long time before we see the shape of an idea.

The script of *Shakespeare in Love* is filled with these processes. Some of the references show how the creative process starts out in one place, and ends up in another. It builds on ideas, either ideas from our own experiences that are enhanced through the process of rewriting, or ideas that are stolen from somewhere else. Much of the humor in the film comes from the unique way that ideas wend their way into our creations. By playing on these ideas, the writers suggested the leaps by which Shakespeare's ideas could have been developed.

Will tells Henslow, the manager of the theatre, that he still owes him for the play of *One Gentleman of Verona*, a play that, of course, became *Two Gentlemen of Verona*.

As Will is walking down the street, he overhears a Puritan preacher, Makepeace, haranguing the townspeople, and asking God to smite the two theatres that breed lewdness and rebellion and idleness and wickedness: the Curtain, owned by the famous actor Richard Burbage, and Henslowe's theatre, the Rose. "I say, a plague on both their houses!" he says, and Will listens, finding it a useable line which soon is inserted into the finished play of *Romeo and Juliet,* referring to the two houses of the Capulets and Montagues (p. 8).

When Will goes to the Whitehall palace as Richard Burbage and his company are preparing for a performance of *Two Gentlemen of Verona*, comedian Will Kempe finds a skull in a prop box, and holds it up, a scene which does not go unnoticed by Will, who will use it several years later in his play, *Hamlet*.

Like many writers, Will has his own writing ritual, designed to spur on the Muse: the special mug by his desk, given to him by the folks at Stratford on Avon, the ritual that begins his writing, "he spins round once in a circle, rubs his hands together, spits on the floor. Then he sits down, picks up his pen, and stares in front of him" (p. 20).

Part of the creative process includes the search for the Muse, that creative presence that seems to sit next to writers when the work is flowing. Henslowe sees the best recourse to Will's moodiness would be to encourage him to write a new play. Will has written one scene for a new play, called *Romeo and Ethyl, the Pirate's Daughter.* It is a comedy, although Will admits a misbegotten comedy, but it seems to fit Henslowe's desires for a comedy: "Fluff, by-the-numbers, young lovers, a Sea Captain, a Bandit Chief, confusions of identity, a marriage at the end..." (p. 13). But the writing of the play doesn't go well.

Where is the play? "It's all locked safe in here," says Will, tapping his forehead. Like many writers, Will knows that the play is already written, he just has to get it down on paper. Of course, there are little problems — the story isn't worked out, he thinks it's a comedy and it becomes a tragedy, and the Muse doesn't seem to be around to help him. But no matter.

The search for the Muse is explored for much of Act One. Will has his psychoanalyst to help him — Dr. Moth — who is many things to many people: a mystic, an astrologer, a holder of numerous degrees hanging on his wall, a dispenser of pills and potions. Dr. Moth conducts his sessions with Will on the couch, and times his sessions with an hourglass — giving Will the full hour, rather than the fifty-minute hour of most modern therapists. Just like our therapists, Dr. Moth listens, and responds with the famous lines: "interesting... most interesting" (p. 10).

Will's troubles include far more than writer's block. Poor Will has lost his gift for words, and with his gift, his other problems have increased: a failed marriage, children whom he rarely sees, impotence with fat Phoebe and Rosaline and Aphrodite and Black Sue. To help him, Dr. Mother gives him a bangle. "Write your name on a paper and feed it in the snake." Then, "the woman who wears the snake will dream of you, and your gift will return. Words will flow like a river." And then the final command to all patients, "I will see you in a week" (p. 12).

Like many writers, Will is always writing, seemingly deeply into his next project, even though it's still locked in his brain. And, like many writers, the idea of writing is stronger and more wonderful than the writing itself, which is pure struggle for him. "Are you writing?" asks Burbage. "Yes he is. A comedy, all but done, a pirate comedy, wonderful" (p.14).

When Will feels a scene coming on, he runs to his room to write. And, when it comes, the writing is furious and fast, ending with the excitement of his own cleverness. "Scene One! By God, I'm good!" And yet, doubts come back. Spurned by the woman he thought was his muse, Rosaline, he throws all the pages into the fire. How easily all our work comes to nought.

Like many writers, Shakespeare discusses his play with many others. Not just Burbage and Henslowe, who ask about it, but with fellow writer, Christopher (Kit) Marlowe, whom he sees in a tavern. And like many writers, he builds on these discussions to figure out his play.

MARLOWE

I have a new one nearly done, and better. *The Massacre at Paris.*

WILL

Good title.

MARLOWE

And yours?

WILL

Romeo and Ethel the Pirate's Daughter
    (beat, sighs despondently)
Yes, I know.

MARLOWE

What is the story?

WILL

Well, there's a pirate...
    (confesses)
In truth, I have not written a word.

Like a good writer friend, Marlowe helps him out, encouraging Will's own creative process to get the juices flowing.

MARLOWE
Romeo is… Italian. Always in and out of love.

WILL
Yes, that's good. Until he meets…

MARLOWE
Ethel.

WILL
Do you think?

MARLOWE
The daughter of his enemy.

WILL
(thoughtfully)
The daughter of his enemy.

MARLOWE
His best friend is killed in a duel by Ethel's
brother or something. His name is Mercutio.

WILL
Mercutio… good name. (p. 29-30)

The writing process is part of a constant process of searching for and sometimes finding the Muse, and letting her inspire us. Norman and Stoppard express the relationship between our own contemporary understanding of art and the artistic process, and the process that Will must have gone through as a young man, starting in the Elizabethan theatre.

ADDING THE INSIDER JOKES

Shakespeare in Love abounds with insider jokes about the film industry, particularly the Hollywood film industry, with its profit motive, its manipulations, its competition. The play begins with Henslowe, "a businessman with a cash flow problem" (p. 1) who believes he can solve his money problems as well as escape the clutches of Fennyman to whom he owes money. His idea — to produce Will's new play, *Romeo and Ethel the Pirate's Daughter*, which Henslowe sees as a "can't miss" commercial success. Like modern day producers who believe that the presence of a star ("we got Russell Crowe", "Tom Cruise has committed!"), a good chase scene, and a few special effects makes a winning formula, Henslowe has the winning formula figured out for the Elizabethan theatre. It's a comedy, a crowd-pleaser, with all the elements of the most popular entertainments of the day: "mistaken identities, a shipwreck, a pirate king, a bit with a dog, and love triumphant" (p. 3). Henslowe believes all will work out. He just has to make sure that Will delivers on time.

The Insider Writer Jokes

In Los Angeles, everybody seems to be a writer, just as in the film of *Shakespeare in Love*. When the Boatman takes Will across the river, he reaches for his own manuscript and says:

```
                     BOATMAN
             (reaching under his seat)
     Strangely enough, I'm a bit of a writer myself…
```

As he produces the manuscript, he adds,

```
                     BOATMAN
     It wouldn't take you long to read it, I expect you
     know all the booksellers… (p. 67)
```

Like many Hollywood producers, Henslowe considers the writer the least important part of the film. When Fennyman asks about Will: "Who is that?", Henslowe answers "Nobody. The author" (p. 49-50). Then Alleyn asks of Fennyman, "Who are you?" Fennyman gives the answer that many self-important film investors give, "I am the money!" (p. 51).

In the Hollywood film industry, competition abounds, with continual discussions and arguments about who is better than whom, or who is considered "the flavor of the month" or the "writer of the year."The savvy writers of *Shakespeare in Love* draw on this conflict by showing how Will is often embarrassed and discouraged by the constant comparisons of his work and Marlowe's. Marlowe was known as the great writer of his age. And Fennyman's references to Marlowe continue to demoralize Will: "It was mighty writing. There is no one like Marlowe" (p. 53).

As for the profits, well, it's the old Hollywood formula: Promise the writer a good back-end deal where he'll get a share of the profits, knowing that in the entertainment business, after all the creative financing, "there's never any..." (p. 4). In the case of *Shakespeare in Love*, there are many costs to the producer which have to be refunded before the writer makes any money, costs such as the cushions to warm and soften the backsides of the groundlings.

And besides, writers are not supposed to think about the small things like money, but the big things such as writing the successful play. Henslowe asks Will, "What is money to you and me?" Of course, to producers, it's everything. To writers, well, they are supposed to be in it for love of the art.

The Insider Jokes about Producers

There are many stories in the film industry about the person with clout, whether writer, or actor, who elevates his or her staff to producer status. Although Henslowe had been producing at the Rose Theatre for a few years, Fennyman, as the money man, achieves producer status, as well as taking the part of an extra in *Romeo and Juliet*. This idea resonates with many of us in the film industry, who know about the proliferation of producer credits, which sometimes includes the names of lovers, friends, relatives, or simply the person who brought the script to the attention of the producer and demands a credit. Some of these unlikely people become very successful just as Fennyman and Henslowe do with the success of *Romeo and Juliet*. Barbra Streisand's hairstylist, Jon

Peters, was helped along the way by his relationship with her. He became the successful producer of over forty-one films, from *A Star Is Born* in 1976 to *Flashdance, The Color Purple*, and *Batman*. Like the producer, Wabash, who began his acting career with a small part, Peters began his film career in 1956 when he played an extra in *The Ten Commandments* — a boy on a donkey crossing the Red Sea. Like Wabash, the director Joel Schumacher began as a window dresser at a New York department store, and went on to become a costumer for Woody Allen and then the a big-time director of such hits as *Batman and Robin, Batman Forever,* and *The Client*.

There is a joke in Hollywood that everybody wants to be doing something different than what they're doing. Writers really want to direct. Actors really want to produce. And everybody wants to write the Academy Award–winning script.

Of course, sometimes there are those who are successful enough in Hollywood to demand the right to play other roles in the movie industry. Directors Alfred Hitchcock and Quentin Tarantino usually acted a part (often very small) in their own films. Actors Kevin Spacey, Mel Gibson, and Clint Eastwood direct. Actress Carrie Fisher became one of the most sought after re-writers in Hollywood. Actor Tom Hanks became a producer and director. Actor Robert Redford directed, and then decided to produce something even bigger than one picture and started the Sundance Film Festival.

Shakespeare in Love plays with this idea which the writers knew about, being Hollywood insiders, showing that if someone has enough money to invest in the play, or if favors are owed, he may be able to get a job in the show. When the stutterer, Wabash, tries out for a part, Henslowe immediately gives it to him. Will is outraged, until Henslowe explains the situation. "My tailor. Wants to be an actor. I have a few debts here and there" (p. 33). And like

Streisand's hairdresser, amazingly enough, Wabash turns out to be up to the part, and when the spotlight is on, and it's all up to him, he comes through like a true star.

The need to satisfy favors with a producing credit accounts for the long list of producing credits at the beginning of many films. For *Romeo and Juliet*, the credits are also myriad:

By permission of

MR. BURBAGE

A

HUGH FENNYMAN PRODUCTION

OF

MR. HENSLOWE'S PRESENTATION

OF

THE ADMIRAL'S MEN IN PERFORMANCE

OF

THE EXCELLENT AND LAMENTABLE TRAGEDY

OF

ROMEO AND JULIET

With Mr. Fennyman as the Apothecary

(p. 126)

The Insider Jokes about Actors

In an industry where actors count their lines and hope to be the one who gets the girl at the end and lives happily ever after, the worse fate is to have a role where the character gets killed off. Every actor knows that the lead actor gets to overcome all obstacles to live another day, and not be the one who is gotten rid of, whether in the beginning, middle, or end of the play. As the very successful actor, Ned Alleyn, prepares for his role, he's told by Will about the greatness of his role of Mercutio: "you have his duel, a skirmish of words and swords such as I have never written, nor anyone. He dies with such passion and poetry as you ever heard" (p. 62). Alleyn: "He dies?"

Will Kempe, the comedian, like many actors, wants to expand

his range. He asks Will to write him a tragedy. Like the romantic figure of Tom Cruise playing the villain in *Collateral,* Bill Murray playing drama (although unsuccessfully) in *The Razor's Edge* after his break-out role in *Ghostbusters,* the beautiful Nicole Kidman playing the depressed and unattractive Virginia Woolf in *The Hours,* and Sylvester Stallone deciding that he'd like to move from his first starring role in the porno film, *The Italian Stallion,* to the more serious work of *Rocky,* Kempe too wants to expand his talents. He wants to move beyond his usual comic roles, asking, "When will you write me a tragedy, Will? I could do it" (p. 13).

Like some actors who can only see the film in terms of their part in it, various characters who have a part in *Romeo and Ethel, the Pirate's Daughter,* define their role as the lead. For Ned, the play is about Mercutio, a conclusion that Will reinforces to keep Ned in the role. For Ralph, who plays the Nurse, it's about the Nurse. For Fennyman, the apothecary, who has an important cameo appearance, Fennyman sees it as so important that the billing for the play announces "With Mr. Fennyman as the apothecary" (p. 126). And like every actor who wants to be at is his best, Fennyman begins thinking about the costume, "I have a blue velvet cap which will do well, I have seen an apothecary with a cap just so" (p. 114).

And like the man on the street in Los Angeles, who often recognizes an actor but can't place him, or who defines himself by who he saw once, the Boatman is also fascinated by actors. When he sees Will, he says:

```
                BOATMAN
    I know your face? Are you an actor?

                WILL
            (oh God, here we go again)
    Yes.

                BOATMAN
    Yes, I've seen you in something. That one about a
    king.
```

```
                        WILL
      Really?

                        BOATMAN
      I had that Christopher Marlowe in my boat once. (p.
      36-37)
```

Playing with Clichés:

The writers of *Shakespeare in Love* play with the many clichés of plays and films. "Follow that car" has been used in myriads of mystery and action movies. When Will gets into the boat to pursue Thomas Kent, he says "Follow that boat" (p. 36).

Sometimes there simply is a play on words that have become a cliché:

```
                        HENSLOWE
      The show must...you know...
                        WILL
      Go on. (p. 134)
```

In Norman's early drafts, he rephrases the famous quote from *Sunset Boulevard,* which is "everyone thinks the actors make up the words as they go along" and instead says "everyone thinks the actors make up the words as they walk about" (p. 8).

The writers reference their knowledge of the film and theatre business: "The natural condition is one of insurmountable obstacles on the road to imminent disaster." And how does it usually end? "Strangely enough, it all turns out well," says Henslowe. "How?" asks Fennyman. Henslowe has the answer: "I don't know, it's a mystery" (p. 23).

In writing such as *Shakespeare in Love*, the writer is not writing clichés, but using them for humor and sometimes for insight. The writer is having fun with words and the ways that words have been set up in our mind, but can be twisted to create new resonances. And, of course, the writer knows what is a cliché, and what is not.

I have worked on innumerable scripts where the character scores a point and yells out, "Yes!" Or where the dating montage ends with the characters walking into the sunset on the beach. In these cases, the writer doesn't recognize a cliché and believes that this is original work. But when the writer has a good understanding of the stereotypes in stories, they can convert them into something fresh and original by coming at them from a different perspective. This is, of course, highly creative work, and means that the writer understands that part of the creative process is simply having fun finding new combinations of old ideas. Like a kaleidoscope, the creative writer's mind is always re-shaping, refracting, and finding new ways to use what is found in everyday life.

WRITING, AND REWRITING, THE SCRIPTS

I must admit to some bias when I began to explore the evolution of *Shakespeare in Love*. I was familiar with Tom Stoppard's name. I had seen his play, *Rosencrantz and Guildenstern Are Dead* many years ago, perhaps at the Cleveland Playhouse or on stage at another very reputable and skilled theatre company. I knew that many times a writer has a creative concept that is rendered into a good script, but then gets rewritten by a more experienced writer with greater abilities. Since I was not familiar with Marc Norman's name, I presumed this was true in the case of *Shakespeare in Love*.

I was surprised to read an early draft of *Shakespeare in Love* and find it to be an astonishing work of great creativity and skill. I soon learned that Norman had written several produced works. Among his many film credits, he adapted *Killer Elite* for Sam Peckinpah and worked on the original *Oklahoma Crude* with Stanley Kramer. Yet the greatness of this work comes from the combined talents of two highly skilled writers. How did this come about, and where did the story begin?

Norman's early drafts tell a similar story to the final *Shakespeare in Love*, although with some clear differences. Norman's second draft tells this story: Henslowe, the owner of The Rose, owes Fennyman money and comes up with the idea of presenting a play, written by a playwright who he can guarantee can create one within two weeks — William Shakespeare. Will is working on a play called *Romeo and Juliet*, which is a comedy, but very little has been written. As Will and Henslowe discuss the matter, they go to Whitehall Palace where Will's play, *Two Gentlemen of Verona,* is being performed. There he observes the beautiful Belinda, (later named Viola), Wessex, Belinda's brother, Edgar, and the Queen. He notices that Belinda knows all the lines of his play. She notices Will, the playwright. Wessex notices Will watching Belinda and doesn't like it one bit. Wessex tries to pick a sword fight with Will, but the Queen forbids swordplay. If they don't stop, they'll be arrested.

Henslowe talks Will into writing a comedy for him, "fluff, by-the-numbers, young lovers, a Sea Captain, a Bandit Chief, confusions of identity, a marriage at the end..." (p. 13). Will agrees to the partnership which will save Henslowe's theatre.

When he begins auditions for *Romeo and Juliet*, various actors read from his work but he can't find a Romeo. They finally look for their Romeo at a children's theatre company, where he sees Thomas. Although Thomas only has a small role in the play, Will realizes he has found his Romeo. During auditions, Will reads the part of Juliet with Thomas as Romeo. When the script calls for them to kiss, after a moment of hesitation, they do, and Will is astonished by his feelings about the kiss. He believes he might be gay, and struggles with this idea.

When rehearsals begin, Thomas begins to suggest changes in the script to make it more real, including having the two young lovers go to bed immediately. Although suggestions from an actor would be considered an insult to a playwright, since Will is enamored of Thomas, he decides that sex on stage won't do (after some consideration), but listens to Thomas' desire for him to make the love more real between Romeo and Juliet. Thomas and Will practice their kissing scene, and Will finally admits that he loves Thomas. He then realizes that Thomas is Belinda, when the moustache comes off and the wig is removed, which puts his identity at ease.

During Act Two, Will goes to Whitehall disguised as a friar to see Belinda. He finds her, goes to her chamber, and accuses her of betrayal since their theatre could be shut down if anyone knew there was a woman performing on stage. Belinda unexpectedly takes off all her clothes, and Will and Belinda make passionate love all day, into the night with the Nurse guarding the door.

Rehearsals continue, and during Act Two they stroll about as two men, and later stroll about as two women, talking to women about what women want.

She tells him that she is to marry in September and he tells her that she's his muse.

Will and Belinda, meanwhile, continue to make love in all kinds of spaces. Will hides Belinda in his wardrobe when they're interrupted.

As the wedding between Wessex and Belinda nears, she doesn't want to marry him, but Wessex has the power to close the playhouse. Belinda finally agrees that she'll marry him, if he won't close down the play. She also agrees to be in the play, once, playing the part of Romeo. Will realizes that the soul of love is tragedy, not comedy, and reworks the play. But when Sam (Juliet) sees that he dies at the end, and that this is no longer a comedy, he quits the production. Thomas returns, and Will and Belinda agree: Belinda will play Juliet, and Will, Romeo.

During Act Three, the play is performed, brilliantly and success-fully. As Will and Belinda kiss backstage, Wessex sees them, Will draws his sword, and just as Will is getting the better of the fight, the Queen stops them. Belinda is told that she must leave with Wessex, and a voice over informs us that The Curtain became the foremost theatre for the next fifteen years, with another voice over at the end that tells us about William Shakespeare's later years, retired, wealthy, home with his wife and daughters, dab-bling in real estate and roses.

Clearly, the basic story beats were already present by the second draft of Norman's script.

As the script continued to develop there were important changes.

In the early drafts, the gender issue was one about homosexual-ity — was Will's attraction to another man because Will's identity was truly homosexual? This question was kept alive for about 16 pages, approximately 15 minutes of screen time. In the final film, the issue was kept alive for two pages. In the film, Thomas kisses Will in the boat as they journey across the river. Will is clearly attracted to Thomas, and shocked by the kiss, but immediately afterwards, the boatman tells him that this is Lady Viola. Will immediately follows her and their love affair begins immediately.

In Norman's first draft, there is an ongoing throughline about a reunion that is to take place between those in the theatre from Stratford who have moved to London. Will wants little to do with it. The throughline is a reminder of Will's background in Stratford. As the rewriting continued, the reunion was cut.

The early drafts of *Shakespeare in Love* use a voice over of Henslowe, who tells the story about Shakespeare and about his reversals of business fortunes and how he resolved them through Will's play. The use of the voice over gives more emphasis to Henslowe, since it becomes his story, as he tells Will's story. Stoppard removed the voice overs of Henslowe, thereby making the story more immediate, showing us the story as it was lived, rather than telling it through the point of view of a supporting character.

Other characters were introduced as the script was further developed. Webster, the street urchin, was added, based on the actual playwright, John Webster, who loved all things gory and violent. Christopher Marlowe is added, with his small subplot and the addition of the competition between two playwrights. Some characters were further defined, such as Wabash, who was given a stutter, and who becomes the narrator of the play of *Romeo and Juliet.*

The theatre competition between The Rose and The Curtain was further developed, adding the character of Burbage and his company, with his generous gesture at the 2nd turning point when he offers his theatre for the performance of *Romeo and Juliet.*

Throughout Act Two in the film, there are additional scenes, showing the intersection of the love story of Viola and Will with the love story and rehearsals of Romeo and Juliet. The scenes of one push the scenes of the other, adding shading. We see how the reality of love pushes the play's exploration of love. The play is able to show the true nature of love because Will and Viola are living it.

In the early drafts, Will's problem was not writer's block, but his desire for love. Will's need for a muse to write, and of Viola as the muse, was also further developed, showing that Viola was the muse for writing and the muse for love.

The film creates a humorous cut from the first scene with Henslowe talking about Will, as the playwright who will make him money which he can then pay to Fennyman, to a scene of Will supposedly working, although in reality, only practicing his signature. In Norman's early draft, the humor is there, but with a different focus. Henslowe has promised that he will bring in "the finest playwright in the field. He's very fast, very cooperative... he will write and I will bring forth on these boards, I swear, a resounding success in, (swearing again), two weeks" (p. 3). Fennyman asks him, "who is this nine day's wonder?" (p. 4), and then we CUT TO Henslowe pounding on the door of a house where Will has been kicked out of his apartments by a very unhappy and irate landlord and his voluptuous housewife. We then see Henslowe looking all over London for Will — at the tavern where other playwrights are scribbling their newest work and turning to each other for inspiration, e.g., "What rhymes with 'castle'?" asks Playwright One; "Asshole" says Playwright Three (p. 4). But Will isn't there. Finally Henslowe finds him on London Bridge, but instead of turning to the subject of the first scene — Shakespeare's play — we learn that it's not writer's block which is the problem, but that Will can't find the soul of love. In the film, the cut is condensed and immediately leads us to Will, creating humor through the reversal of expectations. When Henslowe goes looking for Will, whom he believes is hard at work on a script, the scene then cuts to Will practicing his signature. The idea of finding the soul of love is kept in the film, but it isn't the driving motivation, it's a result of trying to write a play about love.

This change keeps the focus on the subject which is the major storyline of the script: creating a play. The process of writing *Romeo and Juliet* leads Will to understand the nature of love. Before, he was content to find a lusty muse for each of his plays. Unconsciously, he was looking for something deeper about love and truth. He just didn't know it.

Will is more introspective and angst-ridden about love in Norman's draft. In the film, he's more angst-ridden about his writer's block. In Norman's draft, he talks about seeking love "with widows" (p. 5), "vanity, shallowness." Henslowe thinks that Will is speaking about finding the right woman, but Will says "I was speaking of myself. I am love's fool... I put sluts on...". He recognizes that he is the problem. He doesn't even know where to look for love. Will says "I pretend to know about love... I could not tell you one thing about it, except it rhymes with 'dove'." (p. 10).

Many of the elements which were strengthened in later drafts are already embedded in the material in the second draft. On page two of Marc Norman's early draft, Fennyman says, "I went to the theatre once — I didn't like it." In the film, we see the remarkable transformation of Fennyman who moves from someone who sees the theatre as an investment which has some possibility of bringing him the money owed to him by Henslowe, to a man who becomes entranced and enamored by the magic of theatre. This is the start of Fennyman's transformational arc, which is further strengthened in the film when Fennyman gets the part of the apothecary in the play, and becomes a star, at least in his own eyes.

Norman's draft contrasts a number of different ideas about theatre: the preacher Makepeace considers it a "rebellion of morality," a "wicked theatre of corruption" (p. 6). Henslowe sees theatre as a business opportunity and as entertainment for the masses, provided, of course, that there is a dog in the play. Viola sees it as truth-telling, as moving, with beauty, to the very heart of life itself. Will sees it, at the beginning, as the expression of his muse and later as a place for truth-telling. Ned sees it as an expression of his talents, and a way to show off his talents. Burbage sees it as the place for his competition to shine, provided they have good material, preferably a play by Marlowe or Shakespeare. Wessex doesn't like it much. Queen Elizabeth recognizes that the plays are made for her. These ideas, which are all introduced in Norman's script, become further sharpened as the development process continued.

In Norman's draft, Richard Rowley is the leader of Lord Pembroke's Men, a prosperous theatre company that performs for the Queen. In the film, Burbage is the leader of The Curtain theatre, which seems to get all the advantages (p. 7).

In Norman's draft, Will is a less savory character. He has had sex with the wife of Rowley, as well as with widows and whores and countesses. He says "I put sluts on pedestals, degrade honest women. I kiss the candle and blow out the girl..." (p. 5).

In Norman's draft, Belinda is twenty-five and has a brother, Edgar, who is described as an "overdressed boob" (p. 8) and is a friend of Wessex. Edgar desires what Wessex desires — that Belinda will marry Wessex. Wessex, in the Norman draft, is a far more dangerous man. He "found his first wife in bed with a lover... one sword did the work of two" (p. 12).

In Norman's draft, Wessex fights Will with a real sword on the street, challenging him for having looked at Belinda. In the film, Wessex doesn't realize, for some time, that Will is the person who has been cuckolding him with Viola, and when there is a sword fight it isn't with Wessex but on the stage with fake swords between the players of Henslowe's company and Burbage's company since Burbage is angry that Will didn't give him the play.

There's the addition of other characters in Norman's draft, who were then cut. John and James were actors who are willing to do anything for a role, even getting money in order to bear false witness at a trial and pretend to be wounded. When Will offers them a role, they strip off the bandages from their fake wounds and join his company.

More time is spent auditioning for the play in Norman's draft, with actors reading from *Romeo and Juliet*. In the film, the role of Marlowe as Will's competition was added, and actors read from Marlowe's *Dr. Faustus* for their audition. The scene in the film builds and gains humor through the Rule of Threes — three actors read from Marlowe, from the same scene, until Thomas Kent comes on the scene and reads from *Two Gentlemen of Verona*, Will's previous play.

As in many scripts, the title keeps changing, depending on what actor he has to talk into playing the part. In Norman's early drafts, the title is already *Romeo and Juliet*. Stoppard played with the title, first by choosing a title for Will's play that obviously just won't do: *Romeo and Ethyl, the Pirate's Daughter*. The title is discussed several more times, as Will chooses a title, according to whomever he wants to produce or act in his play. Will knows that many actors only think of their own parts, and consider themselves the center of the universe. To keep them in the play, he tells Burbage (the producer) the title is simply *Romeo*. For Ned, who he wants to play Mercutio, the title is *Mercutio*. Will is not above spinning the information to get the result he wants.

STRUCTURING THE STORY

Each of these insider jokes, insights into the creative process, and clichés, add layers to the story. *Shakespeare in Love* is further layered by the intricate connections between its plot and subplots. We can break down the structure of the film by looking separately at the "A" story (the main storyline) about the creation of the play and the various subplots which further dimensionalize the story.

In the case of *Shakespeare in Love*, there are two issues that are part of the overall idea of theatre. On the one hand, the film is about William Shakespeare writing his very famous, breakthrough play, *Romeo and Juliet*. The basic storyline for this is that he is asked to write the play in Act One. He writes it in Act Two. And it's performed in Act Three.

But there is a larger issue that is part of the writing of the play — the nature of the theatre itself. Can theatre show the true nature of life and love? The play of *Romeo and Juliet* proves the larger issue, and sets up the possibility that great theatre does more than just entertain. It is implied in *Shakespeare in Love* that this will be then be true for all theatres (and therefore all films) after *Romeo and Juliet*. Although a case could be made that the Play Story and the Theatre Story are really the same story, by analyzing the structure of these two stories, we can see that they each, at times, have different structures.

The Play Story, which gives direction and urgency to the film, is the story of Will trying to finish the play so Henslowe can put on the show of *Romeo and Ethel, the Pirate's Daughter*. Will is having a dreadful time coming up with his story. The genre changes, the storyline changes, the characters go through changes.

The structure of this storyline is tight and strong. This plotline begins by setting up the problem immediately when we see that Henslowe doesn't have the completed play, and without the play, he doesn't have the money he owes Fennyman. If Henslowe doesn't come up with the money immediately, his feet will be burned in hot coals. But there's a problem. Will has writer's block and can't find his muse. Immediately, there's a conflict and a necessity. All of this occurs within the first five minutes of the film.

During the Development of Act One, Will is able to finish enough of the play to begin casting and Thomas Kent arrives, reading beautifully and clearly perfect for the role of Romeo. At the 1st Turning Point, at 32 minutes into the film, Will becomes inspired by Thomas, begins writing feverishly, and right after that, the play is cast. During Act Two, Will continues to write, and the actors continue to rehearse.

At the Midpoint, the play begins to take shape through a series of decisions about the play that further define it. Since the film is 117 minutes long, we would expect the Midpoint scene to be about 57-60 minutes into the film. At 58 minutes into the film, Will recognizes the true nature of the play he's writing — it's a tragedy and the lovers are fated to be apart. At the 2nd Turning Point, at 92 minutes into the film, the play is ready to go on but Viola has just been married and is ready to sail for Virginia. As she leaves her wedding, she sees the flyer for the play, escapes from the groom, and hurries to the theatre. Crowds arrive. Wabash prepares to go on stage, stuttering his lines until the moment he's on stage, and suddenly his voice is forceful, clear, and all is off to a good start. At the climax, at 107 minutes, the play is a great success, with all the appropriate and much-yearned for response from the audience — tears, stunned silence at the brilliance of what they've just seen, followed by great applause.

We can analyze the Theatre Story separately. In this analysis, we're looking for turning points which open up the idea of theatre to a new level. The set-up is essentially the same — Henslowe needs a play, and expects Will to give it to him, but Will is having trouble writing. But the issue here is bigger — the Queen, and Henslowe, want a play that is farcical. Like many writers, Will is trying to find the larger story: the truth. He is jostled about by the ideas of others, but can't find his own way. The 1st Turning Point of the play story could be seen as 33 minutes into the film, when Will delivers his pages and Henslowe reacts to the changes. Something different is beginning to happen here, and Henslowe isn't sure that he's pleased. At 63 minutes into the film, at the Midpoint of this storyline, a wager is made about whether a play can show us the truth and nature of love, which deepens the play, and clarifies, for Will and for us in the audience, what this play is really about.

A case could be made that the 2nd Turning Point occurs at 78 minutes when both Henslowe and Fennyman approve the new play, since it leaves open the question about whether the audience and the Queen will accept it. But there's a larger change in the nature of theatre later — at 97 minutes into the story, when the concept of theatre is changed again, as Viola makes her entrance as Juliet — clearly a real woman playing the part. And at 110 minutes into the film, the Queen announces that the play has set out to do what the Queen thought a play could never do — show the true nature of love.

By the end of the film, we know that Will has succeeded in all the plotlines related to the play. He has achieved what he set out to do — to create a successful play.

The structure of this play story, in shorthand, would look like this:

SET-UP: Henslowe needs a play. Will has writer's block. (1-8 minutes)

ACT ONE DEVELOPMENT: Will continues to try to write. He starts writing *Romeo and Rosaline* but destroys his draft. Casting begins. He auditions Thomas Kent. He's inspired by Viola and writes feverishly. (8 minutes to 29 minutes)

1st TURNING POINT: Will is inspired/begins writing. Right after, casting and rehearsals begin. (30 minutes)

MIDPOINT: Leading up to the Midpoint, *Romeo and Juliet* takes form, finds its genre. (58 minutes)

2nd TURNING POINT: The play is ready to go on. (92 minutes)

CLIMAX: The play is a success with the audience. (107 minutes)

The theatre story, in shorthand, would look like this:

SET-UP: Henslowe needs a play, but Will is having trouble finding his story.

1st TURNING POINT: Henslowe isn't sure about the pages that Will is turning in. (33 minutes)

MIDPOINT: A wager is made about whether a play can show the true nature of love. (63 minutes)

2nd TURNING POINT: Viola plays Juliet, clearly as a woman. The nature of the theatre is changed again.

CLIMAX: The Queen clarifies that the play has proved the true nature of love. (111 minutes)

RESOLUTION: Will starts writing the next play, keeping Viola alive in his imagination. (116-117 minutes)

Notice how tightly structured this "A" story is. In a well-structured script, we expect the Catalyst to be in the first 10 or 15 minutes of the film. It is. The 1st Turning Point is well placed. Usually a 1st Turning Point occurs about 25-35 minutes into a film. This one occurs at 30 minutes. The entire film is 117 minutes long. We expect the Midpoint scene to be around 60 minutes into the film — and it occurs shortly after that. Usually a 2nd Turning Point occurs somewhere around 85-95 minutes into the film. This one occurs at 92 minutes. Usually the Climax is about 3-5 minutes from the end of the film. Although the strongest Climax seems to be earlier than this — at 107 minutes, the Queen's declaration which clarifies that the play has achieved what it set out to do is about 6-7 minutes from the end.

The shorthand for the love story is:

SET-UP: Will sees Viola at the theatre, mouthing the words to his play, *Two Gentleman of Verona*. He's immediately attracted to her. (13 minutes)

1st TURNING POINT: Will discovers that Thomas is really Viola after they kiss. (45 minutes)

MIDPOINT: Viola must marry Wessex by order of the Queen. (59 minutes)

2nd TURNING POINT: Viola marries Wessex. (91 minutes)

CLIMAX: Viola must leave Will, a teary good-bye. (115 minutes)

In subplots, the Turning Points will vary, sometimes coming five or ten minutes after a turning point of the "A" story. In this storyline, which could be considered the "B" story, the structure is close to the structure of the "A" Story.

Generally, for a movie to work well, the "A" and "B" stories need to be very tightly structured. Smaller subplots can then have more leeway with their structure.

The structure of the actual play of *Romeo and Juliet* is not quite as close to the "A" and "B" story structure, but still has a clear set-up, turning points, and climax.

SET-UP: Rehearsal of scene when Romeo meets Juliet at the dance. (41 minutes).

1st TURNING POINT: Romeo is clearly in love with Juliet. They have their first kiss, and are clearly falling in love. (51 minutes)

ACT TWO: They fall in love and pursue their forbidden, secret love.

2nd TURNING POINT: Juliet is going to get married to someone else. Romeo must leave his beloved Juliet. (100 minutes)

CLIMAX: They both die. (103-104 minutes)

The story of *Shakespeare in Love* continues to layer its storylines with smaller subplots as well. There's the subplot about the competition between the two theatres, Henslowe's Rose Theatre and Burbage's more famous Curtain Theatre. The competition operates on two levels. On the one level, Burbage is simply more famous. We learn in Act One that his players perform for the Queen at court, that they have had a very successful run of *Two Gentlemen of Verona*, and that Henslowe hopes to match their success. But we learn that there is also competition for Will's newest play.

At the 1st Turning Point, Burbage pays Will for the play, as does Henslowe, and at the Midpoint, Burbage discovers that Henslowe is producing Will's play and is deeply into rehearsals. He's furious, and with his men, march upon the Rose Theatre and confront the other players, with swordfights and the throwing of props.

At the 2nd Turning Point, the Rose is closed by Tilney and they have no theatre for their play. But Burbage, in a great reversal, shows his generosity and offers his theatre to Henslowe and Will. In Act Three, the play is performed at the Curtain, not the Rose.

Structuring Small Subplots and Throughlines

By bringing in the conflict between the two theatres, *Shakespeare in Love* is also able to explore not just the play itself, performed in a theatre, but a deeper sense of theatre. For those of us who have worked in the theatre, performed in the theatre, perhaps written or directed theatre, we all know the magic that can happen when all is going well — the hushed audience, the spectacle, the wild applause. This comes across by showing a small subplot about the transformation of Fennyman, the man who has had little to do with theatre but has become a producer because he has the money. He watches rehearsals, and is curious, then watches, fascinated. Ah! The excitement of swordplay, the beauty of staged love, the tenderness of first love, and, when he gets a part, he pursues it with all the care and study and discipline of the best professionals. He plays it with the deep conviction that is part of the wonder of theatre, when theatre is not just about play or just about spectacle, but about truth.

The film continues to be layered with other subplots. Christopher Marlowe is considered the great playwright of his generation. He's introduced in Act One, first by mentioning his work, and then when Will meets him at the bar, Marlowe says he too is writing a new play.

At the 1st Turning Point, Wessex believes that there is another suitor to his betrothed, Viola. He asks Will (who's disguised as the chaperone of Viola) who he is. Without missing a beat, Will grabs at the first name that comes to mind — Kit Marlowe. At the 2nd Turning Point, Will learns that Kit has been killed in a tavern, and is deeply and profoundly shocked by this revelation. Will believes that Wessex killed Kit because of his lie about Kit. At the Climax of this small subplot, Will learns that he had nothing to do with Kit's murder, and Will is comforted.

There is a small subplot about the wager that Queen Elizabeth sets up, when she first meets Viola and wagers that a play cannot show the true nature of love. Will, as the chaperone Wilhemina, wagers 50 pounds, and Wessex is forced to match the amount. At the end of the story, Wessex loses and Will now has 50 pounds that can free him from being a contract player and become a partner at The Curtain Theatre. In the exploration of this wager, the play, indeed, shows the true nature of love which is part of the theme of the play.

There are several other subplots in *Shakespeare in Love*.

The Wessex and Viola Story is set-up when the father sets up the marriage (27 minutes).

At the 1st TURNING POINT, Wessex clarifies that they will wed (40 minutes) and it is clear that there is no way out.

At the MIDPOINT, the Queen inspects Viola. (62 minutes). She gives her approval.

At the 2nd TURNING POINT, they get married. (91 minutes)

At the CLIMAX, she must go with him to Virginia. Even the Queen cannot negate this marriage. (111minutes)

There are also some *throughlines* that move throughout the script.

The NED AND HIS PLAYERS THROUGHLINE is set-up when they come to the Rose Theatre and Will gives them a part, with Ned playing Mercutio. During the middle of the script they rehearse, and in the third act, they perform.

There are also a few story beats about Viola's parents who begin this small throughline by first telling her that she must get married, whether she wants to or not. They then leave for a short vacation and then the third beat of this small throughline shows them returning for her wedding to Essex.

PLAYING THE RELATIONSHIP OF SCENES

When constructing a script, a writer is not only thinking of the content of each individual scene, but of the relationships of one scene to another. The writer can use the cuts for humor or surprise, or the movement from scene to scene to advance the story quickly, or reveal insights by the relationship of one scene to another.

Playing the Cuts

Humor, surprise, and reversed expectations are often played out in a film by playing the cut from one scene to the next. Sometimes it's played by showing that what is said in one scene is contradicted in the next.

In the first scene, Henslowe tells Fennyman that he is sure that Will is completing the play, "at this very moment." In the next scene, we CUT TO Will's room, which has all the accoutrements of the writer — the favorite mug, the crumpled rejected writing tossed on the floor. The scene begins when we see Will studiously writing, expecting that he is doing exactly what Henslowe said he was doing — completing the play. But, upon closer inspection, Will is doing one of the many tasks that writers do when the muse is far away. In this case, he's practicing writing his signature.

Although many cuts reverse expectations immediately, such as in a horror film when a character says "the monster is gone" and everyone breathes a sigh of relief, and then immediately CUT TO the monster at the window, in this case, the expectation is kept for the first few seconds of the scene, and then reversed. We are pulled into the scene with one expectation — since it looks as if Shakespeare is writing, just as Henslowe said, and then the joke comes within seconds when we realize it's another writer's joke. Writers have the most enormously clever methods for avoiding work. And Will is no exception.

Relating the Scenes

Scenes never exist in themselves, but in relationship to each other. One scene might intercut another, perhaps contrasting with the scene, perhaps showing a relationship of two scenes. Or a scene might not be played out completely, but another contrasting scene intercuts, to advance the story quickly, to add urgency to the story, to deepen the story or to add the element of surprise. *Shakespeare in Love* moves back and forth with scenes that show the reality of life and true love, and the way that the reality is translated to the stage.

Much of Act Two shows Will and Viola as lovers, and then shows how their experiences push the writing, and rehearsing, of *Romeo and Juliet*. These scenes, together, create a shorthand that moves their story, and the writing of the play, forward quickly.

When Will first meets Viola, he sees her in the crowd. He moves closer, asking, "by all the stars in heaven, who is she?" (p. 42). As she begins to dance, they come closer, then farther apart. This scene pays off not in the next scene, but about twenty pages later when it forms the basis for the rehearsal of the dance scene in the play of *Romeo and Juliet*.

Later, when Will and Viola first make love, they are awakened by the sound of a bird.

```
                    WILL
    ...the morning rooster woke me.

                   VIOLA
    It was the owl. (p. 71)
```

This becomes the basis for the nightingale and lark scene which is rehearsed on page 116.

As Will starts to leave Viola's home, he sees her balcony, and Viola and Will begin their own balcony scene, which is then interrupted by the Nurse, just as it is in *Romeo and Juliet*. The true life balcony scene leads, immediately, to a scene of Will's room at dawn, where "his quill has already covered a dozen sheets. He is inspired" (p. 47). However, the actual rehearsal of the balcony scenes comes on page 78, almost thirty pages later with further rehearsal on pages 82-85.

Intercutting the Scenes

Some scenes form a montage of true life leading to a rehearsal of the play. These scenes are often next to each other, smoothly flowing one into another to show the passage of time and to reinforce the writing process:

Will begins writing, and then gives the manuscript to Viola who begins reading the line, first in her bedroom, then at the theatre:

```
INSERT MANUSCRIPT: 'But soft, what light through yonder
                    window breaks.
                    It is the east and Juliet is the sun."

VIOLA'S VOICE OVER speaks the line.

                    VIOLA (V.O. )
        But soft, what light through yonder window breaks?
        It is the east and Juliet is the sun."

                    VIOLA
                (reading)

        "Arise fair sun and kill the envious moon…

VIOLA is in bed reading the lines from the manuscript
page. WILL is in bed with her, reading with her.

                    VIOLA (CON'T)
        Oh, Will!

                    WILL
        Yes, some of it is unspeakable.

She has to speak through WILL's kisses, he is nibbling
```

at her neck and shoulders and she has to bat him away
with the pages.

> VIOLA
> (continuing reading)
> "It is my lady! O it is my love!
> O that she knew she were!"

THE ROSE THEATRE. STAGE. DAY.

VIOLA continues the speech, edge-to-edge, now in rehearsal,
with SAM as JULIET sighing on the balcony above her.

> VIOLA AS ROMEO
> "The brightness of her cheek would shame those
> stars…

The scene then continues CROSS CUT between the STAGE
and VIOLA'S bed (p. 79-80).

The scene continues to move back and forth, as Viola reads Will's
new lines in bed, and then they're rehearsed. Back to bed. Back
to the theatre. The scenes are a montage with dialogue. Will says
to Viola, in bed, "Stay but a little, I will come again." And Viola
"slaps him playfully for his vulgarity, and then kisses him" (p. 83).
This is followed by SAM AS JULIET saying the same lines.

And as the rehearsal continues, with the beautiful lines, in all seri-
ousness, suddenly SAM stops the action to voice his complaint:

> SAM
> I cannot move in this dress! And it makes me look
> like a pig! I have no neck in this pig dress!
> (p. 85)

In the middle of creation of some of the most beautiful lines ever
written, comic relief comes into the action. This takes courage
and a confident writer to know that the overall tone won't be
destroyed.

Intercutting through Parallel Journeys

Sometimes the script uses intercutting to show parallel journey storylines coming together to collide. Whereas the above scenes led one to another, and were all related to the writing of the play, sometimes scenes intercut to build tension and conflict.

Burbage has just discovered that Will has given his *Romeo and Juliet* play to Henslowe, even though Burbage had paid two sovereigns for it. He's angry about it, and leads his men, the Chamberlain's Men, to cleave a path through the crowds on the streets of London, ready to confront Will at The Rose Theatre. His journey — of going to the Rose Theatre, is intercut with the rehearsal of the fight scene of *Romeo and Juliet*, which continues, not knowing of the impending threat.

In the theatre, the fight scene between Romeo and Mercutio is being rehearsed.

NOL AS BENVOLIO

"By my head, here comes the Capulets"

Of course, it's not really the Capulets who are advancing, but Burbage's angry men.

Suddenly six more men and a dog invade the stage, ready to fight.

Burbage and the Chamberlain's Men have arrived to avenge Burbage's honor with swords, clubs, and a bucket (containing pig swill) (p. 98-99). And the fight begins, with Fennyman very happy to see such excitement. "Wonderful, wonderful!" Fennyman says. "And a dog!" (p. 100).

EXPLORING THE THEME

The theme is, of course, about Love. It's about finding love, about the true nature of love, about the obstacles to love, about love found and lost. The theme is reinforced by the Queen's wager, that a play cannot convey the true nature of love. This is further reinforced as Shakespeare learns about the true nature of love during his relationship with Viola, and also uses his play of *Romeo and Juliet* to explore the theme. At the end, the Queen clarifies that the theme has been proven through the beauty of the play.

Before Shakespeare, there had been poems about the nature of courtly love, such as *Sir Gawain and the Green Knight*. There had been plays about the struggles of love, such as the Greek plays about jealousy and betrayal (*Medea*) and about lust (*Hippolyta*). There were Roman comedies about mistaken identity and plays performed by traveling actors, who played the perky young lovers, Pierrette and Pierrot. But plays were not expected to tell the truth. Queen Elizabeth tells us that playwrights teach us nothing about love (p. 94). Love and truth are enemies. So a wager is made, whether Shakespeare can create a play to "show us the very truth and nature of love" (p. 95).

Will seems to know little about true love. Trapped in a marriage without love to a woman who lives far away, Will seeks his muse in lusty relationships with whores, whose passions he hopes will inspire him to write about love. He has bedded "Black Sue, Fat Phoebe, Rosaline, Burbage's seamstress, Aphrodite" (p. 10).

Before *Romeo and Juliet*, Will explored the subject of love in the light-hearted *Two Gentlemen of Verona,* and after *Romeo and Juliet* he explored the misunderstandings and the gained wisdom of love in *A Winter's Tale*, love, jealousy and betrayal in *Othello,* the passions of mature love in *Antony and Cleopatra*, the corruption and integrity of love in *Measure for Measure*. Here, in *Romeo and Juliet*, he is exploring young love, love that struggles against social barriers, love that can overcome revenge. When the play is finished, Queen Elizabeth says that he has, indeed, proven that plays can peer deeply into the nature and truth of love.

What does the play of *Romeo and Juliet* and the film of *Shakespeare in Love* tell us about the nature of love? How does this theme layer the film so that we in the audience, who have loved and lost, loved and found ourselves, recognize certain eternal truths?

The Course of True Love Never Did Run Smooth

Both the play of *Romeo and Juliet* and the film tell us that there are obstacles to love. The world, our society, our class, even ourselves conspire against us to be able to love truly and freely. In *Romeo and Juliet*, one's duty to satisfy parental goals runs against the lovers' own sense of duty to the soul. Romeo and Juliet can only express their true love for each other if they "deny their parentage" (p. 80). A Montague and a Capulet can never be in love — their two warring families forbid it. Will/Romeo says "a broad river divides my love — family, duty, fate" (p. 88).

Yet love, true love, "knows nothing of rank and riverbank" (p. 66). Great literature through the ages is often about love crossing the artificial barriers put up by culture, society, class, occupation, religion. The conflict occurs, not only because the barriers are strong, forceful, obstinate, but because our souls search for the truth while the obstacles ask us to deny ourselves. "Love denied blights the soul we owe to God" says Will as he explains that our soul demands that we follow that spark. It is a sin not to (p. 66).

And, as the play explores the nature of love, it finds another contradiction and struggle about love. Just as we sense the spirituality of love that embraces that which is true, and connects us to something larger than ourselves, we also know that there is that in love which can tempt us, limit us, and bring us down. In *Romeo and Juliet*, in the middle of great passion there is also a discussion of sin. To kiss, for them, is a sin — against parents, perhaps against God. Yet, it is sin that can be forgiven: "Thus from my lips, by thine, my sin be purged" (p. 74). While the soul expands between the Lover and the Beloved, to do this means that sometimes it crosses the social boundaries of class and parentage. Sometimes it crosses the boundaries of traditional morality. It raises the question of whether following our love is always right, or can be wrong. Does it lead us to that which is greatest within us, or that which is weakest within us?

Our authentic selves recognize that everything within us reaches for the Beloved. Our reality recognizes that everything outside ourselves can put up obstacles between the Lover and the Beloved, particularly if the Beloved is not considered an appropriate match. Yet, our hearts are willing to risk everything for love. "For one kiss, I would defy a thousand Wessexes" says Will (p. 67). Yet, even for a thousand kisses Viola can't defy her betrothed whom she doesn't love. Even Queen Elizabeth, with all her earthly powers, cannot remove the obstacles that separate Will and Viola.

There are other obstacles. Will cannot overcome his own marital situation. He is married to a woman he doesn't love, a partner in a forced marriage with a woman he had gotten pregnant. For Viola, her marriage to Wessex is forced because of Wessex' social need for her dowry, and the family's need to wed Viola to a man of a high social station.

Yet, in spite of all the obstacles, one cannot deny one's love — the beauty of the Beloved. Think about how many love poems and love songs describe the Beloved. From the Song of Solomon with the yearning for the Beloved, to I Corinthians in the Bible ("Love bears all things, believes all things") to Robert Burns' "my love is like a red-red rose" and Elizabeth Barrett Browning's love which loves to the "depth and breadth and height" or Amanda McBroom's song "The Rose" ("Some say love, is like a river").

There is no way to adequately describe the Beloved, except by similes with that which is the most beautiful, the most true, the highest that the soul can attain. What is love like? It is like opposites: "sickness and its cure together, like rain and sun, like cold and heat" (p. 65). It is the best and the worse, the harshest and yet the gentlest, that which we trust, and that which we mistrust.

Will speaks of the beauty of Viola's eyes, for he was "born to look in them and know myself" (p. 65). The beauty of lips for "The early morning rose would wither on the branch, if it could feel envy!". Her bosom, "as round and rare as golden apples!" (p. 66). She is more fair than the moon, her song deeper and softer than the lark or nightingale (p. 79). Her cheek, so soft, if only his glove could be upon that cheek. Will, like us, searches for the words, the exact words, to describe the beauty of the Beloved. Of course, his words usually hit the mark better than ours.

Promises of Love

Shakespeare in Love also explores the promises of love. What does love promise? To be true. To follow one's love wherever he may go. To be willing to go far from the home we love. To do what love asks of us.

Yet, what do we fear about love? That love is but a dream (p. 84), a brief candle, a sweet note that disappears. That love is not true. That the beloved will betray us. When Viola leaves Will after learning that he is married, she runs, desperate and in despair. Yet, she encounters deeper despair when she believes that he is dead, and when she finds him alive, her love is so deep and expansive that she feels "I never loved you til now" (p. 112).

The wager about love is not only about finding the true nature of love, but recognizing its mystery and its secrets. In its truest state, love expands the soul. Love engenders more love. "My bounty is infinite," says Juliet (p. 82).

When love asks us to be as expansive as our feelings of love, it asks that "If you love… you must do what she asks" (p. 64), even if that means saying goodbye. That which we love must be allowed to be free, to make choices, to acknowledge the reality of our world.

Part of this idea of love is a recognition that this love cannot be ruined, killed, or distorted. We carry within us the memory, the emotion, and the mark of that first love. "You will never age for me," says Will to Viola (p. 153). The great tragedy of love is the killing of love. The death of love may come from "never to have loved at all," for one's heart never to have expanded to embrace love. And the great tragedy of love is to have allowed, or been forced to, abandon one's love because of the rivers that divide in reality, although they never divide in love. "Never a story of more woe, than of Juliet and her Romeo" (p. 145). Never a story of more woe, than any love that has been compromised, abandoned, distorted, sabotaged, or limited.

Our understanding of the true nature of love can find a resonance in the multi-dimensional descriptions of love that we find in *Romeo and Juliet*. It can be both tender and harsh. Hot and cold. Sweet and bitter. Passionate and yet, when we feel betrayed, turns us to cold stone. It is the sweetest of all emotions, the most expansive, and yet sometimes the most limiting. It can be both death-defying and death-embracing. And yet, to compromise love, is to allow our souls to wither. We carry within us the spirit and recognition of that first love that will never age, and that, if allowed, blossoms within us to lead to other great loves.

Love, for Will, and often for us, also leads to creativity. It is a Muse. Will equates love, sex, and creativity, as he discusses the loss of his gift with his therapist, Dr. Moth: "It's as if my quill is broken. As if the organ of the imagination has dried up. As if the proud tower of my genius has collapsed" (p. 10). Will recognizes that many great works of art have been inspired, sparked, and blossom through the creative muse, which carries the spark of love.

The writers of *Shakespeare in Love* explore this rich theme through the love relationship of Will and Viola, through Will's play of *Romeo and Juliet,* by contrasting the love of Will and Viola with the lack of love between Viola and Wessex, and by showing both the comedy and tragedy of love.

Developing the Theme of Identity

One of the most dramatic, strongest themes in drama is the theme of identity. This is to be expected, since many of us ask ourselves two very important, basic questions: "Who am I?" "What is the meaning of life?"

In my book *Advanced Screenwriting,* I mention that most films have identity themes. The three films analyzed in this book are not exceptions and show how prevalent these themes are. Of course, one can find other themes to define these scripts. I prefer to start with the theme of identity (if it's part of the script) since it helps me tune in to what the script has to say about the human condition. Since drama is, in my opinion, the art form that best exemplifies the many aspects of humanity and best explores the human condition, a film usually looks closely at what it means to be human, and what are the problems and challenges and yearnings that we encounter in our journey through a story.

In many films, the theme revolves around a single protagonist who is challenged to either figure out, or affirm, his or her identity. In *American Beauty,* the protagonist faces a mid-life crisis and has to find his authentic self. In *Capote,* we see a man who is fascinated by evil, but has neither the moral nor spiritual resources to know how to deal with it without being sucked in by it. In *Brokeback Mountain,* we see two men desperate for intimacy, and yet who won't admit who they really are. In *Titanic,* the main character falls in love with someone who is clearly below her station, and yet her true identity emerges as a result.

Shakespeare had already played with the identity theme in his previous plays, often by playing with the idea of gender-bending — male actors playing female actors who disguise themselves as males. In *Two Gentleman of Verona*, Julia disguises herself as a male in order to move about freely and in order to follow her Beloved. In *Love's Labour's Lost*, the women disguise themselves with masks, and playfully toy with their suitors who confuse them with each other. In *The Comedy of Errors*, two sets of twins are continually confused with each other.

Shakespeare paired the theme of identity with the theme of love, often exploring the idea of who was supposed to marry whom. In a number of plays, he explored the rules of class, and even the rules of birth order as obstacles to marriage. In *The Taming of the Shrew*, beautiful and lovely Bianca is not allowed to marry until her shrewish older sister marries first. In *Love's Labour's Lost*, it is appropriate for the lovers to wait a year to marry, since their Prince has recently died and there needs to be a year of mourning.

All of these plays were preparation for Shakespeare's exploration of appropriate and non-appropriate love in *Romeo and Juliet*, and preparation for the over-riding theme of love and identity. Romeo finds true love with Juliet, after believing himself to be in love with Rosaline. Juliet, who has no wish to marry, suddenly in the midst of her passionate love for Romeo, insists that he marries her tomorrow.

Developing the Theme of Sexual Identity

Building on the themes of the plays of Shakespeare that came before *Romeo and Juliet*, the first writer, Marc Norman, updated the identity theme by exploring the idea of sexual identity. He plays with the idea of what it would mean for Will to be falling in love with Thomas, and not understand what that means to his own idea of his sexual identity, and his own idea of love.

In the early drafts, the exploration begins when Thomas does not do a good job when first auditioning for the part of Romeo. Will compassionately steps in, and reads the part of Juliet to Thomas' Romeo.

As they reach the cue for the kiss, both are hesitant and tense.

>   WILL
>   He kisses her here...

Both swallow. But there are lines left in the scene.

>   WILL
>   Then have my lips the sin that they have took.
>
>   THOMAS
>   Sin from my lips? O trespass sweetly
>   urged./ Give me my sin again...

They confront the cue again. They hesitate — their lips approach. It's not that one commits before the other, but both at the same moment. Their lips meet, linger — then part.

ANGLE AUDIENCE

A knowing glance from Fennyman... he knew all these theatre types were fruits.

ANGLE WILL AND THOMAS

Not breathing, regarding each other.

ANGLE GROUP HENSLOWE

He's been silent, but now he realizes Will's picked his Romeo. He begins to applaud loudly. Peter joins in.

ANGLE WILL AND THOMAS

Both still frozen. Will's voice cracks again.

```
                        WILL
        That  was  very  nice…

                        THOMAS
        Thank  you…
```

(p. 22 from script)

Notice the moment of gender bending here. Shakespeare is shocked and baffled by his response to Thomas. The kiss was — well — an experience that he both wanted to, and didn't want to, repeat. For the next sixteen pages, Norman explores what happens when one discovers that his (or her) sexual identity is different than expected. First, Will goes back to his room, but can't write. Instead of working on his play, he finds himself tracing out the word "Thomas" and then violently crossing it out. (This same idea is used in the film, although Will practices his own signature in the film, not writing Thomas' name.)

He ponders this: "Thomas. You wrote 'Thomas.' You wrote a boy's name…" (p. 24).

Later, Will then confesses to Henslowe that he's "contracted an attraction" to Thomas.

Henslowe, always trying to understand says "Spiritual? Magnetic?"

```
                        WILL
        Erotic.  Phillip,  I  love  him.
```

Henslowe tries to help him work through this.

```
                        HENSLOWE
        You're  fond  of  him.

                        WILL
        More  than  that…

                        HENSLOWE
        He  reminds  you  of  yourself,  starting
        out.  It's  brotherly  —  you're  confusing
        the  emotions…
```

```
                    WILL
It's not brotherly. I have brothers — I
don't want to kiss their neck where
it joins their shoulder. I can't
work, I can't sleep. I'm changeable,
fumbling, full of tears, full of smiles,
now like him, now hate him — all the
symptoms… I want to penetrate him.
```

For Will, this is a sin. "I can burn in hell" (p. 31–32).

For Henslowe, this is a troublesome problem since it means that they won't have a play next Friday.

Will then considers his identity.

```
                    WILL
You've lived thirty years of your life
and never known who you really were.
Will Shakespeare? Oh yes — minor
playwright, liked boys. How history will
remember you — wrote plays, yes, noted
mainly for his pederasty…
```

He then sees a gay bar, and wonders "Is that your future…?" (p. 33).

As Will considers suicide, "he flings himself over the bank into the river" only to discover that the tide's out, and he's standing in ankle-deep mud (p. 36).

Then Will realizes that to be true to himself, he has to accept wherever true love can be found. "You love him — and you must follow love. And therefore begin the rest of your life…" (p. 35).

Will murmurs a prayer of forgiveness, and then finds Thomas.

He and Thomas then walk together, and he discusses the love scene he's working on, about "a man in love with another." He reflects on how that changes the nature of love. Through his confession, we understand that he realizes that some love between a male and a female may rely more on trickery, bullying, and manipulation. This forces him to re-think the nature of love.

```
                        WILL
    I can't have him do what a man might
    with a woman, bully her into love,
    pretend indifference, praise his best
    friend to make him jealous — as man,
    he knows all a man's tricks… (p. 36).
```

Finally, Will admits to Thomas that "It's you. I love you…" (p. 37).

Will makes his choice. He surrenders to this love, knowing that he might burn in hell for it.

They kiss, but Will notices something is wrong. "There's something on his upper lip. He touches it — he comes away with Thomas's moustache on his fingers. Thomas wheels to flee — Will grabs his shoulder, gets a handful of hair. It's a wig. Will stands there, thunderstruck, while Thomas, with a sob, pulls off the wig and shakes out her blonde hair" (p. 38).

This entire section in Norman's play takes about eighteen pages, as Will tries to come to terms with his identity. In Tom Stoppard's script and in the film, it takes place within two minutes. On p. 65, as Will and Thomas are traveling together on a boat, Will tells Thomas about his love for Viola who is going to marry Wessex. As the boat bumps the jetty by the De Lessepses' house, the bump throws Thomas into Will's arms. "She kisses him on the mouth and jumps out of the boat."

For a moment, Will is surprised. Two lines later, he discovers that Thomas is really Viola.

Why the change? Audiences, particularly heterosexual audiences in America, are often not comfortable with homosexuality. By putting the emphasis on homosexuality for over fifteen minutes of screen time, it would tip the theme into other areas. Audiences could easily believe that this story is about Will coming to terms with his homosexuality. They might have trouble with Will's conclusions — that no matter what sex Thomas is, it would be all right with him because of his love for him/her. Although there was good exploration in Norman's script, with humor, emotional confusion, and some rather profound themes of identity that were part of this exploration, Stoppard used the moment for humor instead, and then immediately put the focus back on the theme of heterosexual love.

Exploring the Theme of Female Identity

In Marc Norman's script, the theme continues to be explored by looking at how Belinda's true identity includes the freedom that few women have. Belinda (who later is renamed Viola) explains to Will how she decided to dress up as a boy, because "who was more free in London than a young boy?" (p. 42).

```
                    BELINDA
      I'd see people in the street, selling
      butter and carrying water and rowing
      boats — and they were free…
      Because I am so different, yards from
      other girls, somebody tells me go
      one way, I'll crawl on my knees to
      go the other, and your plays moved
      me, their lovers, and there I was,
      my wish come true, and curse my wish
      because I was with him, his Romeo
      but what if he discovered me, I'd
      disgust him, he'd reject me, because
      many do, nobody knows me truly… (p. 43)
```

Later, Belinda and Thomas walk around as two males, and see how others respond to them. Some look and some stare, which leads to a discussion between Will and Belinda about how they each are different — Will because "a line of poetry would make me shiver" and Belinda because "when the girls did needlepoint and the boys went to fence and ride... I went with the boys" (p. 57). They discuss their worse fears — for Will it's failure, for Belinda, it's confinement. For Will his worse fault is selfishness, for Belinda, it's loneliness (p. 59).

Viola then suggests that Will dress up as a female, to find out how women relate to each other when not in the presence of men. Will discovers that the women speak of the basic feminist question: "What is it that women most want from a man?" For some, the answer is liberty. For another, patience, kindness, tenderness and encouragement (p. 64-65).

And with each discussion of identity and of love, they understand, more deeply, what Juliet wants — "her liberty, to make her own choice of man" and "Romeo's total attention, his absolute consideration" (p. 66-67).

But their dreams of liberty are not to happen, for the upcoming marriage to Wessex includes all their opposites — surrender, marrying for profit, and "like the mare, [Belinda]... will be broken" (p. 67).

Whereas Norman focused on the more feminist themes of liberty and choice, and the gay themes of "who am I?" and "how does whom I love change my identity?", Stoppard focused more on the themes of heterosexual love, although Stoppard kept the idea of Will dressed as a woman when he dresses up as the chaperone, Wilhelmina, and goes to court with Viola as her engagement is announced.

Like the writers of *Shakespeare in Love*, any writer needs to think about the target audience, and how far to go with edgier themes. Stoppard pulled back on Norman's exploration, recognizing that this wasn't the main issue of the story he wanted to explore, but also that the gay theme was not yet, at least for American audiences, a mainstream theme.

INTEGRATING SHAKESPEARE QUOTES

Both writers drew on their knowledge of Shakespeare to add quotes from other plays to the script. Will uses words with Henslowe that Shakespeare would later use in *Hamlet*: "Doubt that the stars are fire, doubt that the sun doth move." To which Henslowe replies, "Talk prose!" (p. 6). Will refers to mandragora, a medicine that helps sleep, which the historical Shakespeare also refers to in *Othello* and *Antony and Cleopatra* (p. 28). Will says "wonderful, wonderful" (p. 29), which Fennyman also says during the Third Act. Shakespeare uses this line in *As You Like It*, "O, wonderful, wonderful, and most wonderful, wonderful!"

The writers also had to create language that fit the period, while still being accessible to contemporary audiences. The language had the flavor of the Elizabeth period, and, at times, I thought I recognized the line, but was unable to locate the reference. Sometimes they would spin a line around a line from some other play.

Sir Robert, Viola's father, sells Wessex on the idea of marrying his daughter by saying, "She will breed" (p.42). In *As You Like It*, Rosalind says "she will breed it like a fool." Sometimes the writers used simile, much like Shakespeare did, "It is like trying to pick a lock with a wet herring" (p. 11) or "You lie in your meadow as you lied in my bed." (p. 112).

Sometimes the writers used the Rule of Threes in a line, such as when Shakespeare says "I am unmanned, unmended, and unmade, like a puppet in a box" (p. 63). Other lines relied on common terms used at the time — "stop your prattling" (p. 87) or speaking of the "vagabond" — or created language using common elements that would be familiar to those in London, and then created lines that were more poetic. Everyone in London would have been familiar with the Thames — with its width and its tides. This knowledge was worked into the dialogue by the writers: "The tide waits for no man, but I swear it would wait for you!" (p. 90). "Love knows nothing of rank or riverbank" (p. 66). "A broad river divides my loves" (p. 88 and p. 90).

Writers use ink, so lines were used the had double meanings, as: "Where is that thieving hack who can't keep his pen in his own ink pot!" (p. 99). The writers played with the idea of the nightingale and the lark, so famous in the love scene in *Romeo and Juliet*. Will mentions "none of your twittering larks! I would banish nightingales from her garden before they interrupt her song" (p. 66).

Other lines simply sound Shakespearean: "She has been plucked since I saw her last..." (p. 95). "Have a care with my name, you will wear it out," says the Queen (p. 147). "Indeed, I am a bride short!" says Wessex (p. 149). "How is this to end? As stories must when love's denied — with tears and a journey" (p. 150).

I thought I had heard the lines of Queen Elizabeth in some other Shakespeare play: "Have a care with my name, you will wear it out". I thought I recognized the lines, "I swear by my breeches" and "He was the first man among us. A great light has gone out." And "How is this to end? As stories must when love's denied — with tears and a journey." But these are original to Stoppard and Norman.

The writers knew their subject matter well, finding the style and tone and flavor of the Shakespearean period, while still keeping it accessible to contemporary audiences.

RESEARCHING THE STORY

Most writers write about what they know about. Lawyers, such as John Grisham and Scott Turow, write stories about the law. Doctors, such as Robin Cook, write medical stories. Both Norman and Stoppard, although not Shakespearean scholars, were knowledgeable about Shakespeare. Marc Norman had an M.A. in English Literature and had read all of Shakespeare's works. Tom Stoppard had seen most of Shakespeare's plays, and was the writer of the play, *Rosencrantz and Guildenstern are Dead*, which was about two minor characters in *Hamlet*. Director John Madden had taught Shakespeare at Yale and directed several of Shakespeare's plays.

But they needed knowledge of more than just Shakespeare's plays. To write this script, they needed knowledge of the historical period. They then could begin to play with historical dates and facts, being careful not to go against what was known, but playing with areas that were not known.

Norman chose to set the film in 1594. When Stoppard did rewrites, he changed the date to 1593, the year that Marlowe was believed to have been killed in a tavern brawl. Although there is no record that Shakespeare met Kyd or Marlowe, since Shakespeare's star as a playwright was just starting to rise when their reputations were solid, nevertheless he might have met them since they all worked in the London theatre. The writers used this possibility to create a small subplot between Shakespeare and Marlowe. By placing the events of the film in that year, there was an opportunity to create a twist in the story, giving Will further emotional depth and complicating the action when he believes that he is responsible for Kit's death.

After Marlowe's death, Shakespeare became the foremost playwright, although there were many other playwrights, perhaps as many as three hundred writing at the time. Most of them are no longer known. Since the exact date of the writing of *Romeo and Juliet* is unknown, changing the date to 1593 was a valid change.

There was other historical information slipped into the plays. John Webster, the little boy who feeds live mice to cats and loves the stabbings in Shakespeare's plays, is based on the playwright John Webster, who grew up to write *The Duchess of Malfi, The White Devil, The Devil's Law-Case* and *A Cure for a Cuckold*, all tales filled with blood and gore. Director John Madden called him the Quentin Tarantino of his day.

During the time of *Shakespeare in Love*, the Curtain and the Rose were two rival theatres. The Curtain opened in 1577 and was run by Richard Burbage, one of the most famous actors from one of the most famous theatre families of his age. The Rose opened in 1587 and was owned by Philip Henslowe. In 1595, the Swan opened. The famous Globe Theatre, which is often paired with Shakespeare, didn't open until 1599, after *Romeo and Juliet* was produced. These characters were integrated into the story.

The theatres performed during daylight and for most of the year, except for winter. The theatres had no roof over the middle section, where the groundlings (the lower class of the audience) stood to watch the play and the richer members of the audience were covered, sitting on benches in the galleries. John Madden used this knowledge by planning to shoot a rainstorm during the performance of *Romeo and Juliet*, showing the groundlings soaked, but mesmerized by the performance. When he realized that this would mean drying out 300 costumes before shooting the next day, he cut the rainstorm.

The theatres were opened, and then closed, for any number of reasons. The Master of the Revels (Tilney in the film) was in charge of determining whether the theatres would be closed, or opened. He made that determination based on any number of reasons. Theatres could be closed if a play contained sensitive political and religious subject matter or depicted a living person. We see this research used when the character of Tilney decides to close The Curtain, when he discovers that Thomas, the actor, is really a woman. And he decides to open the theatres, when he feels it is safe in spite of the plague.

The theatre was considered lewd and unnatural. Preachers harangued against it on the street corners. "A plague on both their houses" (p. 8) says Makepeace, referring to both The Curtain and The Rose. And at the end, when Makepeace is swept up by the crowds into the theatre, he is one of the most enthusiastic audience members, having had his own transformation during the course of the play.

Plays were performed for the pleasure of the Queen, and she was one of the main reasons why the theatres stayed open. She loved drama. In *Shakespeare in Love,* this information gained from research is incorporated into some of the Queen's dialogue, when she reminds Viola that the plays were for her: "They are not acted for you, they are acted for me" (p. 93).

There were also children's companies performing plays. Children, with their high-pitched voices, acted out adult dramas of love and revenge. In Marc Norman's early drafts of *Shakespeare in Love,* Will seeks his cast at a children's company, hoping to find a youth to play Romeo. He finds Thomas Kent performing at Whitehall. Later, this scene was cut and Thomas comes, instead, to audition at The Rose.

The Life of Shakespeare

Not a great deal is known about the life of William Shakespeare, which allows the writer some leeway, provided that it doesn't contradict known facts. Shakespeare was born in 1564 and died in 1616. He married Anne Hathaway in 1582 and had three children: Susanna, and the twins Hamnet and Judith. We don't know when

Shakespeare went to London, but we do know that a number of theatre companies performed in Stratford between 1579 and 1587. Perhaps Shakespeare moved to London because he began performing for some of the theatre companies in Stratford.

By 1592, his plays were performed successfully at The Rose, and The Rose's owner, Philip Henslowe, reported in 1592 that his theatre had done well with the plays of *Henry VI*. Henslowe became a focal character in *Shakespeare in Love* as the theatre producer commissioning Shakespeare's plays.

Romeo and Juliet is usually considered to have been written in the mid–1590s. In *Shakespeare in Love,* the writers date this play the same year as the death of Christopher Marlowe, in 1593, which is possible. They also imply that the previous play to *Romeo and Juliet* was *Two Gentlemen of Verona*, which fits an accepted chronology. They then go slightly beyond accepted chronology by implying that the next play was *Twelfth Night*, although some scholars date this play closer to 1600 or even shortly afterwards.

In Norman's second draft, Henslowe says that he will start a new company, which becomes the players at the Rose Theatre. Although we don't know the exact date when the company was established, there is sufficient evidence to suggest that it may have begun in 1593, and that *Romeo and Juliet* may have been one of its first plays, if not the first play. The writers used this date as the time for their film. In 1594, in the Norman draft, Will and Henslowe are already partners in the theatre. "We've had success together — we've made money," says Henslowe (p. 6). In 1593, Henslowe and Will were just becoming partners, thereby showing the action that started their partnership. In 1594, Shakespeare became a shareholder in The Lord Chamberlain's Men, along with Will Kemp and Richard Burbage. At the end of the film, Will receives the fifty pounds necessary to join this theatre company.

All of this information, gained from research, was used as a basis for the many flights of fancy that the writers used, as they conjectured what his early life might have been like in London.

USING WHAT THE AUDIENCE KNOWS

Shakespeare is good subject matter. Tom Stoppard has said, "Shakespeare is the playwright on whom one can count as being, to one degree or another, lodged in the consciousness of one's audience. On the other hand, it's rather helpful to the people who are telling the story that so little is known about William Shakespeare because it means that you can use quite a lot without contradicting other things that might have been known about him."[1]

Director John Madden also found this same freedom working with this material. In an interview with Gemma Files, he said, "You can't take Shakespeare himself too seriously, even when you're making a film called *Shakespeare in Love*. For one, we don't even know who he was, really — and for another, if you made a rollicking romantic comedy during which you acted as though he were this untouchable icon, the whole project would be pretty well stillborn. So we treat Shakespeare himself fairly lightly as a person. But the work... his work... that, we take very seriously indeed."

Madden recognizes the essential question that needs to resonate throughout the film: "If only from an historical point of view, the film can't be about whether or not Shakespeare and Viola's love will triumph overall... because we know it won't. So the real question becomes whether or not Shakespeare will succeed in turning the personal joy and pain into a play which will live on long after both of them are dust. [It's about]... the journey from *Romeo and Ethyl, the Pirate's Daughter*, a money-maker with jokes and a dog, to *Romeo and Juliet*, the Western world's classic romantic tragedy."

Madden wanted to reclaim Shakespeare for the masses. "In his

1 "Interview with Tom Stoppard," *www.filmeducation.org*, Interview Transcript.

own time, he wrote brilliantly and effortlessly for the entire social spectrum, and we need to reclaim that, to let the movie audiences, now one of the largest audiences around, experience first-hand the intoxication of his language, the depth of accuracy of his characterization.

At the end of the review, Gemma Files said that Shakespeare changed the "face of literature forever by crossbreeding poetry, psychological insight, and pure, unabashedly populist entertainment". Files sees "the world's most effective aphrodisiac... as creativity." All of this comes through beautifully in the film.

CREATIVITY AND STUDY GUIDE TO
SHAKESPEARE IN LOVE

(1) What did the writers need to know about Shakespeare to write this story? What did they already know before they tackled this subject matter? What additional research did they need to do? Where did they take liberties with what is known about Shakespeare? What did they add and/or imagine to what is known that does not contradict what is known, but is not known for sure?

(2) How much do you know about Shakespeare? Is there research you know that you could have fit into this story? How would you do it? Write the scene. (For example, might you have a scene where his daughter comes to London, or his wife? Would you have other playwrights in the bar?)

(3) Read Shakespeare's play of *Romeo and Juliet*. Are there other scenes in that play that you could intercut with a scene of Will and Viola?

(4) In a good script, it is said that even bad actors can read the dialogue well because it's so well written. Read some of these scenes of *Shakespeare in Love* out loud, and see how easily, or how

---

2 Gemma Files, "Doing the Bard: Rethinking Shakespeare and Falling in Love," review of Shakespeare in Love, Eye Weekly, December 17, 1998 (*eyeweekly.com/eye/issue_12.17.98/ film/shakes17.php*).

difficult, it is to read it well. Do the words flow? How did the writer create the flavor of Shakespearean speech? Feel the rhythm of the dialogue. Once you feel the rhythm, expand on the scene by writing additional dialogue that might have been written for the scene, to see if you can write a scene in this same style. Is it difficult? Or once you feel out the rhythm, does it flow easily?

(5) What did the writers need to know about the structure of the Elizabethan theatre in order to create certain scenes in this film? How many scenes take place at the theatre, and in how many different locations? Do some additional research on the theatre buildings, and then draw the theatre (whether The Curtain, The Swan, The Globe). Are there other locations in the theatre that would have worked well for a scene?

(6) Have you ever experienced the loss of the Muse that Will experienced? What exercises that you did, or therapists you went to, or love that you found, helped you regain it?

(7) Do you know any insider information about show business — whether about actors, producers, directors, or writers? Is there any additional insider information you could have added to this film?

(8) What did you learn about the nature of love from this film? What do you learn about the nature of love from reading *Romeo and Juliet?* Do you agree with their conclusions? Have they left anything out?

(9) How do you feel about Stoppard dropping most of the homosexual theme? Do you think this was censorship? Or wisdom? Did it add, or subtract, from the final film?

(10) Were you disappointed in the ending? Did you feel that Viola and Will should have lived happily ever after, together? Which of Shakespeare's plays show a shipwreck? What do you think happened to Viola, as a result of her relationship with Shakespeare?

Interview with Marc Norman

Getting the Idea

The idea really came from my son, Zack. He was taking an
Elizabethan theatre class at Boston University. Now, my
kids have always been movie addicts. They saw early on that
being the children of a freelance writer, it was in their self
interest to come home with an idea. And when they were
little kids, they gave me little-kid ideas. But as they got older
and more sophisticated, their ideas got better. Zackary called
me up one day out of the blue and said, "I got this idea of
young Shakespeare starting out in Elizabethan theatre." And
I thought about it for a second and said "That's brilliant!" I
said that it satisfies me on some many levels. It's fresh. It's
esoteric. It's obscure. It's the kind of thing that I like, but I
have no idea how to do it. I knew it was a great idea and the
fact that one of my kids came up with the idea probably kept
me at a task where I might have otherwise given up. Because
there were years there where nothing was happening with
this idea. It was fallow. It was not going anywhere. So I kept
at it and in the end it worked out.

Researching the Story

The research was really necessary because I felt the subject at
first was so daunting. There is so much that you have to get
right. I was aware that there is three hundred years of second-
rate fictional writing about Shakespeare. Shakespeare doing
this, Shakespeare doing that, Shakespeare on a flying saucer.
I mean everyone has seen Shakespeare and done something
fictional with it, which is fair game, but in my opinion it was
all second rate and I didn't want to do second rate which

made me raise my own bar because in some ways taking on this subject was more ambitious than anything else that I had done. So research can be a way to postpone writing. It's procrastination at some level. But it's this wonderful procrastination because you get to be a graduate student again. You get to go to libraries and read, which is probably how most writers start out. I was an English major at Cal, I had taken some courses in Shakespeare. Also I had a kind of liberal arts understanding of Shakespeare and I had seen a lot of the plays, but I couldn't in any way consider myself an expert, so I had to first read all the plays. Then I had to read the major work about Shakespeare, to get into his world and to find out what issues about Shakespeare other people had brought up. At this point I had no idea what the story was going to be about. All I had was a tantalizing area that I kept on telling myself would, with enough time, yield something great, but I wasn't sure I was going to find it.

After I read the basic stuff, it lead me into Elizabethan theatre and in some ways it was even more interesting than the Shakespearean stuff, cause when you really look at Shakespeare himself and get kind of rigorous in terms of what you can say for sure about him, it's really only a couple of pages. There's a couple of signatures on a will. There are a couple of reminiscences from people who knew him, which may or may not be self serving and may or may not be accurate. And that's it. He was a person who apparently took great pains not to be a public person, took great pains to preserve his privacy. So doing research about Shakespeare the man was kind of frustrating because all you can do is to get into this expert's speculation versus that expert's speculation. Then you get into the whole minefield of whether Shakespeare existed, which I think is a silly one. I didn't go there at all.

But when I started to get into Elizabethan theatre, now there's something you can get your teeth into. In fact there are artifacts of that world that have remained. Henslowe kept a diary so we know what he paid Shakespeare, we know what he paid Marlowe, we know what he paid actors, we know what he borrowed, how much money he grossed, we know how he operated. And looking at that research I began to see something I don't think was original with me, but maybe original in terms of doing a movie about Shakespeare. The Elizabethan theatre was Hollywood. It was show business. In fact, those young guys in the space of maybe twenty years invented modern entertainment and that is show business as we know it. And everything we know about show business — the passions, the back stage rivalries, producers, agents, temperamental stars — everything we think of as show business, they invented, down to the contract. They in fact invented the contracts that we still use today in the motion picture business.

And that idea was the first aperture into the story. It took me about a three-year period between the time I first got the idea and the first writing. I kept coming back to the Shakespeare project and basically every time I came back to it with a new idea, it wasn't good enough. It just would have been another one of those second-rate, clichéd shards of fiction at the foot of the pedestal of Shakespeare.

During those three years I was coming up with potential approaches to the story and throwing them out because they weren't good enough. But after I did the research on the Elizabethan theatre, the first sort of glimmer of an idea came to me — that of Shakespeare in the entertainment business, which was a business that I knew. And I came up with the notion of making this a backstage story.

Then I realized that that was at least one connection between me and Shakespeare. In the early 1590s, Shakespeare was a competent playwright, he would rhyme "love" and "dove." He could do the obligatory scenes, he knew the rhythms. He had been an actor. He knew plays on some level — he knew the form, he knew the style. And he had written some plays and they were well received but not really seen by the audience as anything remarkable. He wanted to do something remarkable, but he didn't know how. When I thought about that as a character problem, I fell back on the old school cliché in Hollywood which is the character meets a girl and the girl changes his life. And I liked that. I liked the notion of Shakespeare being a poet and writing about love when in fact he was a fool in love. In fact he didn't know anything about it and it was tormenting him because he simply had not figured out his relationship to women and where he fit in with a woman. And the third leg of the triangle, and again these ideas occurred fairly quickly in sequence, was if you want to have a story about Shakespeare and a girl, and you want to do a story about Shakespeare backstage in Elizabethan theatre, you don't want to keep splitting your focus between the backstage theatre and some field outside of town where they're making love. You want the unity of place, you want them to be in the same place, so they can't be in the same place, because there were no girls in the Elizabethan theatre group. Boys played girls. So it almost became fated that the story would be about a girl who disguised herself as a boy because she wanted to be an actor and then Shakespeare fell in love with a boy who turned out to be a girl. And those are kind of the three legs of the tripod. When I thought about Belinda, which was her original name before she became Viola, she was the perfect girl for a writer. She was beautiful. She was independently wealthy. And she knew everything Shakespeare had written by heart. What more could you want? What more could you ask for? And once I had those ideas, it felt right, like I had what I needed to go ahead. And after those ideas kind of coalesced, the script came together fairly quickly.

What Is the Story About?

Most people saw the story as being about writer's block but I never did because in some ways I don't believe in writer's block as it is normally understood. I don't believe the writer wants to write something and he doesn't know what to write. My understanding of it is the writer wants to write something excellent, there are all kinds of things he could write, but they're not good enough. He's trying to do something better than he's ever done and he doesn't know how. But how does a writer, how does anyone creative, raise themselves up a notch? It's all self motivated. It all comes from the inside. There's no external thing you can do to make it happen. You have to put yourself into the mind of it happening and hope that something will trigger something, So for me, Shakespeare was a young writer who had achieved a nominal level of success, as good as everybody else that was writing in Elizabethan theatre, but he wanted to achieve something better than that and he didn't know how. The story is how he writes *Romeo and Juliet*, which was, in terms of my fiction, arguably his breakthrough play that really catapulted him into something unique in Elizabethan theatre.

Making Shakespeare Accessible

I was aware that I was doing a story on an esoteric subject that would have to find its way in a very competitive marketplace and I was worried that the screenplay might not be readily understandable. I was working with the Elizabethan language and wondered if I could make it familiar enough to people so that teenagers sitting in the balcony could get it. One of the rules that I made for myself was that I didn't want to make any esoteric references to Elizabethan literature or the historical Shakespeare. Because I didn't want someone in the audience saying, for example, "Who is that kid with the mouse?" So I eschewed all insider jokes. But when Tom did the rewrite, he threw them in, all of them. And the audience loved them! If you talk to people who've seen *Shakespeare in Love*, they remember the little kid with the mouse. I have to tip my hat to Tom, he was right. I was being so rigorous about this and Tom went for these rather broad gags about Shakespeare and people loved them.

I had a sense that Shakespeare's rivals were college kids down from Cambridge and Oxford who would normally have gone into the priesthood or military or civil service or something. They had written plays in school because part of their curriculum was studying Latin. They studied the Romans and Greeks. They studied plays by Plautus and Seneca, so they knew how plays worked. They studied Aristotle who said that comedies are about young lovers and end with a marriage, tragedies are about men who dare the gods and go beyond their station and they die. You don't mix and match. One is one and one is the other and most of Shakespeare's rivals took that to heart. So when you look at Elizabethan plays in that period, there are comedies about young lovers who get married and there are tragedies about someone who goes too far and dies.

Shakespeare did what I think was a unique thing: he starts off with *Romeo and Juliet* as a comedy and not only a comedy but also a parody of a comedy. Romeo's first lines are about Rosaline who has broken his heart. He's the silliest, most cliché swooning lover, and then he meets Juliet and sees her and it's love at first sight but she belongs to the rival family. If the play remained a comedy, that would cause complications and disguises and mistakes and things like that and in the end the two families would be resolved and there would be a wedding. Shakespeare takes the idea and goes in a different direction. He says that this love is so threatening to both families that it must be destroyed. The only way the young lovers can be together is in death, that the young lovers in essence dare their gods with their love and must die for it. And I have to think that this was seen as sort of a breakthrough by the Elizabethan audience. I have to think that the reason that the audience responded to *Romeo and Juliet* so well and why that play was done over and over and over and over again for the next 500 years was because it treats love as something wonderful at first but that becomes so serious and overwhelming to life that its only solution is death. And I think Shakespeare knew what he was doing and of course what I did was take the comic point of view that he was going through something similarly serious and overwhelming in his own life.

Ideas that Didn't Remain in the Script

In my earlier draft, Shakespeare is convinced he is falling in love with a boy. I thought in order for Shakespeare to have this creative leap that I wanted him to take, he had to have all of his habitual sensibilities shaken. He had to have what we call consciousness raising and it had to come out of left field, from where he did not expect it. And to me it was the premise that here's Shakespeare at the beginning of the movie, complaining to Henslowe that he doesn't know anything about love. He admits that he's had women, but they're always the wrong woman, and he does stupid things and winds up being a fool. And then he finds this powerful attraction to this young man and he has to confront himself and ask, "Who am I? Is this what I want? Does this explain why I've been such a fool about women? What does it mean, because I've never thought about myself this way. It sends me to strange worlds and embarrasses me and makes me self conscious and scares me, but in the end what can I do but follow it, because that is what my heart is telling me to do? How can I tell my heart no?"

So he makes that commitment and decides to follow up wherever the passion takes him and Thomas turns out to be a girl. To me what was important in my draft was that Shakespeare made this commitment to follow love wherever it took him and then that was what opened him up to the possibilities of *Romeo and Juliet*. Because what I decided was missing in Shakespeare up to then was an ability to be unconventional in love. He had been too conventional. He had been like all of the other Elizabethan playwrights — he's been copying their clichés, using their same formulations. And once he was free to come up with his own formulation, that gave him that play.

Well, there were people involved in the production that were disturbed with that idea. They thought it was homophobic but I felt it went beyond gender. I think it's a statement about love in general and can be applied to any gender. It's about the heart, but I was overruled.

Understanding Shakespeare's Writing Process

Any writing is a lot of experimenting. Writers know about this process. You start something and you live in a state of anxiety. You feel something, but you don't know if it's there or not. All writing is an experiment. You never know if it's going to work. So Shakespeare begins writing something basically just for money, just to satisfy a contract, just to get out of trouble, and because of what happens to him, the writing starts to get better. Writers know even without external things happening to them, there are times when the work starts to take over.

The characters start to come up with their own voices. The characters start to say "I don't want to do that, I want to do this!" And the writer acknowledges that's a better idea.

So the writer begins to get into this workshop experimental relationship with his characters. Which may sound kind of nutty because we're dealing with ideas, not real people. But in fact the character is beginning to become real. All Henslowe wants is the play. He doesn't care if it's good or bad. He's a businessman. So here is this schmuck writer who is constantly changing the play because he's going through some sort of ethereal, esoteric process. This drives Henslowe crazy. And that sort of speaks to the relationship, the eternal relationship between writer and producer. Especially when the writer is doing well. Producers should learn that when a writer is in this kind of state to back away and let him do it because there is a chance that something good will happen to it, but in fact all it does with producers is make them totally crazy.

Some people say that writers have motors that drive them, in other words a secret set of life experiences and dreams and fantasies and secrets that inform their writing. They really shouldn't tell anybody about them because it won't mean anything to anybody, and if you let it out it kind of spoils the fun. One of the motors of this movie that few people identified is that it's about creativity.

For me, the movie is about the mystery of creativity and how it happens. How it happens in one case, not how it happens all the time. How it can happen. And in that sense I was very influenced by the movie you mentioned, and that was *Amadeus*.

I cry whenever I watch that movie because it is so brilliant and it is so beautiful. And what the beauty is for me, is its take on creativity. It's the beauty of how beautiful things happen to us flawed, crippled, twisted little people. And that to me is the magic of creativity — that we fallible, prone-to-error people come up with such beautiful things now and then.

My Writing Process

I begin by writing random notes to myself. I just take a clip board and a hunk of paper and I start putting down anything that occurs to me. And I date the pages and put them aside. And I'll do this until I have a stack maybe two inches high. Just random pages. I'm not consciously looking for core ideas. I try not to force them. I operate basically on the basis of trying to postpone decisions as long as I can. I may come up with an idea early on that turns out to be a great idea, but I don't commit to it. I say, "What else can you think of? What else is possible?" And I do that until I reach a point of frustration, till I'm so full up with the subject that I have to start making decisions. And I'll go back through all those stacks of notes and I'll cull out what I think are my best ideas. And sometimes I'll only have a portion of what I need which means I have to go back into the process and do it some more. But when I have the core ideas, then I'll go to index cards for scenes, and I'll block scenes.

I've got a wall in my office that's made of cedar, and it takes push pins very well, so my office is a bulletin board, and I'll put up the ideas for scenes on index cards. I'll move the cards around. I am looking for shape and structure and flow with those cards. I'll start looking for where my act endings are. I don't look for internal builds and turning points since they seem to just occur. And once I have a close-enough version of the screenplay up on the wall I'll start writing it. The writing is the easiest part because you've done most of the work.

Subplots occur because you need a counterpoint theme. I sometimes think of writing as music and I think the best training for screen writers is to think of a screenplay as chamber music. Because chamber music is for something like two, three, four, or five voices at the most. Screenplays are too. Screenplays are pieces for two or three or four or five voices, and not more. Chamber music shows how themes are stated and counter themes are introduced.

When I think of theme, I think of "Wouldn't it be nice if this idea got worked out?" And you start to play around with it. And all you're doing now is really moving scenes and characters around. You have forgotten the theme because you're into a kind of the carpentry of the screenplay itself. And then you step back and look at it and you say, "Oh, I have worked out that theme." Or you step back and you say I haven't. I wanted it to be about this and I look at it now and I don't see this happening, so you tear into it some more. So you go through a long process of writing and rewriting. The draft that I show people that I call my first draft is usually my sixth.

By the time I've written thirty pages of screenplay I'll start taking notes on the rewrite. But these are just notes. Usually I try to get through a first draft before I start changing things.

Working with Clichés

One of a writer's jobs is to get past clichés and yet a writer always comes up with clichés to begin with when he begins to consider a project. The good writer goes through the process of snuffing out the clichés and hopefully coming up with something better. When I first started writing the Shakespeare dialogue it was "Thou hast done this." I mean it was cheesy Shakespearean dialogue because all I could come up with was the cliché version of that. I kept on throwing that out and then I began to get a sense of the sound and rhythm of the movie's language and using certain Latinized words that might sound strange but would explain themselves because the root was familiar. By giving the language a kind of pentameter swing, I could make the language that the characters were saying off-stage somewhat like what the characters were saying on-stage, so it would seem like it came out of the same root language. It was a lot of trial and error.

Since I was doing a backstage show business story, because my tongue was calibrated to my cheek to a certain extent in terms of Hollywood parody, to me it was fair game to use modern clichés of show business and put them back in time. If you buy into the general notion that the Elizabethans were inventing show business, then they would know the clichés we know.

It's an old cliché of playwrights, for example, that the audience thinks the actors make up their own lines as they go along. They don't want to think that a writer is supplying these puppets with words and telling them what to do. There's a line in Shakespeare about the audience coughing over all his best lines. These are just common backstage clichés that you can assume began back then.

Shakespeare was not above using clichés. When you work in a deadline business you tend to rely on clichés if you need to get something done by Thursday as opposed to something brilliant. And Shakespeare was in a deadline business. The Elizabethan playwrights would steal from each other because they needed 150 pages by Thursday. The whole point being that *Romeo and Juliet* for Shakespeare was something new, fresh beyond cliché. And to me, the applause at the end by the audience showed they were seeing something that they have never seen before. To me, it was like what I felt when I saw *Star Wars* in 1977.

Somehow the bar had been raised and that narrative in movies would not be the same any more. They would all be altered by this from then on.

Building on Shakespeare's Past Work

I pretty much limited myself to the plays that Shakespeare had written before *Romeo and Juliet* because they were what he had done. They were what he knew. If *Romeo and Juliet* is an elevation up a rung of the ladder, he has to build on what he had done before. And we have to see what's different from what he had done before.

When Tom did the rewrite, he fell in love with the notion of Viola being Shakespeare's lifetime muse, and providing him with other plays including *Twelfth Night*. I never gave her that function. I think it is fine that he did that. In some ways it gave the piece an ending. I always liked my ending where Shakespeare's dad showed up. I always had a problem with Tom's original ending — a bizarre ending in which Viola is shipwrecked and she comes ashore on the coast of America and there is New York City with the Twin Towers and the Empire State Building. They shot and re-shot this last sequence and they finally got the ending right in the cutting room.

Exploring the Puritan Conflict

Puritans basically ran London in terms of politics. Puritans were the alderman and mayor. And they were constantly trying to shut the theatre down for religious reasons. They saw actors as immoral, as idolatrous, as violating all kinds of social contracts. They saw the theatre as places where lewd acts took place in the audience, and whores would proposition guys. They saw the theatre as lies. The only reason the players could fight off this onslaught of negativity was that Queen Elizabeth liked plays. She was amused by the players.

In the Elizabethan social fabric everybody had a place and a job description. You were a butcher. You were a milk seller. You were a bookseller. You were this or that. Actors had no legal standing. They were considered vagabonds. Which means somebody outside of the social contract which means civil laws really didn't apply to them. Actors needed some protection and some legal standing, so what they said was, "We are actors rehearsing plays to perform before Elizabeth. We must have theatres, and we have to have theatre companies, and we have to work all year on these plays. And of course we have to feed ourselves, so we have to put on plays for money, but it's all for the sake of Elizabeth." So the queen was in some ways the reason Elizabethan theatre existed.

Playing with Subplots

During the rewrites, the reunion plot was cut. I always liked that subplot — there was a very successful character who knew Shakespeare back in the old Stratford days, and who implied that of his graduating class, Shakespeare was the one who'd never made it. Everybody else had done pretty well, and everybody liked Shakespeare. It was too bad that he never really found his way.

Another exploration that was cut was a scene of Belinda helping Shakespeare learn about love. I was exploring how that insight affected his writing on *Romeo and Juliet*. He had to keep probing deeper into love, to find a definition that satisfied him. Then he'd find a deeper insight that was even more revealing than what he'd found before and he'd put that in the play. And then he'd come to an even deeper one. So the play on screen would progress as a kind of an exploration that goes further and further into an exploration into love. And there was this parallel between Shakespeare learning these things through his relationship with Belinda and the play becoming more and more sophisticated, more and more insightful about love.

Looking at that idea now, it feels kind of schematic. It feels kind of mechanical. And I probably would have changed that in future rewrites.

The Rewrites

Tom did his major rewrites in 1992, and later, when John Madden came on the picture, around 1996 or 1997, when Miramax decided to put it into production, John worked with Tom on further rewrites, but I think they were minor rewrites.

Tom brought in a lot more insider jokes. Tom made it on some level more popular, more a sort of audience-pleasing movie and I have to say I applaud him for it. I think it was a good idea because I think it helped the project.

Although I wasn't happy about Universal bringing in another writer, when we saw the premiere of the film, I said to Tom, or perhaps he said to me, "I couldn't have done it without you." He needed my script and I needed his rewrites for it to turn out the way it did. I think that's incredible!"

The Production Process

We tried to get the movie made in 1992. I was a co-producer, which allowed me to keep my oar in the production. My task as I saw it was basically to help make the picture turn out as well as I could. Ed Zwick was the director at the time. Julia Roberts was committed to play Viola, we were all over in London, we had offices, they were building sets, cutting costumes, we were four weeks away from shooting, but we couldn't get an actor for Shakespeare. Nobody worked. The actors we wanted didn't want to do it. The actors who wanted to do it, we didn't like. Julia Roberts was getting nervous. She had committed to the movie but we couldn't provide her with a Shakespeare and she was getting self-conscious about this. She suggested Daniel Day Lewis but he had said "no" six months before. She said to us, "Let me try talking to him." She called him up in Dublin. She said, "Hello, I'm Julia Roberts and I'm doing this movie called *Shakespeare in Love*. I know they've approached you and I know you've turned it down, but I'd like to come talk to you and see if I can talk you into it." He said, "Well, you're welcome to come, but I'm not making any commitments." So she went over to Dublin and they spent time together that weekend. I don't know what happened between them, but I do know at the end of the weekend he said, in so many words, "It's been very nice meeting you, but no." And Julia Roberts got on a plane and flew to Los Angeles — she walked off the picture and the production collapsed. Now she had a contract with Universal to do the movie. Movie stars are not supposed to walk off movies. Could Universal have sued her for all the money they had already laid out? Sure. Did Universal want to? No. They wanted to do other movies with her. So the picture fell apart and Universal at that point abandoned the movie. They were willing to put it in turnaround but in addition to turnaround costs, they put in the costs of all that money they had put into preparing the movie that hadn't gotten made, and that was around four million dollars. So that was four million dollars hung on the turnaround price that would not appear on the screen if anybody else picked up the project and decided to make it.

Moving Ahead, Slowly

For the next five years Ed Zwick and I and other people who were interested in trying to mount the picture, went from company to company to try to make a deal. And company after company would say, "Sure we like this script, it's good," but since the movie had all this money laid against it by

Universal, they wouldn't commit. And Universal wouldn't work out any deal, any arrangement. Not only did Universal not want to make the movie, they didn't want anybody else to make the movie. Because if somebody else made the movie and it was successful, they would look like morons. So they basically tried to kill its chances of ever getting made. And miracle of miracles, Harvey Weinstein of Miramax decided to go ahead and pick up the project even with that financial liability against it.

When we were getting ready to film the script, for the second time in 1998, we had exactly the same problem we did in '92. We could not find a Shakespeare actor. We had Gwyneth Paltrow for Viola, but every male lead we talked to wanted to mess with Shakespeare. Tim Roth says, "I'll play Shakespeare but I want him to be an alcoholic." Then somebody came up with Joe Fiennes. And Joe Fiennes had just finished the film *Elizabeth,* but he'd done very little film work. And John Madden talked to him, and John came away saying, "I can make it work." And nobody quite knew if they believed him —we basically all relied on John's judgment. And I remember being on the set and watching John work with Joe and Gwyneth on their scenes together. And Gwyneth was like born in a trunk. I mean Gwyneth is a natural performer. Gwyneth is so brilliant and gets it so right. She's right on the first take. Second take she's done. Joe Fiennes would take ten takes, twelve takes to begin to start getting into the scene. And Gwyneth worked with him. She would keep her performance level high. She helped him along with a generosity you don't usually see in performers. And John worked with Joe in an intense way that finally carried it off, because I think Joe Fiennes was great.

Winning the Oscar

I had a sense we would win for Best Screenplay, since we had won the Golden Globes and the WGA Award, but everyone presumed that Steven Spielberg would win for *Saving Private Ryan*. But I would go to Oscar parties, and people I knew would say to me, "I voted for your picture, but Steven's going to win." I'd say yes, that was probably right. And then others would tell me the same thing. After a while, I began to wonder who was voting for Steven. I had a sense we could win the Best Picture Oscar. When I finished my first draft I thought, "This could win an Academy Award because it's such a shameless valentine to show business. It's a tribute to the power and need for entertainment, which is the business we're all in. It's, on some level, a love song to the entertainment business."

INTERVIEW WITH DIRECTOR JOHN MADDEN AND ADDITIONS FROM CO-AUTHOR TOM STOPPARD

(Note: Tom Stoppard declined to be interviewed for this chapter but did agree to an email exchange. His interpolations are taken from earlier interviews, as credited, and from email exchanges with me. He also edited the interview and included some corrections, comments, and additions made to the preliminary text.)

Bringing Tom Stoppard on Board

TOM: I had an arrangement at Universal where I was looking at what they had in development with a view to finding something for myself. I started reading Marc's screenplay about 1992 and the first scene I liked a lot which remained the basis for the movie's opening scene. I also liked — and used — a scene in which the Admirals' Men disrupted their rivals' performance by hurtling a beehive into the theatre (although this never got into the final draft). But I didn't want to do the picture at first. It took a while to find the right mood for it and for me. I always insisted and do so now, that Marc deserves the credit for having the foundational idea (young Shakespeare in love), but I didn't "get" his script. As far as I recall, it used bits of *As You Like It* and there was a gay angle.

I realized that Marc had this foundational great idea which was to write about Shakespeare not as a genius, but as a young writer trying to make his way and tumbling into beds and predicaments. And I suppose, perhaps because it was an English subject, they thought an English writer would be a good idea — somebody who lived in London and knew the in-jokes from the London theatre.

You probably recall the first thing you see of Will Shakespeare in the movie is he's practicing his signature, and I just loved that. But I have to make an embarrassing confession: I told several interviewers that this came from Marc's original, but my mind was playing tricks on me. It turned out I'd read it in a book *No Bed for Bacon*, written years ago by a friend of mine, Ned Sherrin, and Carly Brahms. Ned shrugged it off, kindly and typically.

Further Research

TOM: [Around this same time] there was something fortunate that happened. The foundations of the original Rose Theatre were discovered in London at that time.... Then a woman wrote a book about the Rose Theatre. So I had the advantage of that going on. Not that it matters to the audience, I suppose, but the bare bones of the context of this movie are, broadly speaking, historically accurate. Ned Alleyn, played by Ben (Affleck) was indeed the leader of the Admiral's Men at the Rose Theatre. Henslowe was a real person who owned the theatre. Burbage was England's most famous actor, and he had his troupe at the Curtain Theatre across the river.... Christopher Marlowe did get killed in a tavern brawl in that year. So, to some extent, the film is there to be enjoyed on an extra level by people who happen to know the historical context."[3]

Getting Started Again

JOHN: Originally Ed Zwick, who had first commissioned the script from Marc Norman, was going to direct, with Universal financing and distributing the picture. Fairly quickly Julia Roberts became attached to the film as the part of Belinda, the part which later became Viola. They got a substantial way down the road into production while still trying to identify the actor to play Shakespeare.

From the beginning, the plan was to make it in England. Zwick had auditioned a number of the actors whom I subsequently auditioned and who ended up in the movie, but they couldn't identify the person to play Will. From what I understand, they considered Daniel Day Lewis for the part, but that didn't happen and that made Julia wobble. But whatever it was, they couldn't quite arrive at the right configuration and so the film stopped, but by that time they had spent quite a bit of money on it. They had already started to build a set, but it was my under-standing that Universal was nervous of this project without a bankable star, since they thought people would neither care about Shakespeare nor be interested in a film about him. So the piece then went on a shelf with a very heavy price tag around its neck to the tune of about five or six million dollars, which was the cost of the development and the money that had been expended on production and fees and so on. It stayed there for a number of years, until the script came to Harvey Weinstein's attention at Miramax, and he thought it one of the best scripts he had ever read and made an audacious offer for it.

---

3 "Rhyme and Reason: A Conversation with *Shakespeare in Love*'s Marc Norman and Tom Stoppard," *Written By* The Magazine of the Writers Guild of America, West, March 1999, pgs. 24-25, and email from Tom Stoppard to Linda Seger.

Ed Zwick at that point moved from being director to producer, because Harvey was intent on making the film for much less than had originally been envisaged. And I suppose one step towards that goal was to offer it to a director who wouldn't be as expensive. Harvey Weinstein and I first developed a relationship with my first film, *Ethan Frome*, which he had bought for U.S. distribution, and we had just renewed our acquaintance when he acquired *Mrs Brown*, a film he was very taken with, and I think he suddenly thought, "Well, Madden might be perfect for *Shakespeare*." And I think they had already offered it already to quite a long list of directors. So they gave it to me.

This would have been in about April 1997. The version I read appeared to be Tom Stoppard's second draft; I don't remember the date of the draft clearly, but it was certainly some years old. It was not at all clear to me that the script was being offered when I read it — quite probably they were waiting for an answer from somebody else — but I remember distinctly the thrill of discovery reading it: its cleverness, its wonderful momentum, the way it appropriated Shakespearean techniques and themes, the outrageous jokes, the poetry, the magic spell it cast. I couldn't quite believe a script like this could be countenanced as a movie. But it felt like a world that I knew, a sense of humor I knew, and this feeling persisted all the way through the making of the film. I thought this would be irresistibly and exquisitely enjoyable to anybody who shared an affinity for that world, who had been a part of theatre, who knew Shakespeare, who knew the jokes and what they meant. I kept thinking, "It would be marvelous if other people get this," but that was not my particular concern at that point. All I wanted to do was to make a film that somehow encapsulated the intoxication that I felt reading it, that I felt the whole story was about — and still feel it's about. The studio paying for it had to be concerned whether

the film had the ability to travel and reach a larger audience;
I just thought I had to realize it properly.

Bringing in Their Shakespearean Background: Making It Accessible_

JOHN: I had studied Shakespeare at school and at university and I
subsequently ran a company called the Oxford and Cambridge
Shakespeare Company for three or four years. Later I went to
Yale Drama School to teach Shakespeare and acting and play-
writing and directed Shakespeare while I was there.

TOM: I don't consider myself some kind of Shakespearean
expert. I'm not. I'm an intermittent theatre-goer. I've seen,
I guess, most of Shakespeare's plays and have read the rest
now and again, but it's not an infatuation with Shakespeare....
I had seen Peter O'Toole play Hamlet as a very young
actor at Bristol, where I was a reporter, and I used to write
about the theatre occasionally. That was my first real exposure to Shakespeare. Then writing my play *Rosencrantz and
Guildenstern Are Dead* really made me understand at least that
play (*Hamlet*) by Shakespeare pretty well. (WGA, p. 24)

JOHN: With some trepidation I went to meet Tom, who I imagined to be a somewhat daunting figure. I'd grown up with his
work and admired it hugely and relished his sense of humor.
I had recently seen his play, *Arcadia,* which I thought was a
masterpiece, so I hardly thought of him as somebody you
could approach lightly and suggest changes. But he turned
out to be the most extraordinarily generous and receptive
and unassuming man: a master technician who simply wants
to know what it is you want him to do and what you want to
communicate, who then sets himself the task of doing it.

Tom had said, "I suppose that the first thing I ought to do is to
read the script again; have you got one?" He writes in long

hand and gives the script to Jacky Matthews, his long-time assistant, to put into a database, but he doesn't tend to keep those things around. At the point the original version of the movie had run out of steam, he decided to put it aside and not to return to it, so I sent him what I had read and took to be the script he had written. I arrived at his apartment to discuss it, to be greeted with the news that this was not his version of the script, despite his name being on the cover page. We later discovered two initials in the bottom corner of the cover sheet, a tantalizing indication of the identity of the writer who had rewritten his version — a scenario that seemed, like many others subsequently, to have come straight out of the script itself.

Somewhere between Tom finishing his second draft of the film, and it going into production in the Ed Zwick incarnation, I think it had undergone a "polish" and it had happened without any of us knowing it, including Miramax when they bought the script. Though still unmistakably Tom's, it had become slightly romanticized and been made more polite. Some things that might be thought to be questionable for an American audience, such as the fact the whole movie concerned an affair while this man was married and had children, was sort of swept under the carpet in the script. So, Tom said "Okay, if I'm to do some work — which I'm very happy to do — I'd rather start with the script that I wrote."

TOM: As far as I knew, the script which first came to John was my "final" script for Ed Zwick with changes made by a writer employed for the purpose by Ed. When John asked me to come back aboard, he sent me this script. I told him I'd only work with him on the script as I'd written it, so we went back to that. He hadn't realized that another writer had had a go at it. Nor did I — Ed never told me.

Rewriting the Script — Writer and Director

JOHN: The script was already in amazing shape, in my view, with perhaps the ending — as so often — most in need of consideration. There was certainly still some way for the script to go, particularly in the rendering of the performance of *Romeo and Juliet,* and the way in which this resolved the story of Will and Viola, and this was the area on which we concentrated. We worked on the script quite closely for several months in late 1997. Tom is obviously a genius with structure and particularly brilliant, I think, in set-up — what he calls "the long fuse" — something that is established invisibly very early on in the story that starts to pay off and pay off again as the story develops, so that there is a sense of accumulation, a sense of momentum, and finally a satisfying sense of everything coming together. But Tom is generous enough to believe that a director has to make the script his or her own, and was happy to accommodate my feelings about where it might still need to go. And he remained happy to scratch every itch I alerted him to as we got further down the line into production.

Tom's brilliant conception was to model the story very, very faithfully on the structural and emotional principles of mature Shakespearean comedy. And there's always the moment in Shakespearean comedy where death intrudes, where real pain suddenly collides with this kind of impossibly charming and delicate world, and that pain has to be incorporated into the world of make-believe. In *Shakespeare in Love,* that moment comes in the tavern scene, with Viola's discovery Shakespeare is married, and her realization that this dream that she was living was actually a complicated violation of somebody else's life. And that moment is in turn followed by the news of Marlowe's violent death, which Will imagines to be his fault, so the specter of darkness and death suddenly tips the comedy off balance, and the comedy Will is writing becomes a tragedy.

The focus of Tom and my work was both to balance the comic extremes of the material — Tom claimed he had originally conceived of it as a Zucker brothers farce, a kind of Elizabethan *Airplane* — and to finesse the last act of the film where the first performance of *Romeo and Juliet* interweaves with the story of Viola and Will. The marriage of Wessex and Viola, for example, was added, which eventually became the trigger for the film's resolution, as were other strands — the earlier introduction of Marlowe, for example.

TOM: John Madden is a director who likes to involve the writer very closely at every stage. We were talking constantly and very often we were talking about the tiniest detail of changing a phrase, changing half a line. As with all fiction involving historical characters, the story is taking place in a parallel world. So one is making a fairy tale out of the life of a genius who lived. It's rather helpful to the people who are telling the story that so little is known about William Shakespeare because it means that you can use quite a lot without contradicting other things that might have been known about him.... I think the difficulty with plays and films re the challenge, if you like, is much more to do with dynamics and structure, and when a film is first put together and shown to a group of people, it's always the pacing and the structure which needs adjustment... With films you're manipulating tape. I love the power one can have over the raw material.

One of the things which was enjoyable was to be able to occupy some ground between contemporary, colloquial dialogue and Shakespeare's lines. The characters never quite break into mock Elizabeth but there is a period quality to some of the writing.[4]

---

4 "Interview with Tom Stoppard," *www.filmeducation.org*, Interview Transcript.

The *Twelfth Night* ending, as I remember it, didn't enter the picture until one of the later drafts. I remember changing the heroine's name to Viola because of this. Marc had given her a name which was an eighteenth-century coinage by Alexander Pope, I believe. *Twelfth Night,* supposedly, was not written until about 1601, so it wasn't the next play after *Romeo and Juliet.* That was dramatic license.[5]

Finding the Style

TOM: I loved those Zucker Brothers comedies and I think that when I kicked off on the script I was thinking of it as pure comedy for its own sake. I would like to think that by the time I finished for Ed Zwick, I had found my way to something with more ambiguity, more feeling. But I can't emphasize enough that without John's influence, *Shakespeare in Love* would not have been the film it is, it would not have been complete. Insofar as the film succeeds as a love story on a truthful, human level, it is John's film. I had to be bullied into its romanticism before I caught on.

The Director Takes It Into Production

JOHN: There had always been a lot of nerves at the beginning about whether the mixture of tones could work, but that mixture was something that I was very attracted to and perhaps stupidly confident that I could achieve, so I wasn't initially worried by it. But I think that others were, not least some of the actors who turned the script down on that account.

There is definitely a view in Hollywood that "theatre" is bad box-office, and there were many who felt the script too full of in-jokes for its own good. Equally, there were some who felt that the comic concerns of the story would preclude the romantic, or vice versa. I think there was also a sense from Miramax that they thought an audience might need help

---

5 Email from Tom Stoppard to Linda Seger.

with an unfamiliar subject, and some suggestions were floating around, which I tried to ignore, that the "shrink" scene (where Will is consulting a mountebank (Anthony Sher) about his sexual and creative problems) should be expanded and used as a device to "explain" things.

So the early days of shooting were haunted by some ghosts, and I was trying to remain impervious to the nerves about whether it would all work. I remember watching with some relief a sequence which we had cut together very early on, when Will is showing Viola a scene he's just written, the "balcony" scene from *Romeo and Juliet* — intercut in the film with the scene where Viola as Thomas Kent is rehearsing it — and discovering that the humor seemed to intensify the romantic story, and created something very unusual. A shot of Fennyman — the ruthlessly hard-nosed businessman, and a hilarious and absurd character — falling under the spell of the scene, seemed not to explode the mood, as I had feared, but to make it more magical. We put some music on this sequence and sent it off to the studio, and it seemed to reassure them, and they left me alone for most of the rest of the shoot.

So we settled down into the routine nightmare of trying to get it all done. The nerves never entirely went away, re-appearing for me every morning, but they always evaporated during the day, and I went home at night feeling elated and confident, until I woke up the next morning, and so on until we wrapped.

Rewriting the Ending

JOHN: Miramax had always been concerned about the commercial perspective — not so much at the script stage, but later, certainly. I think it's fair to say Harvey Weinstein wears two hats, like all people who finance movies: one creative and the other commercial. He's a highly intelligent man and very smart about script, so he could immediately see what this script was doing, but at a certain point the other hat, the Ringling Brothers hat, goes on his head. He becomes preoccupied what he feels is going to work — or not work — with an audience. And the idea that the ending of this film would be "downbeat" — that it would involve the parting of the couple — was something that he could understand with one hat on, but not with the one he always found himself wearing at the end.

In the script the parting of Will and Viola felt very touching, and made your throat catch when you read it. But by the time I came to shoot it, and had the feel of the film in my bones, I knew that it was not going to work in the form it was written. I felt desperately uncomfortable the day that we went in to film it, because I couldn't find the right way of blocking the scene. One of the reasons it was wrong was that their farewell was a public farewell. The stage had been cleared up, the Admiral's Men were taking all the props off stage and bumping into each other. Tom had written it instinctively with a sort of sense of the untidiness of life going on and there wasn't really time or space for their farewell. The nurse was kind of waiting to take Viola elsewhere and Fennyman was busy discussing with Henslowe what his next part was going to be, there were a hundred other playwrights waiting to offer their scripts to Henslowe who was, of course by now, successful, and so on and so on. All of these were marvelous little vignettes but for once they were colliding and negating each other. And as a result the actors couldn't find the right way of playing it. At the end of the day I said to the cameraman, "We're not going to print any of this."

I called Tom that night. And I said, "Look, I think we have got a bit of a problem, the end doesn't work. I shot it but it doesn't work and I'm happy to show it to you but I don't want to show it to anybody else." And he said "What's the problem, what do you need?" And I said, "Well it's just not gathering correctly, it's not pulling everything together correctly and I'm sort of groping for it and I can spend an afternoon with you, I can articulate it better, but the first requirement is, I think they must be alone. They must be able to say farewell to one another alone."

So Tom said, "Well I suppose we should try and work out how to do that." I was away and I remember calling him from location and asking him how he was doing, and he said "Well, I can't really say that I've got anywhere except that one phrase comes into my mind, which is the phrase, 'How will this end?', because it's the problem that is facing me. My only kind of instinct at the moment is to incorporate that idea into the script." I thought this was brilliant: to include the problem of the film — how to end it — into the film itself. We puzzled that out, and the answer to the problem finally emerged in the realization that the Queen effectively could rewrite the script, both for the lives of her subjects and for us in the movie. We had added Wessex' and Viola's marriage to the script, but now found that there was a tempting loose end: Wessex had "lost his wife in the playhouse," and the Queen had to restore to Wessex the bride she had approved. This suggested at least the text of a different farewell between Will and Viola. But mechanically we had to find a way of allowing such a scene to occur, which was not easy. It particularly wasn't easy because we had already shot the huge set-piece where the Queen takes the stage and delivers her verdict, and there was absolutely no way due to the budgetary restraints of the film that we could reassemble all of that or restage it.

We decided to have Wessex accost the Queen outside the theatre — though we had shot her exit from the theatre interior, we had yet to shoot her exit outside, and her progress to the puddle where a dozen courtiers would lay down their capes ("Too late, too late"). In response to Wessex' immortal plea that he finds himself "a bride short," the Queen sends Master Kent back into the theatre to fetch out Viola so he can claim his bride, which of course turns the story round one more corner and gave us the simple mechanical opportunity of restaging their farewell in the empty theatre. At first this scene took the form of an impossibly poignant last embrace, with Viola leaving Will standing dejected on stage. Burbage arrives and asks him if he would like to join the Chamberlains' Men and the money that Will won from his wager with the Queen — that true love could be depicted on stage — becomes, in a neat formulation of Tom's, the fifty-pound share that Shakespeare is known to have paid to join Burbage's company. So it was a kind of Casablanca-type ending where the two men walked off down the muddy street with Burbage putting his arm around Shakespeare to console him — the beginning, in other words, of a beautiful friendship. This was the ending we had by the end of shooting, and the one I think is included in the deleted scenes segment on the DVD of the film.

But once the film was edited, and after some research screenings, Miramax still had concerns about the film's commercial potential, and a ferocious argument began to develop between myself and Harvey about the way the movie concluded. Harvey had been hankering for an ending whereby Viola somehow stayed a part of Will's life; the idea seemed to be that we would see her performing in disguise in *Twelfth Night* or something. I always maintained that this was kind of meaningless and left an odd taste because it meant she was some sort of bit on the side that Shakespeare would have for the rest of his life, and ignored the whole idea that she became his muse in favor of one where she became his mistress. We were also, as Tom pointed out, constrained somewhat by biography: Shakespeare did after all have a wife and children.

We were also constrained, thankfully, by the fact that we still could not afford to rebuild the Rose theatre and restage the whole climax of the film. After much discussion, Harvey conceded to our insistence that the film must end the way it was always intended, but Tom and I agreed to re-examine the final scene where Viola conveys the Queen's commission to Will on the empty stage: "The Queen commands a comedy, for Twelfth Night." Tom then wrote an amazing scene built on the principle that Viola somehow coaxes out of Will's misery the beginning of his new play ("Orsino — good name"), becoming in the process both his inspiration, and the model of all the heroines to come. Will's question to her after they have spun the story together is "How does it end?", to which Viola responds: "I don't know, it's a mystery." I remember him sending the pages over to me and I thought, "Well, game over!"

TOM: I can't remember the order of events which got us to the ending of the film. I think John protected me from much of the pressure he was being subjected to on the issue of the boy getting the girl and living happily ever after. It seemed obvious to me that if we expunged Will's wife from history, we'd look like idiots and be rightly punished for it. It was always in my mind that the heroine's name — Belinda — would have to be changed because I was pretty sure the name didn't exist in 1600, and there came a moment when turning her into "Viola" from *Twelfth Night* suggested a way forward toward a bittersweet ending. When Viola in Shakespeare's play gets washed up from the shipwreck she asks a sailor, "What country, friends is this?" The sailor replies, "This is Illyria, lady." I wanted the sailor to say to our Viola, "This is America, lady" and then to have a ghastly Manhattan skyline superimposed on the distance — which just goes to show that at a certain point the pencil should be taken out of my hand.

Casting the Film

JOHN: It's true to say that Harvey had some very strong ideas about who he thought would be appropriate casting for the film, based not just on their talent, but also on their box-office visibility. He had made what some observers thought to be a reckless investment in the script, and was perhaps understandably anxious to give himself the best chance of recouping it. So I met a number of people who fit that bill, without feeling I had found anyone plausible. And I was contending with the thought that the picture might not happen at all if we could not agree on the right casting of the two leads. That was what had happened, after all, the first time around.

The subsequent search was a very long one — May to October 1997 — and I auditioned large numbers of people for both parts. I had insisted on auditioning everybody because I felt that the requirements that the material imposed on the actor were so particular that it was impossible to know if an actor could meet them on the basis of a meeting alone, a process into which the director is forced if the actor has enough clout. This instinct began to be borne out when some extremely good actors who one would have thought would have been contenders just did not seem to have an affinity for the material. Some were quick to realize it after they had auditioned.

Strangely, I had auditioned Gwyneth Paltrow some years before for another film, and felt on the basis of that, and her performance in the Austen adaptation, *Emma*, that she was perfect casting for Viola, but understood from Miramax — who were her biggest fans and mentors — that she had passed on the film already. Whatever the reason for that decision, she later thought better of it, and inquired whether the part was still un-cast, which it was. So we had a Juliet, as the film has it, but we still had no Will.

The first time that Joseph Fiennes had auditioned, I did not spot his potential. I was looking in the wrong direction and somehow went past him. But as the casting director and I kept re-visiting our options, we felt that Joe was so right in every respect that it deserved further exploration.

Tom had been working on some new material, including the scene where Will encounters Marlowe and is dismayed to have to recount to him the plot of *Romeo and Ethel, the Pirate's Daughter.* We called Joe's agent and said, "We want him to read some new scenes but I don't want him to work on them." He had worked very exhaustively on a scene in his first audition, and on reflection I wondered if that had served him well. I got some tremendous reservations from Joe's agent that Joe would feel he was not doing the job if he didn't come in prepared, but I said no, I wanted him to come in and work cold with me. So he came in and we talked for a morning about the script. He is an extremely sweet and intelligent man. Then I sent everybody else out, and it was just him and me and a camera, which I operated, and we worked on the scenes together and I remember thinking "this is really good." Later, when I went home and watched the tape, it seemed obvious. Somehow the new scenes released him, and his humor was so deft, and his touch so light.

In so much of the story Shakespeare is the butt of the joke, which is something that had really bothered some other actors who were trying to deal with it. Joe had no difficulty dealing with that at all. And he was just very clever. Suddenly I could see this working, so I told Miramax and I brought him and Gwyneth together to read and they clicked. She adored him and he came with the Shakespearean credentials that I think she sort of admired, and took some comfort from. She had not seem daunted particularly by the challenge of the movie — she had grown up with theatre because her mother, Blythe Danner, was a very busy actor then working primarily on stage — but she later revealed how daunted she had been.

With those two parts cast, the picture became a go picture. The other roles were easier to cast. Judi Dench agreed immediately to play Queen Elizabeth, having just played Queen Victoria in *Mrs Brown*, worried only that she would give exactly the same performance but in a different frock. Geoffrey Rush thought it the most brilliant script he had read, and didn't have to think about it at all. Colin Firth (who had been considered for Will in the film's original incarnation, and credits himself — as the last person to audition — with being the man who finally made Julia Roberts drop the project) took some persuading, but then grabbed the role of Wessex. Ben Affleck put himself on tape to pitch for the role of Ned Alleyn, and I had my pick of an amazing pool of British character actors for so many of the other roles: Imelda Staunton, Anthony Sher, Martin Clunes, Tom Wilkinson, Jim Carter, Mark Williams.

Shooting the Film

JOHN: We started rehearsing in February for a month, and it was a sort of Shakespearean indoctrination for some of them. I worked with Viola, and with all of "the Admiral's Men" because I wanted the Admiral's Men to feel like an organism. We worked on scenes, but only loosely, wanting to leave spontaneity for the shooting, concentrating instead on the Shakespeare/Wessex duel, the dance, and the big fight, all of which needed careful choreography. I was spending from 10 until 3 in the rehearsal room, and then after 3 o'clock I was going off to the theatre planning the shooting and getting stuff together for production. We started shooting in March and finished in mid-June and then we cut it for about a month and went off to America with it for the first time in mid-August. We went back again in late September. Then in October we re-shot. Then we finished the film at the very end of November. We showed it to the press about a week later and it was released at the beginning of December in two cinemas in L.A. and two in New York. To our surprise and delight it started to get wonderful reviews and we started to widen out after Christmas.

TOM: I thought we just got away with the exterior re-shoot, with all the actors crowding outside the theatre. And just-married Gwyneth fleeing from Wessex's coach was a bit audacious. But then, the Bard sometimes had to get himself out of tight corners. In a paradoxical way, getting those final pieces of jigsaw into place against the clock was the bit I enjoyed most. It's an essential and true part of moviemaking. It puts you to the test in a way which doesn't happen when all the pieces fit neatly first time.

STORY BEATS FOR *SHAKESPEARE IN LOVE*

Act One/Set-Up

1 min.   In 1593, two theatres vie for London's audiences: Burbage's Curtain Theatre and Henslowe's Rose.

Set-Up/Fennyman

2 min.   Financier Fennyman holds Henslowe's feet to the fire — literally — giving him three weeks to come up with an overdue payment. Henslowe has no fear, sure that Shakespeare will finish and stage a new play for The Rose.

Set-Up/Theatre Story

3 min.   The play is "Romeo and Ethel the Pirate's Daughter," which Fennyman insists Henslowe open in two weeks to generate the payment funds.

4 min.   Shakespeare, meanwhile, struggles to write — dawdling and doodling.

Set-Up/Will and the Play Story

5 min.   Shakespeare tells Henslowe that he's blocked and lonely, needs a muse.

Henslowe explains their dire dilemma vis-à-vis Fennyman.

6 min.   Shakespeare asks Henslowe for payment; Henslowe holds out.

7 min.   Shakespeare visits his Counselor, alludes to sexual dysfunction and writer's block.

8 min.   Shakespeare reveals that he's banished from the wife he had to marry — who lives 400 miles away — has dallied with local women but is alone now.

9 min.   Counselor gives Shakespeare a charmed bracelet in which to insert his written name and give to a woman to elicit her "muse" charms.

Set-Up/Burbage Throughline

Shakespeare visits Burbage for payment, pits him versus Henslowe.

10 min.   Burbage gives Shakespeare an advance to write. Shakespeare's latest comedy is performed for the Queen.

0:11 — Shakespeare dallies with Rosaline, Burbage's mistress, and gives her the bracelet.

0:12 — The Queen howls at the play's farcical comedy. Henslowe urges Shakespeare to write another play featuring love and farce.

Set-Up/Will and Viola Story

Viola is in the play's audience.

13 min.   Viola is profoundly moved by the play's romantic soliloquy. Shakespeare continues trying to write.

Act One Development

14 min.   At her family's grand manor, Viola discusses the play with her Nurse, laments that women should be allowed to perform in the theatre, reveals that she's rich and seeks romance and adventure.

15 min.   Viola rhapsodizes for love, wishes she could be an actor but it's not allowed.

16 min.   Fennyman pushes Henslowe to make things happen. The theatres, closed for plague, are reopened.

17 min.   Henslowe promises Fennyman that the new play is in-the-works. Shakespeare, inspired by Rosaline, rewrites his play as "Romeo and Rosaline."

18 min.   Shakespeare finds Rosaline in a tryst with another man, is crushed and destroys his new draft. (REVERSAL)

19 min.   Shakespeare and Henslowe recruit people to audition for the upcoming play.

    Marlowe and Shakespeare talk shop about playwriting. Shakespeare is embarrassed at his current effort; Marlowe offers helpful story advice.

21 min.   Shakespeare joins Henslowe to audition a motley group of would-be actors, choosing the least awful of the bunch for the play.

22 min.   End of auditions but no lead actor found. Viola, dressed as a boy and calling herself Thomas Kent, arrives late and auditions with great talent and passion, grabbing Shakespeare's attention.

23 min.   When Shakespeare asks Viola to remove her hat, she bolts and Shakespeare chases her.

24 min.   Shakespeare chases, sees her leave via boat, follows to her family's estate.

Set-Up/Viola and Wessex Story

25 min.   Viola dashes in, nearly late for the dinner during which her father will arrange her marriage to Lord Wessex.

26 min.   Shakespeare arrives, asks for Thomas Kent, hangs around to wait, leaves a story idea to deliver to him. Viola reads the idea and vows to play the lead role.

27 min.   Shakespeare joins the dinner party at the estate and sees Viola without her disguise. Her family plots her marriage to Lord Wessex.

28 min.   Shakespeare is attracted to Viola, intrigued. He learns who she is, that she is out of his league. He is, nonetheless, smitten.

29 min.   Viola dances with Shakespeare, then with Lord Wessex in a romantic triangle's "pas de trois." She's smitten with Shakespeare.

30 min.   Lord Wessex pulls Viola away from Shakespeare, and threatens him. Shakespeare mis-identifies himself as Christopher Marlowe when Wessex demands his name.

31 min.   Shakespeare tries to get to Viola. She professes her admiration. He knows this infatuation will lead to trouble, but proceeds anyway, climbing up to her window.

32 min.   Shakespeare falls from the window, is chased from the estate.

1st Turning Point/Play Story

He writes feverishly now, inspired by Viola and full of new ideas.

1st Turning Point/Theatre Story

33 min.   Henslowe et al react to the changes in the play. Shakespeare rejects the Teenaged Boy Actor who would play the lead part. Fennyman does the tough producer thing.

34 min.   The regular troupe of actors return to town. Ned cows Fennyman, demanding respect.

35 min.	Ned accepts the lead male role in the new play, lured when Shakespeare claims the play's title will be Ned's character's name — Mercutio.
	Shakespeare announces that Thomas Kent will play the lead female role. He gets story ideas from the violence-oriented Teenaged Actor.
36 min.	Viola rehearses the part, disguised as Thomas Kent.
37 min.	Shakespeare coaches Viola/Thomas on acting, inspires passionate emoting.
	Ned clamors for more juicy lines in the play. Shakespeare writes sonnets to Viola.
38 min.	Viola's Nurse buys time for her when Lord Wessex seeks her out. Viola returns from rehearsal, and Lord Wessex tells her that they will wed.

1st Turning Point/Viola and Wessex Story

39 min.	Viola declines. Lord Wessex explains it's not a request; it's a command. They'll wed and move to America. Lord Wessex grabs her; acts the cad.
40 min.	Lord Wessex explains that Viola will be inspected/approved by the Queen on Sunday, and tells her how to behave. Viola writes to Shakespeare — "forget me, I'm engaged — with no way out."
41 min.	Actors rehearse and Ned pushes for more lines, more stage time.
	Shakespeare offers Ned a dramatic death scene, comically accepted till Ned thinks harder about it.
42 min.	Viola (disguised as Thomas Kent) gives Shakespeare the news that Viola must wed. Shakespeare laments, cannot believe it, declares his love for her.
43 min.	Poetic romantic exchange between Shakespeare and Thomas Kent as they wax lyrical about Viola.
44 min.	Shakespeare waxes on. Thomas Kent challenges whether Shakespeare's love is true; Shakespeare responds with convincing sincerity.
45 min.	Overwhelmed, Thomas Kent kisses Shakespeare, then bolts.

1st Turning Point/Will and Viola Story

Shakespeare recovers from being kissed by a boy, then learns that Thomas Kent is Viola.

46 min.　　Shakespeare meets Viola in her room. They embrace and he undresses her.

47 min.　　Viola stands, unwrapped and revealed. They make love.

48 min.　　Post-sex, the pair glow, then start at it again.

49 min.　　Next morning Shakespeare is ready to dally, says Henslowe can wait for his play. Viola urges him to write.

50 min.　　At rehearsal, actors practice with renewed passion for the new material. Viola (as Thomas Kent) shines as an actor.

51 min.　　Ned tries to take control. Shakespeare kisses Thomas Kent during rehearsal; they are obsessed with one another, comically stealing embraces and kisses.

52 min.　　Shakespeare leaves to go write, inspired to compose poetic dialogue. Viola reads it and loves it.

53 min.　　Rehearsal continues. Shakespeare's work is now glorious. He writes *Romeo and Juliet*, inspired by Viola.

54 min.　　Rehearsals/writing/romance continues, with *Romeo and Juliet* reflecting Shakespeare and Viola's situation.

55 min.　　Rehearsals/writing/romance continues, with interruptions, and everything in their lives finds its way into the new play's story.

56 min.　　Ned likes the new play, magnanimously suggests *Romeo and Juliet* as the title. Henslowe is comically unmoved by the new play, wants his farcical romance/comedy.

1st Turning Point/Fennyman Story

57 min.　　Fennyman interrupts rehearsal, but shows new respect for actors and the play.

Midpoint/Play Story

58 min.　　Shakespeare explains the tragic nature of the play — the lovers fated to be apart.

59 min.　　Lord Wessex collects Viola for her visit to the Queen.

Shakespeare must hide and flee, but vows to accompany Viola who has accepted her arranged fate.

60 min. Shakespeare sneaks along, disguised as Viola's cousin/chaperone. They arrive at the Queen's grand palace.

61 min. Viola stands before the Queen. Lord Wessex quizzes Shakespeare for information about Christopher Marlowe. Shakespeare pours on more claims that Marlowe is the rival Lord Wessex must worry over.

62 min. The Queen inspects/quizzes Viola, notes that she attends plays, quizzes her about her interest in theatre, ridicules her and playwrights re love.

63 min. Viola disagrees with the Queen, alludes to Shakespeare's talent for writing truth.

Midpoint/Theatre Story

Lord Wessex sucks up, makes a bet that playwrights have no truth. Disguised Shakespeare takes the bet — playwrights do write truth on the nature of love.

64 min. The Queen declares she'll decide if it's true. The Queen tells Lord Wessex that Viola has just recently lost her virginity.

1st Turning Point/Marlowe Throughline

Lord Wessex now suspects Marlowe. Marlowe, meanwhile, holds back a play from Burbage, demanding payment first.

Burbage Throughline

65 min. Burbage threatens to use Shakespeare's play instead, but Marlowe reveals that Shakespeare gave it to Henslowe. Burbage is incensed, finds Shakespeare's bracelet on Rosaline and is even more incensed.

66 min. Burbage storms rehearsal, challenges Shakespeare to a sword fight. Both sides battle.

67 min. Henslowe pleads for peace as the fight rages on. Shakespeare and Viola hide, kiss, lament the fate that is unfolding to keep them apart.

68 min. The fight ends with Burbage knocked out. Fennyman treats the actors to a celebration at a tavern/brothel.

69 min.   Viola is shocked to be at a brothel.

2nd Turning Point/Fennyman Story

Shakespeare gives Fennyman a part in the new play as the apothecary.

70 min.   Henslowe urges Shakespeare to include a happy, comical end to the play.

2nd Turning Point/Will and Viola Story

He reveals that Shakespeare is married and Viola is crushed.

2nd Turning Point/Marlowe Story

71 min.   News arrives — Marlowe is dead, killed. Shakespeare is remorseful. Viola leaves. Shakespeare feels guilt over Marlowe's death.

72 min.   Shakespeare, in church, prays. Lord Wessex finds Viola.

73 min.   Lord Wessex alludes to Marlowe's death. Viola misinterprets and thinks that it is Shakespeare who is dead. Viola mourns. Wessex and Viola go to church.

74 min.   Shakespeare arrives at church, accuses Lord Wessex who runs, spooked by what he thinks is Marlowe's ghost. Viola sees Shakespeare alive. They happily reunite.

75 min.   Shakespeare admits his guilt in Marlowe's death, praises Marlowe's talents. Viola confronts Shakespeare re his lies and married status.

76 min.   Shakespeare says Viola deceived him too. Viola vows her love, but the pair are trapped in their fates, kept apart.

77 min.   Actors rehearse the play. Shakespeare writes Juliet's feigned death, and Romeo's suicide, followed by Juliet's revival and suicide.

78 min.   Henslowe and Fennyman approve the play. Ned quizzes Shakespeare re a vital part missing from the play. Shakespeare gives the finished play to Viola.

79 min.   Shakespeare recites the new scene — of love and loss.

80 min.   Shakespeare and Viola recite the lines as they embrace and make love.

81 min.   The Teenaged Actor squeals on Shakespeare and Viola's affair.

Lord Wessex interrupts rehearsal and challenges Shakespeare to a sword duel.

82 min. Swordplay as the actors watch. Shakespeare prevails, Lord Wessex feints, wounds Shakespeare.

83 min. Duel continues. Shakespeare prevails, accuses Lord Wessex of murdering Marlowe. Lord Wessex denies guilt.

Climax/Marlowe Story

Ned reveals that Marlowe died in a tavern fight.

84 min. Lord Wessex orders Rose Theatre destroyed.

85 min. Teenaged Actor points out Viola as a woman. Theatre ordered closed. (DARK MOMENT) Viola is tricked into revealing herself.

86 min. Viola apologizes, explains her motives, and leaves.

87 min. Viola is distressed, depressed. Actors lament the theatre closure.

88 min. Burbage comes to Henslowe et al. to offer his theatre for Shakespeare's play.

2nd Turning Point/Play Story

89 min. Actors et al. prep at The Curtain Theatre. (NEW STIMULUS)

2nd Turning Point/Viola and Wessex Story

90 min. Viola preps to wed Lord Wessex, who plans their trip to America. Shakespeare comes to stop things but cannot.

2nd Turning Point/Will and Viola Story

91 min. Viola and Lord Wessex emerge from church, married. Viola sees a flyer regarding the play performance. The Nurse distracts Lord Wessex and Viola flees.

92 min. Crowds gather for the play. Actors prep. Shakespeare will play Romeo.

93 min. Pre-play mayhem and prep. Shakespeare and Henslowe fret. The performance begins.

94 min. The Narrator freezes up, stutters for an eternity, then dives in to eloquently announce the play.

95 min.   Viola and Nurse near the theatre. The Actor playing Juliet is in trouble — voice has deepened overnight — cannot sound like a woman.

96 min.   Viola arrives to watch. Henslowe reveals the need for a new actor to play Juliet. Viola offers to do it.

97 min.   Lord Wessex arrives at the theatre.

2nd Turning Point/Theatre Story

Viola makes her entrance — clearly a real woman — and the crowd is shocked.

98 min.   The play goes on. Lord Wessex watches, sadly. Shakespeare watches, smitten. Viola shines.

99 min.   Romeo's fight scene. Ned's death scene. The Queen's soldiers near the theatre. The fight scene continues.

100 min.   Romeo is advised to flee and does. Shakespeare asks Viola if she wed Lord Wessex. They lament, then kiss, then rush back onstage.

101 min.   Romeo and Juliet's parting scene.

102 min.   Juliet takes her potion. Romeo gets poison from Fennyman, the Apothecary. Soldiers march, closer to the theatre.

Climax/Romeo and Juliet Story

103 min.   Romeo finds Juliet dead, takes poison and dies.

104 min.   The audience weeps. Juliet revives, finds Romeo dead, kills herself with his dagger.

105 min.   The Narrator finishes the play. The crowd sits in absolute silence. The theatre company holds their breath — a hit or a bomb?

Climax/The Play Story

Climax/Fennyman Story

106 min.   The audience goes wild with applause. Actors rejoice. Viola and Shakespeare kiss, embrace, take their bows.

107 min.   Soldiers reach the theatre and announce the arrest of everyone in the company.

108 min.   Burbage talks back. The Queen arrives, examines Viola as Thomas Kent.

109 min.   The Queen declares it a mistake to accuse Thomas of being a woman, dismisses (wink, wink) Viola.

Climax/Theatre Story

The Queen summons Lord Wessex, declares that this play has proved the challenge and won the wager — yes, a play can prove the true nature of love.

Lord Wessex loses.

110 min.   The Queen approves of Shakespeare and departs. Lord Wessex grovels.

Climax/Viola and Wessex Story

111 min.   The Queen refuses to override Viola and Lord Wessex's marriage vows, tells Viola to do the right thing, say goodbye to Shakespeare.

112 min.   The Queen departs. Viola gives Shakespeare the wager winnings. Shakespeare wants to quit the theatre.

113 min.   Viola urges Shakespeare to continue as a playwright, tells him that the Queen requests a comedy from him next, and gives him story ideas.

114 min.   Viola predicts her future (as she suggests story ideas).

Climax/Will and Viola Story

The pair bid tearful farewell.

115 min.   Farewells continue and conclude. Shakespeare writes.

Resolution

Twelfth Night, wherein all seagoing voyagers drown except for Viola on her trip to the new land.

116 min.   Shakespeare writes, predicting Viola's new life alone in the new land, keeping her forever alive in his imagination.

117 min.   Viola walks alone up an empty shore as Shakespeare writes. Credits roll.

part

◆ *3* ◆

CRASH

EXPLORING THE THEME

When *Crash* won the Academy Award in 2006 for Best Picture, there was an audible, surprised gasp from the audience, as if they knew that *Brokeback Mountain* was a shoo-in, and *Crash* was a long shot. Although certainly many in the audience must have voted for the film, the gasp may have meant that they voted for it, but didn't expect others to vote for *Crash*. Or it might have meant that the vote was split, and *Crash* came up through the middle, between *Brokeback Mountain* and another film, even though no other film had been trumpeted as the expected Best Picture winner.

Why the surprise? *Crash* simply didn't fit the expected Academy Award winner. Usually the Academy Award goes to the big picture, set against a panorama with broad vistas and cinematic beauty — such as *Gone with the Wind, The English Patient, Dances with Wolves, The Last Emperor, Out of Africa.*

Sometimes the big expensive picture wins, that proves that the big risk was worth the big pay-off, such as *Titanic* or *Lord of the Rings.*

Sometimes the picture is big and important, dealing with themes that are sometimes historical: *Schindler's List, Platoon, Braveheart, Amadeus.*

Sometimes the film is character-driven, with a strong protagonist who shines in the starring role, such as *A Beautiful Mind, Driving Miss Daisy, American Beauty, Forrest Gump, Rainman, Gandhi.*

The smaller film may get nominated, as we have seen with *Good Night and Good Luck, Capote, The Full Monty, Secrets and Lies, Babe,* and *The Crying Game.* But very rarely is the winner a small film, with no starring roles, a small context, without a main protagonist, and with little color or spectacle.

Crash is an exception.

WHAT IS THE STORY ABOUT?

Crash is a very complex story, interweaving various storylines that seem to be disconnected with each other, but all relate to the theme of racism. The story takes place Today, and Yesterday, in Los Angeles. It begins with a carjacking by Anthony and Peter, two blacks, who steal the SUV of Rick, the District Attorney who is up for re-election, and his wife, Jean, who represents the life of the upper-class, wealthy white world. This carjacking causes problems for a number of other people. Rick is concerned because the SUV was stolen by two blacks. Rick needs the black vote to win the election, so he promotes a black detective (Graham) and decides to frame a white cop (Lewis) who killed a black cop (Conklin).

Graham is the cop investigating the Lewis-Conklin shooting. Graham is also in a sexual relationship with his Hispanic partner, Ria. Graham is trying to find his younger brother, Peter, the carjacker, who has turned to a life of crime.

The carjacking causes problems for the D.A.'s wife, Jean, who now must have the locks of her home replaced by a Hispanic locksmith she doesn't trust — Daniel. Daniel also works on the locks for Farhad, a Middle Eastern shopkeeper who has been robbed several times. Daniel tells Farhad that the problem is not the lock, but the door, but Farhad thinks he's lying. Toward the end of the story, in a rage over another robbery, Farhad tries to shoot Daniel. But Daniel is saved by his young daughter, Lara, who jumps in her father's arms to save him, since she's wearing the "impenetrable invisible cloak" her father gave to her to protect her from bullets. Through a seeming miracle, she's able to save him, although we later learn that Farhad, unknowingly, had blanks in his gun.

The movie follows another line of stories that revolve around Ryan, a white racist cop, who stops the black television director, Cameron, and his wife Christine, as they are driving home from an award ceremony. He is partially motivated by his rage over how his ill father is being treated by a black social worker (Shaniqua). He does a lewd body search of Christine, which enrages Christine, and she takes it out on her husband who did nothing to stop it. The search also shocks Ryan's partner, Hansen, who asks to be reassigned, which he is.

The carjacking causes problems for carjackers Anthony and Peter, who, by mistake, run over Choi, a Korean who seems to be trying to enter a van parked by the side of the road. They dump the bloodied Choi by a hospital, and then try to sell the stolen SUV to Lucien, but Lucien finds blood in the SUV and won't accept it. Later in the film, Anthony tries to carjack Cameron's SUV. Peter leaves Anthony and hitches a ride with Hansen, who kills him. Anthony goes back to steal Choi's van, and learns that the van is carrying illegal Asian immigrants who are chained in the back of the van. He decides to set them free.

These stories, some of which seem unrelated to each other, intersect throughout the film.

The Cast of Characters

Crash is made up of many characters, from many different ethnic backgrounds. In order for the reader to keep these characters in mind, here is the cast:

Graham (Don Cheadle), the black detective

Ria (Jennifer Esposito), his Hispanic partner who is part Puerto Rican, part Salvadoran

Rick (Brendan Fraser), the white District Attorney

Jean (Sandra Bullock), his white wife

Anthony (Chris "Ludacris" Bridges), the black who steals Rick's and Jean's SUV

Peter (Larenz Tate), Anthony's black partner who is also the brother of Detective Graham

Ryan (Matt Dillon), the white cop

Hansen (Ryan Phillippe), Ryan's younger white partner, who later asks to be reassigned

Farhad (Shaun Toub), the Iranian shopkeeper whose store is repeatedly robbed

Dorri (Bahar Soomekh), his daughter, who is a pathologist

Shereen (Marina Sirtis), Farhad's Iranian wife

Daniel (Michael Pena), the Mexican locksmith who fixes the locks of Jean and Farhad

Lara (Ashlyn Sanchez), Daniel's young daughter. Daniel gives his daughter an invisible cloak to protect her from bullets

Elizabeth (Karina Arroyave), Daniel's wife

Shaniqua (Loretta Devine), Ryan's father's black social worker

Cameron (Terrence Dashon Howard), the black television director

Christine (Thandie Newton), Cameron's black wife who is molested by Ryan

Notice the ethnic mix includes White, Black, Hispanic, Middle Eastern, and Asian characters. Within this group, we can see the upper-class whites (Rick and Jean) and various working or middle-class whites (the police, the gun store owner who sells the gun and the blanks to Farhad); upper-class blacks (Cameron and Christine), middle-class blacks (Graham), and lower-class blacks (Anthony, Peter); middle-class Hispanics (Ria, Graham's partner, the locksmith Daniel, a Hispanic cop that becomes Ryan's new partner) and lower-class Hispanics (Maria, Jean's maid). The Hispanics include Mexicans, a Puerto Rican and a Salvadoran. The Middle Easterners are represented by Farhad's family who are Iranians (Persians) rather than Arabs.

WHAT IS THE STORY *REALLY* ABOUT?

The Theme of Racism

Although the above synopsis is what the story is about, the story is really about racism. *Crash* has a kind of European feel to it, with its small story and strong characters. Like many European films, it's driven by its theme more than its plot. Every choice of storyline, scene, conflict, confrontation, and story movement relates to the theme of racism. Although we often find this type of philosophical, thematic-oriented film in other countries, rarely are American films so driven by one central idea.

Crash explores the many aspects of racism: the stereotypes, the expectations, the injustices, the sadness, the fury, and the dangers.

The film shows how racism is embedded in our attitudes, and our actions, and under highly stressful situations is apt to move from our unconscious and subconscious to the conscious level, spilling out into actions that are based on inaccurate perceptions. The film crashes one perception against another, constantly intersecting stories that force stereotypes to rise to the surface, to be confronted, to do their damage, and eventually, for some, to reach resolution and even transformation. It shows us that the characters are often better than their petty racism which diminishes them, and that sometimes, they're able to get past these racist attitudes. For others, they're not.

The film is set up to first establish the stereotypes in Act One, then to explore them in Act Two, and then to start resolving some of them late in Act Two, and in Act Three.

The stereotypes are presented to us from the very first scene which begins with a car crash. We are told that Koreans look like the Chinese, and are short and can't drive because they can hardly see over the steering wheel. As a result, they cause accidents. Hispanics can't brake properly.

Iranians are outsiders. Mexicans and Puerto Ricans all look the same, even though they're from different cultures. Blacks are low-class gangbangers. Whites are haughty and manipulative.

The film is set in Los Angeles, because of its racial mix, but also because Los Angeles is structured so the races need not mix. It's a car-driven society, where whites rarely have to drive through Koreatown, or Watts, or East L.A. but can take the freeways instead. Other ethnic groups can avoid the areas where they might be stopped, just for being non-whites, as in Beverly Hills and Bel Air. It's a city of distinct neighborhoods where people can easily be segregated from each other. Each can fairly easily stay within their own special world. Without an intersection, a clash of cultures, the stereotypes remain the same.

In the first lines of the film, Graham explains this isolation from each other:

```
                GRAHAM (V.O.)
    Any real city, you walk, you're
    bumped, brush past people. In L.A.,
    no one touches you….
    We're always behind metal and glass.
    we crash into each other just to
    feel something. (p. 1)
```

As the story develops, the character's attitudes toward each other are explored, as they are forced to collide with each other. Sometimes this collision happens in ordinary life, because society can't keep a total separation. People collide through their jobs, as we see with the police force. Sometimes through love and sex, as we see with Graham, the black detective, and his Puerto Rican partner and sometime lover, Ria. Sometimes through a dependence upon the skills of another, as we see when Jean, the D.A.'s wife, and the Iranian shop-owner, Farhad, hire Daniel, the Mexican, to fix their locks, or when Ryan is forced to talk to his father's black social worker. Yet, in the rare moments when they do come together, somehow the stereotypes continue to be clutched, as if one's own identity depends on holding to inaccurate perceptions of another's identity. As with any of the "isms" (ageism, racism, sexism), the stereotype clearly decides who's in, who's out, who's up, who's down.

The film suggests that these stereotypes are held on to, because of the lack of intersection. It takes a crash, of one kind or another, for them to come to the forefront. It takes tragedy, or near tragedy, for a stereotype to be broken.

Breaking Stereotypes

After the story sets up stereotypes, it then proceeds to break them by showing that the characters are more than the expected, predictable, cliché. Cameron is black, but he's a Buddhist.

Peter carries a St. Christopher statuette with him, wherever he goes, even though his activity is decidedly anti-religious.

Daniel is no gangbanger, but a Hispanic locksmith and family man, trying to protect his daughter from violence.

Dorri is a pathologist, and Farhad an American citizen.

Ryan's father ran a business that hired blacks, and paid them an equal wage, at a time when no one had to do this.

Anthony, who seems to be in everything for the money, unexpectedly puts others above financial gain.

Working Out the Theme

When figuring out, and exploring a theme, writers often begin by turning to their own experience. They think about how to bring their personal understandings to the theme to make it personal. They think about and brainstorm their own associations with the theme. And they look for the universal meanings of the events. Writers Paul Haggis and Bobby Moresco were intrigued by this theme, and their encounters with racism in Los Angeles, and brought their own personal attitudes and social consciousness to their exploration of the theme.

Crash has the potential to help us encounter our racial attitudes. It has the potential to not only transform the characters, but to transform the audience as well.

A writer, exploring this theme, might begin by thinking of all their personal associations. The idea began with personal experiences of writer/director Paul Haggis who then further developed it. Believing that the personal can also be universal, the writer's subjective experiences may bring the audience into their own exploration of the theme.

When exploring a theme, a writer can use the technique of journaling, and remembering their own personal experiences with the theme, believing that the personal is also the universal.

For instance, if I were to explore this theme, I'd have to begin to look at my own background. When watching the film, I bring this background back into the experience, and the film means more to me because I can connect with the ideas.

For those of us who didn't grow up in large cities, our interaction with races may be very minimal. I grew up in a town of 2500 people (Peshtigo, Wisconsin), and never met a black person until college, and never had a black friend until after graduate school. But in spite of the minimal interaction, I learned racism. Once when I was small, a black person drove through our town. Yes, only drove through the town, but this was a major event for us kids who had been counting cars and reading license plates to see what state the cars were from. We weren't quite sure what to make of it, but then the car was gone and we simply talked about it for a while. It was an early encounter with The Other, and was confusing to me. I wasn't sure why this event was supposed to be so unusual, but somehow the neighbor kids had already learned that there was something that didn't quite fit here. On some level, I must have learned it as well.

My parents, who were some of the nicest people I've ever met, nevertheless reinforced black stereotypes since we were told to lock our doors when going through the black section of Milwaukee. It was clear we were not safe in "their" company.

I never met someone from a Hispanic culture until college, although Mexicans would come to the area around our small town to pick cucumbers during the summer. We had one Jewish family in our town — everyone else was either Catholic or Protestant, who had plenty of stereotypes about each other to make up for the lack of a racial mix. If someone in our town was "no religion," they wouldn't admit it. We had no Asians (I can't remember when I first met an Asian, but it was either college or shortly after), no Muslims, and only one family I knew from another country — a family who had escaped Latvia during the Cold War and whose daughter became friends with us.

My parents (unwittingly) helped me break some stereotypes, since we entertained Dr. Shri Nehru, Ambassador to the United Nations from India and cousin of the Prime Minister, at our home when I was seven. Dr. and Mrs. Nehru were Hindus, complete with his "Nehru jacket" and her sari, and a bindi on the third eye of their foreheads. I somehow learned, from this experience, that other cultures are all right, but I also developed a class-influenced consciousness — somehow someone from another race who was upper class was better than someone from another race who was lower class. Handsome was better than not handsome. (Think Denzel Washington.) Classy and stylish was better than not classy and stylish. (Think Sidney Poitier.) Talented and sassy was better than not talented. (Think Lena Horne.)

I have found, as a middle-class white woman brought up in the Midwest in the '50s and '60s, that we can easily spend our lifetime trying to break our stereotypes. And rarely will we do it completely. Many times we aren't even aware of what our stereotype is. *Crash* helps us understand them, by first establishing the stereotype, and then breaking it. And no matter what our background is, our racial stereotypes will be part of our interaction with this film.

Racism in our Society

Once a writer explores his or her own individual response to the theme, the writer may also look at how racism is embedded in the structure of society. Writers Paul Haggis and Bobby Moresco read about racism, from a sociological perspective, in order to further understand the theme they were exploring.

Most people have an innate tendency to decide who is In and who is Out, who is Number One and who is on the bottom rungs of the ladder, below the line, and less important. We like to live in our comfort zone, which does not include The Other, The Strange, The Different. This is true in almost any diverse society, whether Paris in the 1920s, Alexandria Egypt and Ancient Rome, or anywhere where many races come together to not just create a melting pot but boiling pots. In American society, the majority make laws, thereby having the power to reinforce these perceptions and keep the majority in, the minority out. In other societies, the minority may rule over the oppressed majority.

Society decides where people can live, who is taxed and who is not, who receives the most benefits from our society, who gets the advantages, and how to keep the bad people out and the good people in, often becoming confused about who are The Bad, and who are The Good. Stereotypes depend on separation. They depend on keeping out The Encounter, The Confrontation, The Meeting, The Relationship. Society has many methods for keeping us isolated from each other. Until something, or someone, comes along to shatter our stereotypes, we can unconsciously continue, making unjust laws and continuing to carry inaccurate perceptions.

The Problem of Language

It isn't just the way we think and the rules we make, but language also helps us continue our racist attitudes.

We still struggle with the terms to describe people. We want to have simple terms so each person can fit into a clear and simple racial box, but people never quite fit into categories so neatly. We try to describe people by their nationality and race, so blacks are called African-Americans, but it's less clear what to call blacks who live in America but aren't African-American. A friend of mine is an African-Canadian, another Jamaican-American. When I asked my Jamaican-American friend what term she prefers, she said to use the word "black" because she is not African-American, and yet she's black.

Calling a black an African doesn't clearly tell us who the people are who are not black but who are, nevertheless, from Africa. When I taught in South Africa, one of my sponsors was an African who was Indian in racial and cultural background. Others in the class were white Africans, but not necessarily Afrikaaners since they had emigrated from the United States.

Hispanic is used to define a people and a culture, but not a race. Chinese might mean an Asian Chinese or it might mean a person from another ethnic group from China.

Then, there are a great many words that are used negatively, by all races, to label races other than their own, such as spic, kike, mick, camel jockey, sand monkey, white trash, round-eyes, long-nose (which some Asians call whites), square-heads (Scandinavians), shiksa, etc. To write this film, the writers needed to be aware of the meanings and nuances of ethnic slurs, such as: homeboy, the oppressor's culture, gangbangers, and rag-heads. You can probably come up with your own list of racial slurs that you've heard.

After a writer explores subjective and social experiences of a theme, the writer may then turn to looking at another aspect of the theme, the theme of identity.

Creating a Social Theme

Crash looks at how our racial identities are molded and set by other individuals and how those identities are deeply rooted in our society. We carry around our attitudes as a result of our lack of touching, and knowing, people of other races, as a result of media images of different races, and as a result of our desire to categorize people quickly.

There is a song in the musical *South Pacific* that says we have to be "Carefully Taught" to hate and fear all those people who are different from us. Although we may have a natural fear of "The Other," that which is Unfamiliar, that fear is often strengthened, rather than diminished, by our family and our society. As children, we are more apt to be fascinated by that which is different, rather than terrified of it. We don't naturally hate each other. We learn to hate each other.

Phrasing the Theme

After a writer explores how to approach the theme, then a writer often finds a way to phrase the theme, sometimes even writing it out and putting the piece of paper in a prominent place, where it can be seen everyday. The theme then serves to keep the writer on track so all elements of the script feed into the theme, in one way or another.

There are many ways to work with, and phrase a theme. Sometimes a writer begins by writing out the word that best tells what the abstract idea is that is being explored: Justice. Integrity. Racism.

Then, add a verb to the word. Is the story about Overcoming Racism? About Shattering Racist Stereotypes? About Conquering our sense of Separation? There is no one right answer, but the best answer will be the one that is best at guiding the writer.

The theme can be worked into a short phrase that says something about the process that the character, or characters, will go through in the journey of the story. Here, the writer has to be careful not to create a statement that is static. Simply saying "racism is bad" will not be workable, since it's a statement that already tells us the end statement of the film, but doesn't tell us the process through which characters go through to understand the statement. It's more helpful to find a statement that implies a process, such as "Seeing one's true humanity leads to resolution" or "Racism diminishes everyone and infects our whole society" or "Butting against our racial stereotypes can lead to reconciliation and compassion."

In Lajos Egri's fine book, *The Art of Dramatic Writing,* he uses this kind of a phrase and calls it the premise of the story. The phrase works well, since it implies the three acts of the story. Act One will show the racial stereotypes, Act Two will show people butting up against them, and Act Three will show, for at least some people, reconciliation and compassion. Using the word "can" rather than "does" clarifies that this will be a film that shows what is possible, although not true for everyone.

By finding a phrase that clearly expresses the three acts of the story, and then exploring the theme in Act Two, the writer then proves the theme in Act Three.

Testing the Theme

The writer may go a step further with the theme — testing it with potential audience members. This might include research, interviews, perhaps some reading of books dealing with racism as well.

In a case such as *Crash,* the writers talked to people who had been the victims of racism. They also researched, interviewed, read books, and analyzed racism from a social perspective. This is one way that writers can test their theme, to make sure it works, to make sure they understand it clearly, and to be able to objectify the theme enough, so it can be discussed and debated and even challenged. This method helps writers see where they're hitting the theme just right, and what they're missing.

THE STRUCTURING OF THE STORY

Crash uses a rare and highly complex structure which I call an Interweaving Structure. Individual stories start their journeys, and then weave in and out of other stories which are connected to them, not by a relationship with plot or characters, but by a relationship with a similar theme. Journeys which seem unrelated to each other begin to find a relationship as the story proceeds and as the threads of one theme begin to intersect the threads of another.

Unlike most films, in parallel journey stories and interweaving structures, there is not one protagonist. In most films, one protagonist goes on a journey, and various subplots intersect and support that journey, but do not function separately from the protagonist's journey. In parallel journey stories, the intersection of the journeys often starts at the 1st Turning Point, or perhaps at the Midpoint, although *Sleepless in Seattle* is a parallel journey story where the two journeys don't intersect until the Climax. In a film such as *Sleepless in Seattle*, there is no real interweaving of the plots, since the story is told almost exclusively through the female's point of view.

The Interweaving Structure is similar to a structure I call the "parallel journey" story, where different characters have storylines that don't seem connected, but, at some point in the story, begin to intersect with each other. Spike Lee used this structure in 1989 with *Do the Right Thing. Pulp Fiction* combines six storylines, which are parallel stories, but it re-orders the stories in a non-chronological order. *Pulp Fiction* won the Academy Award for Best Original Screenplay in 1994. *Traffic*, written by Stephen Gaghan and directed by Steven Soderbergh, uses a series of parallel journey stories that are all connected to the drug trade. *Traffic* was nominated for the Academy Award as Best Picture in 2000. *Syriana*, written and directed by Stephen Gaghan, was nominated for the Academy Award for Best Screenplay in 2006 and *Babel* used a similar story structure to explore three stories and was nominated for an Academy Award in 2007.

Bobby, about RFK and his assassination, wove together a number of stories of people who all were together at the Ambassador Hotel in 1968. The Macedonian film, *Before the Rain,* looked at several different stories which seemed unrelated, until there were occasional intersections as the story progressed. In each of these examples, the connections become clearer as the story moves forward and as more intersections begin to happen, until we recognize the intrinsic connections between what seems to be drastically different stories. All of these structures use a common connecting device for their stories — whether drugs in *Traffic*, oil in *Syriana*, or racism in *Crash*.

Most of the films mentioned above, however, are more like parallel journey stories, where the film shows different stories, which are played out separately from each other, and then very occasionally intersect. In parallel journey stories, two or more characters continue on their separate journeys, sometimes for one, two, or three acts, and then intersect the journey of another character at some point and then may diverge again. Sometimes, the intersection begins at the 1st Turning Point or the Midpoint, and occasionally at the very end, as in *Sleepless in Seattle*. All of the above examples include parallel journeys, since individual characters will, at various times in the story, be on their own personal journey which seems to have little to do with the journeys of others.

In *Crash,* the intersection begins with the first scene and almost every scene has some intersection with someone else's story.

Crash is the best example of the interweaving structure since it puts the focus on the intersections of the stories rather than on the separate parallel journeys. Throughout the film, in almost every scene, there is a connection of one character's story with another story, whether clear or subtle. If you look at the above examples, almost every one of them follows a character for some time as they play out their own story. Many story beats do not seem related to other people's stories.

In *Crash,* every story is played out in terms of its relationship to another story and character.

These structures are similar to, but not the same as, the film *The Hours*, which moves back and forth between three stories whose plots cannot intersect, because they take place in different time periods, although they intersect through the common theme of the women's quest for self-determination. Yet, like *Crash, The Hours* shows thematic connections and connections of character, even though it cannot create the same plot connections as these other films.

How Does This Structure Work?

Rarely is this structure successful. It can be confusing because we're asked to be interested in each story separately, while often wondering what one story has to do with another. *Traffic* and *Syriana* both use a similar structure but take a significant amount of time for their stories to intersect. In *Babel* the intersection is even more tenuous and, according to many reviewers and viewers, doesn't quite add up to a whole.

For both parallel journeys and the interweaving structure, the structure seems to work best when it begins its intersections in Act One or at the 1st Turning Point. *Syriana* and *Traffic* did not begin their intersections until well into Act Two. It is not to say that these films don't work, but in my opinion, they don't work as well as *Crash*, because it takes so long for the audience to see the connections between stories. If the individual stories are sufficiently interesting, we watch, waiting for the moment it all comes together. If they aren't interesting, we tune out, or we may hear, through word of mouth or through reviews, that the film doesn't quite add up, and decide not to see the film.

Crash began its intersections from the ending of the first scene, although the audience wouldn't know why Graham, the black detective, reacted to the sneaker he found on the ground. By the second scene, the story of shopkeeper Farhad and then the story of Daniel, the locksmith, begins implied relationships. By the third scene, the black carjackers, Anthony and Peter intersect with Rick, the D.A. and his wife, Jean, with implied intersections to the stories of Graham who would receive a promotion in order to make sure Rick keeps the black vote in the next election. As the story proceeds, characters continually crash into each other's lives, affect each other's lives, and make connections. With each crash, we find out more about the nature of racism.

The Stories as Individual Journeys

With each crash of culture, the film moves deeper and deeper into the difficult, sometimes tragic, circumstances of people's lives. And we can see that some of these tragedies could be resolved if it weren't for the racism operating that continues to diminish their lives.

Crash tells twelve different stories. This is very unusual, since most films have an "A" story — the major storyline — and perhaps two or three subplots. There are a few exceptions, such as *Tootsie,* with eight subplots, and *As Good as It Gets,* with six subplots. This makes *Crash* a difficult juggling act with some specific challenges. The writers had to make sure that the audience understood each story separately, and also understood the intersection of the stories. The writers had to make sure that each story was there for a specific reason that related to the theme. And the writers had to make the coincidences of the intersections seem credible and possible.

There needed to be considerable economy of writing, to find the core beats to each story, and, at times, to create scenes which contained beats from two or three different stories at the same time.

All of these stories operate more like subplots than plots, since there is no major character in the film. And with each individual story, the crash of characters occurs either at the Catalyst of the individual story, at a Turning Point, or at the Climax.

The film begins with a car crash that happens Tomorrow, and then flashes back to Today to explore the events leading up to this moment. After the film returns to the car crash today, it then moves forward in time to explore the consequences of all the events leading up to the crash.

In the first scene, we enter into twelve different stories, none of them specific at this point in the story, but all of them implied with connections which will become clearer as the film proceeds. I'm numbering the stories so the reader can see them more clearly.

(1) The first characters we meet are Graham and Ria. Although we do not, at first, realize we're in the beginning of several different stories, the car crash implies the *Story of Peter* who has been missing for some time and whose sneaker Graham finds at the crash scene which is also a crime scene.

(2) Their professional relationship as detectives also contains the *Story of Their Sexual Relationship* which we later learn is not going how Ria would like it to go. Yesterday, Graham was booted out by Ria.

(3) Graham and Ria are investigating the murder of a cop (the *Story of the Conklin-Lewis Investigation*).

(4) Graham's search for his brother is related to the *Story of His Mother*, who is on drugs and is desperately seeking her favorite son, in spite of the fact that Graham is the better son.

(5) Graham's investigation of the murder of the cop will connect him to the *Story of the D.A.* whose SUV was stolen, and who is trying to make sure that this investigation does not look racist.

(6) Rick, the D.A., is connected to the *Story of Anthony and Peter* who stole his SUV.

(7) The D.A. is connected to the *Story of His Wife, Jean*, who changes the locks because the house keys were stolen along with the SUV.

(8) The loss of the keys connects Jean to the *Story of the Locksmith, Daniel*, who changes her locks.

(9) Daniel is connected to the *Story of Farhad*, whose locks he also changes.

(10) The car crash was caused by Kim Lee, who was rushing to the hospital to see her husband, Choi Jin Guih, who is connected to the *Story of the Illegal Immigrants*. Choi is hit by a van driven by Anthony and Peter which also connects him to the story of Anthony and Peter, mentioned above.

(11) While rushing to the hospital to see him, Choi's wife, Kim Lee, caused the accident. Her story might be defined as the *Story of Kim's Search for Her Husband* (although most of this story takes place off-screen and is recounted to Choi when she finds him.)

(12) Although we don't see a connection with the *Story of Dorri* until the very end of the film, Dorri is the pathologist that shows Graham the body of his brother, Peter.

These stories are further connected in an ever-widening web.

Through the D.A., Graham will also be connected to Jean's story, since she's the wife of the D.A., although Graham never meets her. And through the death of Peter, Graham is connected to Hansen, the cop who kills Peter by mistake toward the end of the film, although Graham will never know about this connection.

Through her husband, Kim Lee is connected to the story of the illegal immigrants. At the end of the illegal immigrant story, Anthony will set them free, which connects Kim Lee to Anthony's story, although she will never know about this connection.

After establishing the first scene, the film then flashes back to Yesterday, and we begin to see story beats that lead up to the Crash.

Analyzing the Plotlines

Each of these storylines are structured in three acts, although in the smaller stories, a turning point may be dropped out.

By breaking down the structure of each story, separately, we can see that each is a fairly complete story in itself which carries the idea of racism as it collides with other storylines. The following will look at how these structures work, how they carry the theme, and how they interrelate with other storylines.

The Illegal Immigrant Story is set-up in a restaurant where Choi is making a deal and Ryan is on the phone to Shaniqua to talk about his father's pain. We don't, at first, know what this deal is about, but the director puts the focus on him for a moment, to set him up. The deal, we later learn, is a deal to deliver illegal immigrants who are packed, and chained, in the back of a van. But things don't go as expected. At the 1st Turning Point, as Choi is ready to enter his van, he's hit by a van driven by Anthony. He's clearly hurt, and is left for dead. During the second act of this storyline, Choi is dropped off at the hospital by Anthony and Peter, who say they don't want a "dead Chinaman" on their heads, and (off screen) his wife searches for him. Toward the end of the second act, Anthony returns to Choi's van, figuring that Choi's van might be worth something. He steals the van, takes it to his fence, Lucien, who intends to pay him for the stolen van and then discovers the illegals at the 2nd Turning Point. During Act Three of this story, Anthony has to make a decision — whether to sell the immigrants to Lucien, or to set them free. At the Climax, Anthony takes them to Chinatown, unchains them, and sets them free.

A crash of cultures in Choi's story occurs when he is hit by two African-American young men — Anthony and Peter — who look under the car and immediately identify him as a Chinaman. The clash is Black-Asian.

This storyline connects to a small storyline about Choi's wife, Kim Lee, who caused the car crash in the first scene. In Kim's story, she hears (off-screen) that her husband has been taken to the hospital. At the 1st Turning Point of her story (the first scene of the movie), she is hurrying to the hospital and causes a car crash. During the second act of her story, she visits her husband. There is no clear 2nd Turning Point, but at the Climax of this story, she is given the check for the immigrants by Choi and he tells her to cash it quickly. Much of this storyline takes place off-screen, but the story beats are implied through her dialogue, and through the story that we see of Choi.

When Kim Lee arrives at the hospital, she clarifies her search:

```
                KIM LEE
    I thought you were dead - I called
    every hospital. (p. 102)…
    Got in fight with poor woman.
    Call her names…
    I die from worry. (p. 103)
```

In Kim's story, the crash of cultures occurs at the car crash, when she argues with Ria, who is Hispanic, specifically Puerto-Rican/ Salvadoran. Ria has stereotypes about Koreans (they're too short, they don't know how to drive), and Kim has stereotypes about Ria (she doesn't brake, and causes car crashes.) This is a Hispanic-Asian clash.

The crash is the middle of several other storylines that involve Ria and Graham.

The crash introduces us to the professional partnership of Ria and Graham, and brings us into the middle of their investigation of an undercover cop who has been killed by another cop. This is set-up when Conklin, the undercover cop, has been shot (off-screen). We are told, at the crime scene, about what happened:

```
                OFFICER JOHNSON
    Ford pickup and Mercedes driving
    north on Hill. The pickup cuts in
    front. Driver of the Mercedes gets
    pissed, pulls a gun — he doesn't
    realize the guy in the pickup is a
```

```
cop coming off shift.

Name of Conklin. He's a
narc out of Wilshire...

Mercedes takes a shot at him.
Detective Conklin returns fire, one
shot. Mercedes hits the wall,
driver opens the door and falls out
dead. (p. 12)

He says he kept trying to drive
away but the Mercedes kept pulling
up next to him, screaming, waving
the gun. Shot back in self-defense. (p. 13)
```

We see Conklin, relaxed, sure of himself. During Act Two, we learn that Conklin (white) has shot a cop, Lewis (black). We also learn that Conklin had "two suspicious shootings on his record — both black men, both times he was cleared" (p. 74). It looks as if Conklin will get away with this shooting, as he has with the other two.

However, there are complications. Conklin would expect he would get away with shooting a black, as he has done before. But Graham clarifies the problem after seeing that Lewis is a cop: "Looks like Detective Conklin shot himself the wrong nigga" (p. 13). By shooting a black cop, Conklin might be in jeopardy.

The situation becomes more complicated. We learn that Lewis, the black cop, had over $300,000 in cash in the trunk of his Mercedes. Probably Lewis was guilty. But it's better to frame the white cop than the black cop, in this case, because anything that looks like racism won't look good for Rick for his re-election campaign. Graham bets that Lewis was "coked out of his head" (p. 76), but Graham is offered a high-profile promotion in exchange for not mentioning the money, and going along with the LAPD's interpretation of the events. Just to prod Graham a bit more, they show him the warrant for his brother's arrest and say that if he's willing to go along with them, the warrant will disappear. Finally, Graham is willing to give them enough for their interpretation:

```
            GRAHAM
...Given Detective Conklin's
history...I'd say it's clear what
happened last night. (p. 78)
```

And Rick is able to announce to the press...

```
            RICK
...Just after nine p.m. last
night, Detective William Lewis, an
eight-year veteran of the force and
an active member of the black
community was gunned down by a fellow
officer. (p. 79)
```

At the 1st Turning Point of this storyline, Graham and Ria are brought into this investigation. Act Two of this storyline is their investigation. They quickly realize that there are racial implications with this shooting, since Lewis is black, and it is one more shooting of a black that could only be construed as racism of the L.A. cops. During Act Two, the D.A. comes up with the idea to counter the racism charge by giving a promotion to a black cop, and Graham seems to be the best choice — if he'll go along with their interpretation of the event. At the 2nd Turning Point of the investigation, Graham finds $300,000 in Lewis' car, which implies that Lewis, the black cop, is the bad cop. Graham needs to make a decision — whether to tell the truth, or to go along with the decision to frame Conklin to take away any onus of racism. At the Climax, Conklin is framed. By the time the car crash in the first scene of the film occurs, Graham is battle weary from compromising his integrity and from what seems to be the end of his sexual relationship with Ria. At the time of the car crash, he is focused on seeking his brother.

This story can also be seen from the viewpoint of Rick, the D.A. In the set-up, his car is carjacked by Peter and Anthony. At the 1st Turning Point, he has to decide how to deal with the car jacking, since blacks stole his van. He doesn't want any charge of racism, and this is further complicated because he has been investigating the Conklin-Lewis shooting. He makes the decision at the 1st Turning Point to find a black and give him an award. He chooses Graham. At the 2nd Turning Point, he offers Graham the deal, and at the Climax, Graham agrees.

The crash of cultures here is one of black-white: Graham (who is black) versus the white D.A. The black cop (Lewis) versus the white cop (Conklin).

The car crash introduces us to his professional partnership with Ria, but we later learn that he has a sexual relationship with her as well. This story only has a few beats, but can be broken down as setting them up together in Act One of their story, with an Act Two scene of them making love at her apartment, and a Climax when she kicks him out. She kicks him out before the car crash, so by the time of the car crash, they remain as partners, but are no longer lovers.

Graham is also part of the story about his search for his brother, Peter, much of which takes place off-screen. But we follow much of Peter's story as he commits two crimes with Anthony, and we later learn that Peter is Graham's brother.

The "Seeking Peter" Story is set-up off-screen — Graham's brother is missing. We learn about this through a variety of dialogue that mentions this. At the 1st Turning Point (also off-screen), Graham has decided to try to find his brother since his mother has asked him if he's found his brother yet. But Graham is still searching.

We see little of his investigation of his brother, although the warrant for his brother's arrest is used to cajole Graham into agreeing to the D.A.'s interpretation of the Conklin-Lewis shooting. At the 2nd Turning Point, at the car crash, he sees a sneaker and at the Climax, he discovers his brother is murdered and is shown the body by the pathologist, Dorri, and identifies it as his brother. During the Resolution, the mother blames Graham for this death:

```
                    LOUISE
     I asked you to find your brother.
     But you were busy. We weren't much
     good to you anymore, were we? (p. 105)
```

And then Louise gives Peter credit for the good deed that Graham had done.

```
                    LOUISE
     He came home. You know that? My
     little boy. When I was sleeping.
     he bought me groceries. Last thing
     he did.
```

Graham nods, turns and walks past Ria, barely looking at her. Ria watches him go, her heart breaking for them" (p. 105).

After the car crash in the first scene, three other very important stories begin to unfold. One is the story of Farhad who owns a store which has been robbed. The story is set-up by showing him trying to buy a gun after a robbery. Dorri, his grown daughter, buys the gun and also buys ammunition. The actual robbery, which is the Catalyst for his story, is placed off-screen, so we only see the results of the robbery which shows his fear of being robbed again and his desire to protect himself. During Act One of his storyline, he buys the gun, and gets the lock fixed by Daniel who tells him the problem is not the lock but the door. At the 1st Turning Point, his place is robbed again and the lock is broken. This scene is also placed off-screen, but we see the consequences of the robbery, which not only include stolen objects but racial slurs that have been spray painted on his wall. The racial slurs are particularly insulting to Farhad since they call him an Arab, even though he's not Arab, but Persian. During Act Two of his story, Farhad feels helpless and enraged and decides that Daniel is the reason for this second robbery since, in his view, Daniel did not adequately fix the lock. At the 2nd Turning Point, he finds the receipt that Daniel gave him, with Daniel's address. During Act Three of his story, he goes to Daniel's home to seek revenge, and when trying to shoot Daniel, instead he shoots Daniel's little daughter, Lara, who has come running to protect her father. But instead of Lara dying, which is both obvious and expected because of the point-blank range, she is fine. It seems to be a miracle. During the Resolution, Farhad discovers that the gun contained blanks.

This story contains the clash of Middle Eastern culture and Hispanic culture. Farhad is mistaken for an Arab, even though he's Persian, and Daniel is mistaken for a robber and a gangbanger even though he's a loving father who has moved his family to help them escape from the violence of his last neighborhood.

After Farhad's story has been set up, the story moves to the story of Peter and Anthony which also intersects the story of Jean and her husband, the D.A. This story is set-up on screen. Jean and Rick are coming out of a restaurant when they see Anthony and Peter. Out of fear of blacks, Jean clutches on to her husband as they walk toward their SUV. In this case, her fear is well founded, since Anthony and Peter carjack their SUV. In Act One of this story, we see Peter and Anthony driving toward the garage where they'll turn in the stolen van to Lucien who will have it repainted and sold again. At the 1st Turning Point, however, they run over Choi who has been ready to get into his van with the illegal immigrants, although at this point in the story, we don't know that the immigrants are in Choi's van. This upsets the plans, since the van now contains blood, and Lucien doesn't want it.

During Act Two of this story, Anthony and Peter drive, try to rob Cameron, and Anthony eventually goes back to Choi's van and brings that van to Lucien. At the 2nd Turning Point, at the end of Act Two, and during Act Three, Lucien's man, George, discovers the illegal immigrants in the back of the van. Lucien offers Anthony money for the immigrants, but Anthony says no. At the Climax, he releases them.

We can also look at Anthony's story as separate from Peter's story. The beginning of their stories are the same, but they separate at the 2nd Turning Points. During Act One of this story, Anthony and Peter carjack Rick's van. They take the van to Lucien at the 1st Turning Point, expecting to get money for it, but Lucien won't take it because it has Choi's blood on it. During Act Two, they drive around, meet Cameron and try to rob him, and Peter runs off and Anthony stays in Cameron's SUV while Ryan and several other cops corner Cameron as Anthony cowers in the SUV, expecting Cameron to turn him in (which he doesn't do). At the 2nd Turning Point, Peter gets into the car with Hansen, and Anthony takes Choi's van to Lucien, only to discover the illegal immigrants. At the end of Act Two, and during Act Three, Peter's story and Anthony's story diverge into parallel journey stories. At the Climax, Peter is dead and Anthony frees the immigrants.

Ryan's story is connected to Hansen's story and to Cameron's story.

Ryan, for much of the film, is seen as the bad cop. Although we first meet him when he stops Cameron's car, the beginning of his story is actually the set-up of the motivation for his behavior. Ryan's father is ill, and the social worker will do nothing to help, even though she could bend the rules a bit to get the father better care. As a result, Ryan is stressed, and he is taking it out on others. His racist attitudes are pushed to the forefront because of this stress and because the social worker is black. Through this backstory about his father, we learn that Ryan is not what he seems to be. He is not simply a bad cop, but a person who has the ability to be compassionate, and who is coming up against the obstacles set up by the social service system. In this case, the stereotype that blacks are oppressed by whites is reversed, since the social worker, Shaniqua, is the person who is the oppressor of Ryan. We also learn that Ryan's father had a janitorial service where he hired mainly black workers, and gave them a good wage. When a law was passed giving preference to minority-owned businesses, he lost his business, even though he was the person acting from a non-racist attitude. At the 1st Turning Point, Ryan takes his frustrations out on Cameron and his wife, Christine, both black, who are returning from an award ceremony where Cameron won an award for his directing. Ryan, to the dismay of Hansen, searches both Cameron and Christine, taking considerable liberties in the search. During Act Two of this story, the focus shifts to the consequences of this search, which are twofold. It has caused tension in the relationship of Cameron and Christine, since she is enraged that her husband did nothing to stop Ryan. And it has caused tension in the relationship of Ryan and Hansen, since Hansen no longer wants to be his partner.

This central incident, then, is the 1st Turning Point for two different storylines which will develop in Act Two.

The film follows the tension between Cameron and Christine. His anger at her anger carries over to the set, where he's directing a television show. On the set, he's criticized by his producer for the black character not sounding black enough, and Cameron has to re-shoot the scene. This tension continues throughout Act Two of their storyline. At the 2nd Turning Point, after Christine has been saved by Ryan, she apologizes to Cameron, and at the Climax, he resolves the tension by showing tenderness to her, and letting down the guard that had gone up as a result of the incident with Ryan.

In the story of Hansen, the rookie cop, Hansen has been assigned to work with Ryan (off-screen). During Act One of this story, Ryan and Hansen stop a black man (Cameron) and his wife (Christine). When Hansen sees the way that Ryan treats the two blacks, he wants nothing to do with this and asks to be reassigned at the 1st Turning Point. Notice, in Cameron's and Christine's story, the 1st Turning Point is the search. In Hansen's story, his 1st Turning Point is the *result* of the search, which is the desire to be reassigned. Act Two shows the result of him being reassigned. During Act Two, he's by himself without a partner and alienated from the other cops. At the 2nd Turning Point, he picks up Peter, and begins to take out his anger on Peter. When Peter reaches to show him his plastic St. Christopher statuette, which is just like his, Hansen thinks he's reaching for a gun and shoots him. At the Climax, Peter dies, and during the Resolution, Hansen burns his car.

Christine's story intersects Ryan's story again, after Ryan has gotten a new partner. As Ryan and his new partner come around a corner, they see her jeep overturned. Ryan rushes to the scene, and finds Christine, upside down in the car, trapped by her seat belt, as the gas drips from the car to the ground. We can see that in a matter of moments, the gas will catch fire. The urgency of the situation brings up two tensions. Ryan is trying to quickly save Christine. But Christine recognizes Ryan and does not want to be saved by Ryan — anyone but him. There is little choice. In an intimate and tender scene between them, he manages to save her just as the car explodes. Through this incident, we see a change of attitude between Ryan and Christine, and a moment when the audience also changes their attitude toward Ryan. However, we don't know whether Ryan's transformation continues. I spoke to one of my black friends who told me that even after he saved Christine, the blacks did not warm to him since she said, "People often do their duty by day and lynch at night." The transformation may have been short-lived, or may have continued.

Weaving throughout these stories is the smaller story of Jean, the wife of the D.A. In Act One, their car is carjacked and their house keys are taken as well. At the 1st Turning Point, they hire Daniel, the locksmith, to fix their locks. But Jean doesn't trust him, since he's Hispanic, and she figures that he'll arrange for someone else to rob their house later. She intends to get another locksmith the next day. At the 2nd Turning Point, she falls down the stairs, and tells her husband that nobody would come to help her. The fall is shown, but the result of the fall is recounted to her husband, who she couldn't reach after the accident. At the Climax, she recounts that Maria, her Hispanic maid, was the only person who would help her, and we see Maria gently helping her sit up in bed.

Whereas the D.A. story is black–white conflict, Jean's part of the story is a white–Hispanic conflict, which is carried out through her relationship with two Hispanics — Daniel and Maria.

THE COLLISIONS AND CONNECTIONS BETWEEN THE STORIES

Anytime a writer uses parallel storytelling structures, the writer needs to find ways to connect scenes that may seem disparate, because they are on different storylines. In most films, when there is a strong "A" storyline, scenes flow, one from another, in an action-reaction sequence. Occasionally they are interrupted by subplot scenes, but the subplot scenes, if used well, generally push at, and intersect, the major plotline.

When using a parallel structure, there are no intrinsic connections between the stories. As the story unfolds, we can begin to see connections, but usually in Act One, and even sometimes into Act Two, the connections are neither obvious nor organic. It simply seems that we are watching different stories within the same film. If the stories are interesting enough in themselves, and the characters strong enough to capture our attention, we can be patient for some time. But eventually, we want to know that we aren't watching separate films, but one film with connections between the various scenes.

To achieve this, there are four excellent techniques that writers can use to help keep the audience connected to the disparate stories:

(1) The writer can imply connections within the scenes. The implication of some connection helps us anticipate it, and trust that the writer will eventually show us the connection, even though we don't see it immediately.

(2) The writer can create a sense of connections through scene transitions.

(3) The writer can use props to connect scenes that seem to have no relationship with each other.

(4) And the writer can thread a character through several scenes, connecting one story with another.

Implying the Connections

In the plotlines mentioned above, some of these connections become clear because one scene implies other possible scenes. When Graham starts looking, curiously, at the crime scene, we presume that he is connected, in some way or another, with it. He walks beneath the crime scene tape, which tells us that he's official. He looks as if he's on the verge of a discovery, which implies that he's been searching for something related to this scene. His partnership with a woman could, possibly, imply another kind of relationship, although at this point we don't know. The fact that he's a detective implies relationships with other people in law enforcement, so when he has a scene with the D.A., this is not entirely unexpected.

The angry Korean woman driver implies connections with other Koreans in Los Angeles.

Using Scene Transitions

Scene transitions can make us feel that two scenes are connected, even though one does not lead to the next. There is a cut from the SUV that Anthony and Peter have stolen, to the squad car at the scene of the Lewis-Conklin crash scene. So the cut from car to car makes us feel a connection, even though there isn't a relationship between these two scenes.

There's a scene transition where Hansen slams his car door, and then CUT TO Shereen, Farhad's wife, slamming the door to their market which won't close. There's another cut when Ryan "bangs through the double glass doors" (p. 58) to a delivery man entering a Lock & Key Company (p. 58-59). There's a cut from the door slamming, after Graham leaves Ria, to Ryan "waking with a start, thinking he heard something" even though these sounds are in two different scenes (p. 46).

Shaniqua exits a scene where she has bought some cigarettes from Farhad, and there is a CUT TO Maria entering into Rick and Jean's home.

Some of the transitions are subtle, but feel as if one action is leading to another. A scene with Maria and Jean ends, when Maria "grabs a handful of forks and reaches for the cutlery drawer" and then the scene CUTS TO Lt. Joe Dixon who "stuffs some paperwork into a folder, opens his desk drawer and places the folder inside." The Cut moves from something being put inside a drawer to something taken out of a drawer. Dixon then talks to Hansen about his desire to be reassigned.

One scene ends with Ryan kissing his father's forehead and holding him, and the next scene begins with Lara sleeping, nestled close to her mother.

221

Using Props to Create Connections

Connections are sometimes made through props that connect one scene with another. The same locksmith fixes the locks of Rick and Jean and also the lock of Farhad. The locks become metaphoric as well. It is ironic that Jean locks people out when she's so isolated that she truly needs them and that Farhad concentrates on the lock and not the door which is the true source of danger since it lets bad people in.

The stolen SUV weaves throughout several scenes, connecting them. Anthony steals an SUV from Rick and Jean, runs over Choi with it, and then takes it to Lucien, hoping to get money for it.

The St. Christopher statuette connects Peter with both Anthony's scenes and Hansen's scenes.

At the end of the film, Cameron thinks it's snowing, but it's not snow, but ash from the fire of Hansen's car. Soon after, it starts to snow.

Using Characters to Connect Scenes and Storylines

One character intersecting another, even in what seems to be arbitrary or unimportant, helps pull unrelated stories together and implies a connection. Shaniqua's story connects with the story of Ryan and his father. But she also connects with other stories, through the very simple intersections that any character can have by going through their daily lives. We've seen Shaniqua with Ryan. Later, Shaniqua goes into Farhad's market to buy some cigarettes. At the end of the film, her car drives away after Anthony has let out the illegal immigrants.

Daniel's character connects through his profession, since he fixes the locks of both Farhad and Jean.

Toward the end of the film, Dorri connects with Graham, since she's the pathologist who asks Graham to identify the body of his brother, Peter.

THE 2ND TURNING POINT AS THE BREAKING POINT

Although the structure of the film focuses on the individual stories, there is also an over-all structure where the set-up could be seen as the Introduction of Characters. The 1st Turning Point could be seen as several turning points that try to diminish the effects of racism. Rick wants to diminish the effects by giving a black man a medal (page 33). Daniel wants to diminish the effects by giving his daughter, Lara, a magic invisible cloak that will protect her from bullets (page 38). Anthony and Peter diminish the effects by taking Choi to a hospital (page 39). But, ultimately, these don't work, and Act Two then develops the problems further, as they continue to build and spin out of control. The 2nd Turning Point of the over-all structure are moments of near-breaking points for a number of characters, and then the Climax of the film is the snow, which suggests some resolution and cleansing.

The 2nd Turning Point is worth some closer examination. A number of characters come close to breaking. This breaking point then drives them toward a transformation.

Jean's breaking point occurs when she talks to her friend, Carol, and confesses she's constantly angry. Who is she angry at?

```
                    JEAN
    ...the police and
    Rick and Maria and the dry cleaner
    who ruined another blouse and the
    gardener who keeps over-watering
    the lawn and...
    And... I'm just angry!... I realized
    ...it wasn't about having my car
    stolen. That's how I wake up every
    morning... I'm angry all the time.
    (at the point of tears)
    And I don't know why. Carol, I
    don't know why. (p. 95)
```

```
                        JEAN
          (beat/listens)
          Yeah, call me back. (p. 95)
```

It's clear that Carol is not interested in hearing about her anger. Shortly afterwards, Jean falls down the stairs and discovers just how unkind her friends truly are.

For Cameron, it's the moment when he starts losing it with the police and is enraged at them stopping him, once again. He has had it, and rather than being docile this time, he strikes back.

```
                    OFFICER HILL
          Lie face down on the ground, spread
          your arms and legs.

                      CAMERON
          No, you lie on the ground, you spread
          your arms and legs!

                    OFFICER HILL
          Sir, I need you to lie on the ground.

                      CAMERON
          And I need you on the ground!
```

As the tension mounts, Hansen steps in, knowing what is about to happen.

```
                      HANSEN
          You see what's happening here? You
          want to die here? Is that what you
          you want? 'Cause these guys really
          want to shoot you, and the way you
          are acting they will be completely
          fucking justified....
          Are you starting to understand the
          situation here? (p. 88)

                  (to Officer Hill)
          ...I need to let him go with a warning.
```

```
                    OFFICER HILL
...What kind of fucking warning?

                    HANSEN
A harsh warning. (p. 89)
```

And Hansen ends the scene by telling Cameron to go home (p. 90).

For Anthony, it's the moment when he feels so lost that he has to do the final humiliation — ride the bus.

For Farhad it's the moment when he's so enraged he takes his gun to kill Daniel. The breaking point begins when Farhad remembers the receipt from Daniel which contains Daniel's address. Farhad is described as a man destroyed. He "charges the dumpster, pulling out trash until he finds a crumpled blue paper" (p. 66). He then goes to Daniel's bungalow and waits for him, and starts walking toward him with his pistol raised and pointed at Daniel.

```
                    FARHAD
You give my money.

                    DANIEL
What? What money?

                    LARA
Daddy?

                    DANIEL
         (calling)
ELIZABETH! Come get Lara!

                    LARA
Daddy?

                    FARHAD
You pay my store! Give my money!
You pay my store!

                    LARA
Daddy?

                    DANIEL
You go inside, honey. Elizabeth!!
```

But Elizabeth doesn't hear. She's washing dishes and is unable to hear over the running water.

                    FARHAD
        I want money! You give me truck!

                    DANIEL
        It's not my truck!

                    LARA
        Daddy!

                    DANIEL
        Elizabeth!…

                    DANIEL
        Here, I got about fifty dollars –

Farhad grabs the wallet and flings it away, money flying.

                    FARHAD
        Fifty dollars??? I lose everything!
        You give me truck! You give me
        home! You give me everything!

Farhad's whole arm shakes from fear and anger….
Lara suddenly has a horrible realization…

    LARA   DANIEL
    (turns to Mom)   I don't know what you're
    He hasn't got it!   talking about, it's not my
                            house, I don't have that
                            kind of money!

    ELIZABETH
    (approaching)
    Hasn't got what?   FARHAD
                            You lie! Give me
                            everything!

    LARA
    I have it! He hasn't   DANIEL
    got his 'penetrable   You want the truck? It's
    cloak!   not mine! Take it!

Lara almost flies down the walk and across the grass.

```
          LARA                    FARHAD
          Daddy!                  You lie! You cheat me!
                                  You son-of-a…
```

Daniel doesn't see her coming until she's almost upon him, leaping into his arms. Just as Farhad's finger jerks on the trigger - BANG! The bullet hits Lara straight in the back…

```
          FARHAD                  ELIZABETH
          (in horror)             (running)
          AHHHH.                  Lara!!!!
```

Daniel knows she is dead without even looking. The horror registers on his face - and on Farhad's.

But then Daniel forgot something. Lara's wearing her impenetrable cloak. Which is why she's able to lift her head and look into his eyes. -

```
                    LARA
          It's okay, Daddy. I'll protect you.
                    DANIEL
          What?
```

Daniel feels her back, no sign of a wound, no sign of a hole, this is impossible. Elizabeth is right there, throwing her arms around her daughter and husband. Farhad looks at his smoking gun. It falls to his side…Farhad opens his mouth to apologize but can't say anything" (p. 91-94).

And with this miracle, we begin to see the unraveling of certain racist attitudes and a movement toward resolution for some of the characters.

The transformation is also implied for the city of Los Angeles. It starts to snow — an image of cleanliness, purity, covering up the dirty and ready to start again.

MOVING TOWARD RESOLUTION

Using the Sense of Touch

Great writers try to bring in the senses to make their writing more colorful. Obviously, a strong visual sense is necessary to write for film and most screenwriters will create colorful, cinematic scenes that the reader can visualize while reading the script.

Although sound is often brought in by the director, the sound designer, and the composer, many writers include the sounds of the scene.

Very occasionally, writers imply the sense of smell, as in films with scenes of food. *Remains of the Day, Babette's Feast*, and *Like Water for Chocolate* create sensual scenes of food we can almost smell.

Occasionally, writers also add the sense of touch to their scenes. If you've watched many James Bond films, you may remember scenes where he strokes a Bond girl's back with a mink mitten, and you may remember satin sheets and massage lotion and the steam of the steam bath.

Crash uses a sense of touch to make a thematic statement — that people don't touch and that's partly why racism endures. It then brings people in touch with each other to show resolution.

The film begins by talking about touch. In the first scene, Graham says that no one will touch each other, unless they crash into each other. At the end of the film, we see a number of scenes of touching.

When Kim Lee arrives at the hospital to see her husband Choi, "she kisses him repeatedly, barely believing he is alive." Choi "squeezes her hand" (p. 103).

As Anthony drives the van with the illegal immigrants, "fingers touch his head" and then his ear and then "a third hand reaches to touch his head, then a fourth, a fifth" (p. 108).

Cameron gets out of his SUV, "marveling at the 'snow' falling all around him. He touches a flake on his white shirt — it smears black. Ash" (p. 110).

Ryan "kisses his [father's] forehead and holds him" (p. 111).

"Lara sleeps in her parents' bed, nestled close to her mother" (p. 111).

When the immigrants are let out of the van, "ONE... pokes something strange at the vegetable stand. ANOTHER TWO... finger the fish on ice... ANOTHER COUPLE stop at the store displaying bins of CDs — and push a stack back and forth like dominoes... A WOMAN walks... being jostled and bumped by stern-faced pedestrians" (p. 112).

In the city where no one ever touches, everyone is now touching things and people. Have they overcome their racism? No, but they're closer. Intersecting. Touching is the first step.

PLAYING THE TIMELINE

If you read the chapter on *Sideways,* you may remember the title of Miles' novel: "The Day after Yesterday" which is, of course, Today. *Crash* begins Today, and then moves backwards in time to Yesterday, and then moves back to Today to complete the story. This short timeline serves a number of purposes.

The shorter the timeline, generally, the more intense the drama. A number of successful and exciting films have taken place in a matter of hours or days. The *Die Hard* films take place over an evening or a day. *Flight 93* and *World Trade Center* takes place over a day. *Three Days of the Condor* takes place over (obviously) three days, although the novel was *Six Days of the Condor*, but then, everything takes place faster in Hollywood! The television series,

24 with Kiefer Sutherland as a Counter-Terrorist Unit officer all take place over a 24-hour period. *Sideways* takes place in less than a week. By collapsing the time period, the drama is squeezed into a smaller amount of time than usual, and the tensions are played out for their most dramatic effect.

When creating a tight timeline, the action can become unbelievable. Believable characters will not meet, develop a relationship, and fall in love and get married within a day or two, although certainly an attraction can be developed in that amount of time. Usually a crime won't be solved in one or two days. Climbers won't climb Mount Everest in two or three days, and Rocky won't train for the big fight in a matter of days.

In *Crash*, the timeline becomes more believable because these events are happening to different people, and can easily fit within the same time period. In themselves, they aren't necessarily unusual for a short amount of time. It's possible for the investigation of a shooting of a cop to find a number of clues within a day or two. It's possible for a couple — Cameron and Christine — to fight and make up over a short period of time. It's not inconceivable that Farhad buys a gun, gets a lock replaced, and is robbed again within two days. And the fairly constant presence of Anthony and/or Peter in three different vans can certainly take place over the period of a night and into the next day. It is the collision of these events that create the intensity of the drama, more than any event in itself. This heats up the action, because drama is constantly happening as one storyline collides with another.

To establish a timeline, a writer can use the technique of *Sideways* and *Crash*. In both films, the timeline is established on the screen: "Today." "Yesterday," or in the case of *Sideways*, "Tuesday, Wednesday," etc. Sometimes a timeline is established through dialogue. A character might tell us what is going to happen tomorrow: "I'll talk to Jane tomorrow" and then CUT TO the character talking to Jane, and it's clear it's the next day.

Sometimes a timeline is established through dawn and dusk, or morning and evening, so when one scene takes place in the evening as a character is going to bed, and the next takes place the next morning as the character is waking up, we presume that it's the next morning.

Writers need to be very careful if they establish a timeline that they stick to it. The film *The Interpreter* set a timeline of a week, but when I watched it, it seemed that there were too many mornings and evenings to take place in that amount of time. Often, I read scripts that have established a short time line, but when I count the mornings and evenings, it doesn't add up.

In *Crash,* liberties are taken with the timeline, but once we buy into the idea of the film, most of us are willing to go along with the tight timeline. Probably a cop won't meet the same person two days in a row (as Ryan does with Christine), and usually a person won't have more than one encounter with a social worker within two days (since it sometimes takes two days to get one on the telephone), and seldom will a cop be reassigned within a day of a complaint (as Hansen is). Nevertheless, with compressed time, it's possible for these events to simmer and then reach a boiling point quickly.

THE CHARACTERS

There are many different ways to analyze the dimensions of a character. When I first started writing, someone mentioned character dimensions as physicality, psychology, and sociology: What did the person look like? What did they think like? And who were they in relationship to their society?

When I wrote *Making a Good Script Great,* I analyzed characters by looking at the three dimensions of a character — they think, they act, they feel. In *Advanced Screenwriting,* I looked at the layering of characters and looked at their external, their internal, and their invisible (to them) dimensions. In *Creating Unforgettable Characters,* I looked at the consistency and the paradoxes of characters — what was expected of the character given their culture, their occupation, their religion, their race and what was unexpected.

For the purposes of *Crash,* I want to look at the stereotype of the character, the details that break the stereotype, and the emotional wound that the character carries as a result of the stereotype, which in the case of this script, comes from racism.

Each character, for the most part, when first introduced, is introduced in terms of the big character picture — what race are they, and what's the stereotype of that race?

The first two people we meet are the two detectives — Graham, who is black, and Ria, who is Hispanic. Although at first glance, it may seem that Graham is not introduced in terms of his race, his first piece of dialogue implies the racial problem. "People in this city don't touch each other." Although he says it in terms of people in general, it could be construed, very subtly, to have a racial connotation that black men don't touch white women. They're not supposed to. As we learn more about Graham, we see that he's a cop with integrity that is trying to hold onto that integrity, and that he does touch Ria, his Hispanic sexual partner, although she's not happy with the many ways that he disengages from her — by answering the telephone during sex, by his lack of interest in her ethnic background. Although Graham does not want to be judged by his race, he judges Ria by her race. He says she's Mexican, even though she isn't, and lumps her together with the Mexicans who park their cars on their lawns, showing his racist attitudes toward Mexicans and toward Ria.

We then are introduced to Kim Lee, a Korean, who is usually mistaken for Chinese and who is defined by the stereotype of someone who can't drive because she's short. Her husband is constantly called The Chinaman by Anthony and Peter, although he's Korean. And, at first glance, he seems to be an upper-class Chinaman, and is introduced sympathetically to us as the victim of Anthony's bad driving. But we soon learn that he is illegally, and somewhat cruelly, smuggling illegal immigrants in this story who are not Mexicans, but Asians.

When we're introduced to Farhad, he seems to be an angry Arab, buying a gun. It fits nicely into our stereotype of the Arab terrorist, except that Farhad isn't angry over hatred of Americans — he's an American citizen, he's no terrorist and doesn't know how to use a gun, and he's a business owner who is actually Persian (Iranian), not Arab.

Ryan is introduced as the racist cop, but we learn about his tenderness toward his father and his anger at the system that won't help his father. The racism stereotype gets diminished when he risks his life to save Christine.

Hansen seems, from the beginning, to be the good white cop. He's the guy with integrity who is willing to put himself on the line. He's still young and innocent with ideals, yet the stereotype is broken when Hansen shoots Peter, and his innocence is lost. He's the one who kills in this film, not Ryan.

Graham's mother is the drug-taking black, but she's an older woman who is trying to escape from her difficult existence and from the loss of her younger son. Like many mothers, she loves her child, but like many mothers, she never clearly sees her older son, Graham, for who he truly is, and keeps believing that the good deeds done by Graham were actually done by Peter. She continues to believe her son, Peter, loves her, in spite of the painful evidence to the contrary.

Jean represents the rich upper-middle-class white woman, who tries to shield herself from the reality of the world through an expensive car and strong locks on her door. She's fearful of anyone different than her, and when she sees a black, she immediately clutches her husband for protection. But she learns, by the end of the story, that the people who are the same as she is don't come through in her time of need, but her Salvadoran maid does.

Daniel is Hispanic, and is stereotyped as a gangbanger who is expected to use his position as locksmith to betray the whites. Daniel is soon seen as a father who has been a victim of violence, and has moved his family to a safer neighborhood.

Dorri is introduced as the professional daughter of Farhad, who is stereotyped by the leers of the gun-store owner. Although some may stereotype the leer toward another race as believing that the person is "ripe for the picking" (which often occurs with the stereotype of black women and Hispanic women), with Middle Eastern women the interest comes partly because they seem removed from the world, hidden and sometimes protected by the veil. She is the forbidden fruit that the man wants, nevertheless. And that protected status actually makes her more desirable. In the case of Dorri, she's a medical doctor who, obviously, knows something about bodies, and is a pathologist which is a position of authority that demands considerable education.

Conklin and Lewis are introduced as two cops — and at first, we believe that the white cop is the bad guy, and the black cop is the good guy. But we soon learn that it's the opposite of what is expected.

Rick is the D.A., willing to do almost anything to keep his job. He is highly sensitive to the way things look, and particularly sensitive to the race question and how it will play among his black constituents.

Cameron and Christine are first introduced as the upper-class blacks who have made it through the system. They might be thought of as the "Bill Cosby professional type" — classy, successful, beyond racist stereotypes. Yet, they are still prisoners of the racism of others. To Ryan, Christine is part of his sexual stereotype of sexy black women who are, in one way or another, prostitutes that he can feel free to touch. To Ryan, Cameron is not a successful professional, but another black he can push around.

There is also interracial racism between Cameron and Christine. Christine is a light-skinned black, and in the black culture she would be considered more white and more privileged because of her light skin. We learn, from her backstory, that she grew up in a middle-class or upper-middle-class household, and does not have the same understanding of "the plight of the brother" as Cameron does.

Although Cameron is also of a similar skin tone to Christine, he grew up in an urban setting and had to fight his way to the top. He understands that in the white culture, the white man owns the women and if Cameron doesn't like the way that Ryan treats Cameron's wife, he could go to jail or get killed, which would be the modern-day equivalent of a lynching.

Ryan continues to work from his stereotypes, in spite of behavior from Christine and Cameron that belies the stereotype. Christine is introduced as someone who doesn't seem as confined by the stereotype, since she doesn't seem to know her place — to be the docile wife who goes along with mistreatment. She is thoroughly humiliated by Ryan's search and angry at her husband for not doing anything to protect her.

Cameron understands the consequences of racism. Anything he would do to demand respect could lead to jail, or death. Cameron continues to suffer the stereotype at work, where it's clear that he is totally under the command of his producer, who wants the blacks to sound "more black."

Yet, just as we may be adjusting our own stereotype of Cameron and Christine, we are thrown another curve by the writers — the unexpected information that Christine is from an upper-class

Greenwich Village family. She was an equestrian, and Cameron is an award-winning director who is a Buddhist.

Ryan's father is introduced in terms of a stereotype of age. He's an old man who is ill and who is weak and needy and hurt by the social system. We learn that he had been a small business owner with 23 employees, all black. The job was one that many think belongs to blacks — a janitorial service — but he further breaks the stereotype by clarifying that he gave equal pay to blacks at a time when no one else was doing it. He breaks the stereotype again when we learn that he was the victim of racism when the government favored minority-owned business and he couldn't get the contracts he needed.

Anthony and Peter are first introduced in terms of the black gangster stereotype. They're the homeboys. The kids who threaten the white folk. The kids who steal cars. Yet Peter carries a St. Christopher's statuette for safe journeys, and responds to the Catholic image of St. Christopher (even though blacks are usually stereotyped as Baptists or members of the African-Methodist Episcopal church). Peter is the brother of a cop, hates rap music, loves hip-hop, country and western music, and loves to ice skate.

Anthony, who seems quite incapable of doing a good deed, does a good deed at the end, by letting the illegal immigrants out of the van to freedom.

Shaniqua, the social worker, is the stereotype of the Big Mama who tosses her weight around to misuse her authority. She has achieved her status by following the rules, although she is not without compassion. But she won't waste it on a racist such as Ryan.

The Dialogue

In any good film, dialogue serves three, and sometimes four, functions: It advances the story, reveals character, expresses the theme, and sometimes uses word images to make the theme more cinematic.

Throughout *Crash,* much of the dialogue advances the action by having characters make decisions and act on those decisions. Farhad and Dorri act, by talking to the owner of the gun store about guns, and then buying the gun. Hansen decides and acts by asking to be reassigned. Rick acts by making a deal with Graham to promote him. Cameron acts by shouting back at the police in Act Three.

However, the dialogue doesn't simply move the story. While moving the story, it reveals conflict and character. Buying a gun is not a simple action with Farhad and Dorri:

```
                    DORRI
              (in Farsi)
        He asked what kind of bullets you
        want.

                    FARHAD
              (in Farsi)
        The kind that fit in the gun! (p. 5)
```

Later in the scene, Dirk, the owner of the gun store, adds more conflict.

```
                    DIRK
        Yo, Osama, plan the Jihad on your
        own time; what do you want? (p. 6)
```

When Hansen asks to be reassigned, we see that this is not a simple scene, but filled with conflict between Hansen and his superior officer, Lt. Joe Dixon.

```
                    DIXON
        I understand; your partner is a
        racist prick, but you don't want to
        stir up any bad feelings with him. (p. 48)
```

The conflict becomes clearer as we realize Dixon's relationship with Ryan:

> DIXON
>
> ...I am anxious to understand
> how such an obvious bigot could
> have gone undetected in this
> department for seventeen years,
> eleven of which he was personally
> supervised by me. Of course that
> doesn't speak highly of my managerial
> skills, but that's not your concern. (p. 49)

These scenes that advance the story contain strong conflict that puts a bite into every scene, and adds a raw edge to the characters.

Some of the dialogue is metaphoric, creating images that help us understand the theme. *Crash* begins with a car crash, and then uses the physical action of the crash to establish a metaphor of Los Angeles and the need that the story will try to fulfill — the need to have true contact with each other.

Through this dialogue, the writers also establish why this story takes place in Los Angeles, versus, for instance, New York — where people constantly bump into each other.

> GRAHAM (V.O.)
>
> It's the sense of touch...
> Any real city, you walk, you're
> bumped, brush past people. In L.A.,
> no one touches you...
> we crash into each just to
> feel something. (p. 1)

As the dialogue continues, it uses a number of images that establish a metaphor, that helps us understand what is really going on in this story on a thematic level.

```
              RIA
    Graham, we were rear-ended. We
    spun around twice. Somewhere in
    there one of us lost our frame of
    reference. I'm gonna go look for
    it. (p. 2)
```

The frame of reference has to be lost first, in order to be re-found, in a new way. On one level, we might say that this is a story about people losing their frame of reference, and being spun around by events, before re-finding another frame.

Researching the Dialogue

With almost any script, the writer will need to do some research to make a character credible, or to make a piece of information accurate. Although sometimes the writer knows all the information needed in a script, this is rare. The writer is more apt to have to look up information, ask an expert, or observe the intricacies of various professions or situations.

What would the writers need to know in *Crash*? They would need to know how an investigation is conducted and the relationship between the D.A. and detectives and what is needed to get reassigned to another partner and the ways that detectives harass each other.

They would need to understand the differences between various ethnic backgrounds, and know that Iranians are not Arabs but Persians, that there is an active Asian network for illegal immigrants in Los Angeles, and they would need to know how the social service system works.

They need to know something about guns. When Farhad goes into the gun store, Dirk, the owner, explains all the different kinds of ammunition.

```
                    DIRK
Oh, we got a lot of things that
fit. We got long colts, short colts,
ball heads, flat-noses, hollow points,
wad cutters and a dozen more that
all fit in the same size hole,…
```

And then the writers add a bit more character to Dirk, that goes beyond research about ammunition. Dirk continues, after giving Dorri a lecherous smile:

```
                    DIRK
depends how big a "bang" you can
handle. (p. 7)
```

The Emotional Wound of Racism

Each of these characters carry a wound as a result of racism. And most of them have a moment of healing and redemption where the racial stereotype is lifted, even if only for a moment.

Our understanding of emotional wounds can help us understand the writers' insight into the relation of the theme and the character. By looking at the individual wounds, we can see the character's need for healing and resolution.

I first encountered some understanding of the wounds which come from racism when I was in graduate school. I worked with an actress (white) who lived with, but was not married, to a black man. I became friends with her — not close friends, but close enough to spend some time at her home, and have a number of deep discussions. Karen mentioned that her relationship with Ron was loving and caring. Their life together was smoother and much easier than her relationship to her former husband who she loved, but couldn't live with. She told me that in spite of the good individual relationship she had with Ron, everyday something happened in their lives that was racist — whether it was outsiders' attitudes, or internalized attitudes from her or from Ron. It was a constant in their lives — relentless, and it was wearing her down. She wasn't at all sure that she would stay with him, because she wanted simply to get away from it, and considered moving back into her solely white world. Of course, Ron couldn't escape the attitudes, but whites, seemingly, can.

The wounds in *Crash* are complex because they come, not just from racism, but from the basic human experience of struggling with daily existence and normal relationships. In each case when the wound is healed or redeemed or overcome, it comes about because of a breakthrough into the core humanity freed from the box of the stereotype.

Graham is wounded by his mother's lack of love for him. She clearly prefers his brother, in spite of everything Graham does to help her and win her love. Just as Graham refuses to see who Ria truly is, his mother will not acknowledge his worth. She continues to cling to her own wounds, symbolized through her drug addiction and by her love of the dysfunctional son, Peter.

Graham is wounded by trying to make it in a white world. Even when an event seems positive, it still has, within it, the seeds of racism. He is told he will be promoted, but it's because he's black and fulfills the requirement that the promotion must look as if the District Attorney is color blind, even though the motivation is racist. There seems to be no way that he can keep his integrity and still make it in the white world. He has to give up part of his identity to stay within the system. He has to go along with the white authority, take what is handed to him, and within the tight category he's put into, try to find, and keep, his humanity.

Although Jean, the D.A.'s wife, is white, and would probably consider herself not part of a racist system, she makes sure that she fits well into the upper-class white world. She carries certain racist stereotypes, since she is clear about who is beneath her, and who are her equals. She knows who to associate with, who to have as friends, and who to boss around. She makes unreasonable demands of her maid, speaks ill of the locksmith even though she knows nothing about him, and has friends with upper-class white women who truly care little for her. She has no perception of the ways that her upper-class life has kept her from noticing the kindness of her maid or the skill and sweetness of her locksmith.

It may seem that Jean has a choice about whether to be racist or not, whether to fit into a racist system or not. But her inclusion into her white upper-class world can be separatist and exclusionary and is often dependent upon having the right friends, going along with her husband's choices, finding safety and protection within the locked-in confines of her home. She, too, carries the wounds of racism which have built a wall around her and kept her from relating to others based on the integrity of their character, not on their race and class.

For Anthony, nothing really goes his way. And it won't, as long as he fits himself into the racial stereotype of the black gangbanger "thief in the night." He runs over a Korean which threatens to bring him trouble. He can't sell the stolen van, which puts him out of favor with his money source. Peter argues with his choice of music. Cameron freaks him out by going ballistic when he's stopped, again, by the cops. And he's forced to ride a bus, which is a symbol, for him, of humiliation. Why do people put those big windows on the sides of buses? Because, Anthony explains, "to humiliate the people of color who are reduced to riding on it" (p. 53). He has his moment of transformation when he does an act of integrity, courage, and kindness which overcomes the walls of separation between him and the Asian immigrants.

Ryan's racism is overcome when he courageously saves Christine's life. He is bewildered by his response. Perhaps he would have saved anyone's life, but the event itself is complex and confuses him. It reverses the way he has manhandled her in their past confrontation, and instead, replaces his previous actions with respect, a sense of her dignity, compassion, determination, and becomes a moment of great intimacy and tenderness. As Christine is led away, she looks back and her look is described as "angry, grateful — she searches his eyes for answers, some way to make sense of what just happened." It is a look of "hate filled with fear and gratitude" (p. 72). Ryan watches her, "equally confused, overwhelmed and embarrassed by his feelings" (p. 73).

For Christine, the event is also a reversal, placing Ryan outside the box of the expected. This moment of courage and tenderness makes it possible for her to soften toward her husband.

Peter is trying to escape the stereotype and even thinks he has, when he runs away rather than getting into Cameron's SUV. It looks, for a moment, as if he might escape into a better life. He seems to be having a normal conversation with Hansen, who has picked him up when hitchhiking. He's still a victim of Hansen's racism which we may have thought didn't exist. But it does. When Peter reaches inside his pocket, Hansen's conclusion is a racist conclusion — Peter, who is black, must be reaching for a gun, and certainly wouldn't be expected to have the same St. Christopher statuette that he has. The physical wound of Peter becomes a symbol of the emotional wound that Hansen will now carry.

Farhad is saved by pushing his rage to murder, determined to rid himself of the oppressor who symbolizes everyone who misunderstands who he is. In a moment of horror and insight, he recognizes that neither Daniel, nor most other people, are quite what they seem, and that he had as much need to be saved, as Daniel did. The protective cloak protected all of them.

Creating a Transformation

In a short timeline, characters usually don't have the time to change and grow and transform. Yet, sometimes realizations and epiphanies and transformations do take place in a short period of time because of the intensity of the experience.

In *Crash,* many of the characters come to a new understanding or a transformation of attitudes or actions. Ryan becomes aware of his racism and sexism after saving Christine in the car crash. Farhad becomes aware that he's taking out his anger on a father and his precious daughter and is repentant of his actions. Christine and Cameron soften toward each other, as they realize that racism caused their anger, not any intrinsic problem with each other. Anthony is surprised by Cameron's actions, and Cameron's words, "You embarrass me. You embarrass yourself" (p. 91) seem to hit their mark, as Anthony proceeds to do a good deed for the illegal immigrants. Jean softens toward her maid, and says to Maria, "You want to hear something funny?... You're the best friend I have" (p. 108). Jean realizes that friends can better be defined by kindness than by money.

Hansen recognizes that he's not quite the man of integrity that he thought he was, and is left with a sense of vulnerability and confusion, which has the potential to deepen his character. Before his death, Peter found a moment of connection with Hansen, which surprised both of them.

There are, however, some characters that don't change. From all indications, Shaniqua will continue to be inflexible with her social cases. Ria will probably continue to be a good cop, but won't continue her relationship with Graham and probably won't overcome her racist attitudes toward Asians. Ryan's father will continue to suffer, with little change in his circumstances. The D.A. will continue to work the angles and to spin information to assure his re-election. With other characters, it's unclear whether their transformation will hold or not. Will Anthony make any real changes? Will Cameron continue to be under the thumb of a racist producer? Will Jean make new friends, or revert back to her white upper-class life?

Regardless of whether the transformation holds, or to what degree, we do see these moments of grace, of change, of something shifting, even if only for a moment.

REACHING A RESOLUTION

The film gives hints of changes in the characters, and therefore gives hints into the possibilities of some sort of redemption for the characters.

Redemption is a strange word, since it has religious and spiritual connotations, as well as an implication of true change in attitudes and action. By using a word with a spiritual connotation, a writer has the potential to further deepen the script and deepen the resonances that can come from the film. Although the word itself is not used in the film, the spiritual layer of the film is implied with the miracle of the magic cloak, and the angel (Lara) who saved her father from death.

What does it mean to be redeemed? It's a different idea than simply a transformation. It gets to the heart of the vulnerability and possibilities of the human condition. That which was lost, is found. That which was dark, is made light. That which was oppressed, is liberated. That which was bound, is freed.

In *Crash*, there is much in the story that is wearing down the characters. Racism is a heavy burden, and can only be carried on by making sure that characters don't come into contact with each other, don't confront or collide with each other. It depends on stereotypes that are tightly held, and it depends on objectifying the other person, and making the other person less than human.

They are tightly fit into a one-dimensional mold, which can only be broken by these moments of epiphanies where The Other is seen as being as fully human as one's own self.

The writers use an image that breaks into our usual way of seeing things and that force a moment of epiphany. They use a religious image: Farhad has just shot Lara, and by all accounts, she should be dead. Yet, because of the magic cloak that her father gave her to protect her from bullets, and because of her spontaneous willingness to put herself into danger to save her father, she saved all of them. Farhad says:

```
                FARHAD
           (in Farsi)
     She was my firishta.

                DORRI
     What are you talking about?

                FARHAD
     My firishta. You don't know your
     faith. She was my angel. She saved
     me. She saved us all. (p. 109)
```

USING SOUND AND IMAGES CINEMATICALLY

Although the director of *Crash,* Paul Haggis, uses muted colors and the film almost feels as if it's shot in black and white, there are still a number of visual and sound images that reinforce the theme and characters.

Using Sound Cinematically

Most writers use very few sound cues in their writing. Many scripts contain a recognition of realistic sounds that make up a scene (the honking cars, the sirens, the sound of the ocean, the knocking at the door, the tea kettle boiling, the laughter of children), but it's more rare to find a writer using sound as a metaphor and writing it in the script.

Many writers known for their use of music or sound are writer-directors. In *Bugsy,* writer-director Barry Levinson takes sound away and simply shows Bugsy gesticulating, as he comes up with the idea for building Las Vegas. In some films, such as *Platoon,* music is used to create a mood and attitude, as in the scene when the soldiers walk away from the burning village and Samuel Barber's "Adagio for Strings" plays over the scene. In *Apocalypse Now,* Wagner's "Ride of the Valkyries" blasts from the helicopters as the soldiers fly in to bomb a village.

Although most of *Crash* uses realistic sounds, in one of its memorable scenes, sound is taken away to make its impact. When Ryan rescues Christine from the burning car, a Welsh song is sung in the background and most of the ordinary realistic sounds we might expect, such as policemen yelling for help, or the sound of crowds in the background, are taken away. There is occasional dialogue between Ryan and Christine, but the song is in the forefront.

While the action keeps us tense and anxious about the outcome of the scene and provides the needed conflict, the song distances us enough to see other layers of the scene. The scene is shot as a kind of love scene — very intimate, very close, quite gentle. Ryan lovingly reaches over to pull down Christine's skirt so as not to embarrass her. Their faces are close as he tries to undo the seat belt.

                    RYAN
        I need you to move a little, can
        you do that?...
        Are you hurt, anything broken?

                    CHRISTINE
        I don't think so.

                    RYAN
        That's good.

And as the gasoline is ready to explode, Ryan reaches back for Christine one more time, and drags Christine out with him (p. 71–72).

Using Images to Reinforce the Theme

Most of the visuals in *Crash* are realistic, rather than metaphoric. But there are several images that connect scenes and that show redemption.

How does one overcome racism? Through touch. Connections. Meetings. Intersections. Being close enough to see the humanity beneath the race. It is the same path to overcoming any of the "isms" — sexism, ageism, classism, and religious intolerance.

There are three crashes in *Crash*. The first one is at the beginning of the film — it's a crash of several cars, and we see Graham weary as if this is just more of the same. The middle crash, where Ryan rescues Christine, also has several cars involved. With the rescue and the explosion comes the beginning of something redemptive, transforming, that changes perceptions. The third crash is not really a car crash, but a car burning at the end of the film. Hansen burns his car, as if he could, somehow, remove all evidence of hatred, violence, and the troubling nature of racism. The car-burning turns into a bonfire celebration as kids gather around.

These three car scenes are connected with ongoing car scenes that represent Los Angeles. There are many different kinds of cars represented: SUVs, vans, squad cars, passenger cars, Christine's jeep, as well as the bus. These vehicles wind their way through the many locations of Los Angeles, connecting stories that would ordinarily not be connected, and moving people to touch, connect, and sometimes crash into each other.

Fire is used in the scene with Christine, as the fire creeps closer to her overturned jeep. The fire is used with the additional idea of the ticking clock — it seems to be seconds away as it follows the path of the dripping gas, finally leading to an explosion. Fire is used again at the end of the film, when Hansen burns his car to remove the evidence of the murder of Peter. Fire is an image of heat, boiling toward an explosion, causing something to erupt. It is also used as an image of burning away — whether evidence, or burning away a taint, corruption, and old attitudes.

At the end of the film, the city of Los Angeles is also redeemed when it snows. Snow can be a metaphor for making everything clean, pure, and fresh. Like the miraculous moments that overcome racism, snow, which seems to be an impossibility in Los Angeles, is another miracle.

CREATIVITY AND STUDY GUIDE FOR CRASH

(1) Since most people seem to be racist in one way or another, can you define your racist attitudes and where you learned them? Did you identify with any of the racist attitudes in the story? How do you respond to the idea that some of these racist attitudes are based on fact? For instance, some blacks do carjack cars in white neighborhoods, although some whites do also and some white cops do harass blacks?

(2) How did these individual stories touch you? Did you have a favorite? Were you more compassionate towards some of these characters than others? Can you think of some other ways that these characters could have interwoven into each other's lives? Write a scene that brings some together, that don't come together in the film. (For instance, could any of these other characters wander into Farhad's store? Could Shaniqua, the black social worker, intersect with anyone else in the film?)

(3) Define some of the contrasting characteristics that you find *within* these characters. What qualities were unexpected? What qualities did not surprise you?

(4) Why was there so much misunderstanding of each other in this film? What social structures keep stereotypes in place?

(5) What do you imagine would have happened to Hansen after this story ends? Write a scene of how he would reconcile himself to the murder he committed? How do you think that would affect the rest of his life?

(6) Do you think Ryan will change as a result of his experience with Christine? How might that affect his next encounter with someone who is black? Write a scene of what the next encounter could look like.

(7) Do you think that Jean will change? Will she have different friends after this experience? Would her values change? Do you think she'll treat Maria any differently?

(8) How did the racism that all of these characters experience create the wounds that are part of their daily lives? Do you see any hope for them? If so, how has that hope happened and how might it continue to happen?

(9) Look at all the characters and discuss whether they transformed and how they transformed. What would be necessary in their lives to make those transformations permanent?

(10) If you were to write a story about the racism that you see, what elements would be part of that story? What in this movie echoes with your own experience? What is new? What experiences have you had that aren't part of this film?

INTERVIEW WITH PAUL HAGGIS, WRITER-DIRECTOR AND BOBBY MORESCO, WRITER OF CRASH

Coming Up with the Idea

PAUL: I never wanted to make any sort of statement with this film. But things started happening to me living in Los Angeles. And I started asking myself questions that had to do with what happened about America post 9/11. It was about our fear of strangers and how we judge people so easily.

I remember being in a studio lot and walking towards a group of people I knew, three men, two white men, and one black man. The white men were producers and the black man was a director in their employ. And they were having an animated conversation. As I was walking towards them I realized that one of the white producers was telling a joke. As I got closer I realized that it was a racist joke. He was telling a joke to the black director as if to say, "See? We can do this now. Things are different. We can say these words." And before I got close enough to say, "No, you can't," the punch line came, and I saw the black director sort of half laugh, that kind of laugh that's with your mouth but not your eyes.

And the director turned and slapped the guy on the back as if they were comrades and walked back to the stage. I wondered if that man's soul had been eaten at that moment in order to keep his job the next day, and to get next week's assignment. I wondered what price he was paying in what looked like a raceless, classless world where we're all supposedly the same.

Shortly after that transpired I received a piece of hate mail where the person was commenting on a television episode I'd written. He said, "Why is it always the black people who are the victims and the white people who are aggressors?" And he went on to tell the story that Matt Dillon tells Shaniqua in my movie, about how his father had this company and how he lost everything when the city council gave preferential treatment to minority-owned companies. I thought, "Isn't that fascinating!" I'd always thought that racism and intolerance, our worst nature, was passed from one generation to the next. I think a lot of people think that. But here' a man (Ryan's father in the film) who was a good man, but because of the way he fell his son took the opposite lesson that the father was trying to pass on.

I've been intrigued by how we affect strangers without knowing it. So, you're driving along and you cut somebody off and they flip you the finger. And then you yell out the window and whatever, but you go right and they go left. All you know of that person is that they're an asshole. And that's all they know about you. But we know it with great certainty. In that one second. And so I asked myself, "What happens to that person because of that interchange? What do they take with them? Is it something that they've stirred up and they go home and they get angry at their wife? Or might they stop several blocks later at the scene of an accident and save someone's life?"

As Americans, and as people, we judge people very quickly. We see people with swarthy skin and rags on their head and we find it really easy to judge them. And we need to look no further than that. And that always comes back to bite us.

Beginning the Process

PAUL: I begin my writing process by following the characters and then come up with an outline. And I do a lot of reading. I read and read for a year. And then, when I followed this idea and some characters for a bit, I called up a friend, Bobby Moresco, and said "I've got a film line for a story. Do you want to write it with me?"

BOBBY. Paul said to me, "I think this is a movie worth doing. Take a look and see if you want to write it with me." And indeed, after I looked at it, I thought he was right. It was indeed worth doing. That's how it started. I gave him a call back and said, "I'd love to do this!" We didn't know if we wanted to make a television series out of it or a movie. There was a real case to be made for doing a mini-series on HBO, or a television series on a cable network.

PAUL: I passed on a whole shelf full of books to Bobby, mainly nonfiction books. Most were general studies of race and class in America. It was the more specific stories that shook me. A lot of these things didn't make it into the film, but they really helped the way I was looking at the story. I remember there was a little self-published book I found on the internet called *One Time*. I gave it to Don Cheadle. It was the story of a black LAPD officer who joined the force and went to the Academy because he really wanted to do good in the world. He especially wanted to do right by his community of South Central. So he graduated at the top of his class and they offered him a place somewhere else, but he said, "No, I want to go to South Central." After he joined, it only took him a month or two for him to realize how much he enjoyed beating up black people. Now this was a black officer. With so much self-hatred. He judged people, even if those people were very much like him.

BOBBY: Paul had read a lot of books. I read some more and surfed the internet. I did a lot of interviews with people, talked to a lot of people. We did a lot of research trying to understand the nature of what these characters had been through in their lives, and just trying to fill in the holes.

What Interests Us

PAUL: Some people ask how you can write a black family, or

a Persian family, but I think that's nonsense. I think that if
you know the specific given circumstances in a person's life,
and then you don't judge them, then you can write anything
about anyone.

BOBBY: Examining someone's psyche, some part of the human
condition... I think that is interesting. I like to shine a light
on it. Something that says, "Okay, this is who we are. This is
what we do. These are things we hide. These are things we
need to look at if we are going to get somewhere, anywhere."
Whether or not the canvas is racism, social injustice, or any
other number of problems, it's about the human condition.
That's exciting to me.

I think it's a mistake for any writer to sit down and say, "Okay,
I'm going to write a piece now about a social condition and
injustice, and I'm going to teach people about something." I
think that's a big mistake if we do that as dramatists. Instead,
hopefully we ask questions as opposed to giving answers.
Paul was tremendously interested in exploring the idea of the
effect strangers have on each other in a city like Los Angeles,
in ways they don't understand, or even recognize. And for
me, the thing that we pushed for underneath the pages is the
idea of the fear of losing someone you love (like Ryan, Matt
Dillon's character, and his father), the fear of losing things
that you've worked for (like Cameron, Terrence Howard's
character), and the fear of losing the respect that you've
worked for (like Graham, Don Cheadle's character). I was
excited to explore how facing your fears can force a person
to make decisions and rationalizations that maybe they might
not ordinarily make, do things they wouldn't ordinarily do.
You see that in somebody who's ordinarily a good person, like
Cameron, and his fear of losing his wife in that car for just
one moment. Or you see it in Ryan, looking at a black face
that maybe is someone who he's been taught all of his life to

hate. So the idea of fear, how it drives us to places and to do things that we might not ordinarily do as human beings, was really interesting to me. The combination of those two ideas, of Paul's idea of how changes affect other changes and my notion of fear pushing us places that we might not ordinarily go, those became the driving forces in the movie.

PAUL: It's the potential that I think interests me in the characters. I think it's too often in Hollywood films that you go from the potential to some sort of trite ending where the bad guy becomes a good guy and goes on. And the two white people from the north save the black people from the south. It just feels untrue.

The Writing Process

PAUL: Bobby and I met when I was doing a television show called *EZ Streets* twenty years ago which lasted about a second and a half. I took the pilot and was about to shoot it and an actor friend said I should look into this writer and his works. I met Bobby and liked him a lot, but he'd never written for television or movies. I think he had done one spec movie script, but he'd worked in the theatre a lot. He had a lot of experience there. But we just sort of clicked. So we worked together on that series, and then he went off to do some other television shows. And then we got back together to write this.

I like Bobby because he's one of the most annoying human beings on the face of the earth. And he finds me the same. We really are sand in each other's shoes. And that's what I think you need in a partner. You need someone who needles you. You know you get someone who's too much alike, and if you agree too much there's no sense having a second person.

Let me give you an example of the process. We'd be writing along and I'd be on page 22 and Bobby's sitting in the corner reading some pages I'd written or making some notes on his own. Then I said to Bobby, "See this thing here? Page 22. Got this problem. I need something to happen. Nothing going on here. I need to complicate this scene somehow.'"

But then Bobby would say, "Something's wrong on page 4." And he wouldn't let me go forward on page 22 until we fixed the problem on page 4. And he'd be completely right. There was something wrong on page 4. And that was the kind of relationship we had. He just kept making me look at these things I didn't want to look at.

BOBBY: Mostly there is a great advantage to writing with a partner. Hopefully on some level you say, "Hey, what about going over there?" And the other guy says, "You know, that's a good idea, but we should do it this way." So, then you have two people asking questions. William Goldman has a great quote, which is: "Writing is the ability to ask yourself questions and come up with the answers." Most writers stand alone in a room and ask those questions and bang their head against the wall trying to come up with the answers. And it takes a long time. When you're with a good writing partner, you can ask each other the questions. And the other person can come up with an answer. Then you bounce back with another answer. And pretty soon you've got answers to the question.

We are different, Paul and I. It's really funny. We've been working together eleven years on different things, and in all that time we've never ever said how we'll do something. We've never finished a project and asked, "What do you want to do next?" Each project sort of evolves. And every project is different. With this one, we sat in the room together. He types and I don't. I'm in back of him, hollering things and talking. We hash things out with this scene or that, where we're going and structurally what we're after. Then we just start typing again. Sometimes, more often in TV, he'll take an act, and I'll take an act. Then when we're done, we go off and rewrite each other.

PAUL: Often we're in the same room together. But often he'd get so annoying I'd just throw him out of the room and make him go write something downstairs. And then we'd write things separately and get back together, and we'd show each other things. And then edit each other's work.

BOBBY: When we've got a TV show, we work out the acts and the teaser. We know where it's going. We know who the characters are. We know what we're talking about dramatically. We're allowed, then, to separate and go to different rooms. Then we write because we know where we're going. But *Crash* was entirely different. We were writing by the seat of our pants. After we had done all the reading, Paul said to me one day, "You want to write?" I said, "Sure, let's write something." We wrote that first day and never stopped writing. Two weeks later we had a draft.

PAUL: We saw the story as not having secondary characters in the film. Now that's obviously not true, but that was my goal. They seem to play out and anybody who walked into that scene would eventually end up being a main character. So in the case when Sandra Bullock [Jean] says the locks should be changed — at the beginning, that was the only role Daniel had in the story. And then I thought, "whoa... hold on. The locksmith's probably heard these horrible things that Jean said. I wonder how it affected him." So I followed him home. So I just kept following the characters as they'd crash into each other in one way or the other. And then we're going to leave the people we're with and follow the other person. And kept doing that as much as possible. Of course it is impossible to do it with everyone, but I tried my best.

And the other thing I knew from the beginning was I was telling a series of fables. I was going to dress them up. We like our people to be animated characters... lots of fuzzy ears. We don't like them to masquerade as reality. And I really wanted to mix those two things. I really wanted to try and say, "Okay, this could happen to you." And then suck you in. But in telling the story, things are being distorted as well. You can run into the same cop twice in L.A. and the guy who did something horrible to you could save your life. But I wanted to do it over a course of thirty-two hours. And we're going to do our very best to package it in such a way that people don't groan when the sequences happen again. With the cops we had to make sure that it made sense. I said to myself, "Well, I've had three tickets in two weeks by the same cop. How can that be?" Well, because they all stake out the same area. So I said, "Okay, whatever these instances are, they have to occur in the same geographical area. Then I can buy it."

Getting Started

BOBBY: I think the greatest challenge of this material is what we found when we wrote the first scene, which was the first scene in the movie, and we wrote some of that ugly language. When it was done, Paul said to me, "Can we write this?" And I said, "We have to write it. If we're not going to write the truth of how we see these people in these lives and the fear underneath their souls, then why are we writing the movie?" Paul said, "They're going to hate us." I said, "Yeah, I guess we know they're going to hate us." So, the biggest challenge was trying to stay committed to the truth that we saw in the soul of these characters. Lots of critics saw that as a big mistake, saw it as over the top or melodramatic. You know, that's a chance you take. Not everybody's going to get what you're after. Some people didn't.

Everything is a potboiler in this movie. Tensions run high in every scene, and people say things they wouldn't ordinarily say. That's what we're dealing with here. The biggest challenge was trying to get inside the characters' souls and allowing them to say the things they wouldn't ordinarily say. Now, a lot of people saw that as a mistake, as something that made this not a good movie. That may be the case. But that's what we were writing about. That's how we were approaching this piece.

Structuring the Stories

PAUL: I didn't have a classic plot structure. After analyzing it, I don't think I have an Act One or an Act Three. I just have an Act Two. But I'm comfortable calling this an interweaving structure, since it's actually more interweaving than a parallel structure.

When I finished doing the story, and when Bobby and I finished writing the script, we looked at each other. I had no idea if it was a script or not. Or if it was a screenplay. I mean it was 110 pages or whatever. Actually when I faced shooting it, I still didn't know if it was a movie. I figured if ten people paid ten dollars it was a movie. But it disturbed me. It was a dumb thing to disturb me because a lot of people have done this.

The secret to it was just following the characters, and then continuing to put barriers in front of them whenever things would start going too well for them. It was also in asking the characters to ask themselves questions. So we had the two carjackers driving along and maybe talking about life and how the FBI created rap music or whatever, and I looked at Bobby and said, "Nothing's happening here. So, we need to complicate the situation." So, we'd sit around and we'd ask, "What's the worse thing that could happen?" So we go back through the plot and I ask, "Hey, that woman in the first scene who just sort of came in almost as a joke, she was an Asian woman who the female officer could show her hidden hatred for. But let's look at that for a second. This woman ran into the back of a police car. An unmarked police car, yes, but it was a police car. And it was the scene of the crime that was marked with flares and flashing lights. How could she not have seen this car? How could she have run into this car? It's silly. It can't be just saying she's Asian or she's a bad driver. No one's that bad of a driver. She has to have really been distracted. She had to have something in her mind. She had to be really concerned about something, distraught about something. And so maybe her husband was in the hospital. What hospital? That's what happens over in this other scene. They ran over this Asian guy. And I think ok. What was he doing there in the middle of nowhere... on this dark street... in this warehouse district. You just keep asking the questions, and from there the plot unfolds.

We did a lot of forward and backward writing. I'd say in the story I had, 75% of the characters of the story were written one night from two a.m. 'til ten a.m., and the rest were characters we made to allow the plots to work and intertwine more effectively.

Some things I wanted to keep in the background. Some things we can infer. And what happens there in the Lewis-Conklin plot is important because it impacts the Graham and D.A. plot. And it's only important in so far as it's exactly the opposite of what we'd expect we thought happened. And that was based on an actual LAPD incident that took place in the late '90s, a cover up.

All I kept doing was trying to turn the heat up on the characters each time because these people wouldn't act this way unless they were under tremendous pressure. And what I had to do was put these people under pressure immediately. Which is very unlike a lot of films in which you can get to know the person and like the person, and then you put them under a lot of pressure. And in this one I just wanted to say, "Okay, the first time you see these people has to be one of the worst moments of their life. And then things have to get worse." But they get worse in ways that people would never expect them to get worse.

BOBBY: Every project is different. Most of the time Paul and I structure the whole thing out. We have clear ideas of structurally where we and where our characters are going. With *Crash* we threw that out the window. Much of the movie was randomness. You know, the random encounters in city life in Los Angeles with strangers, and how those random encounters affect other random encounters, and how those random encounters ultimately affect people's lives. So, we had all this research and all this talk and all these ideas bouncing around in our heads, but we never structured any of it out. We just started writing. Paul would say, "Do you want to go to the next scene, and in the next scene, we'll go with that other character? Remember that character we were talking about? Let's have him meet her." And then we'd write something. Then he'd say, "Okay, now where do you want to go next?" And we crafted the structure in the writing, which is really crazy. I advise no writer on the face of the earth to write like that. It's really wrong. It should be done the other way around for the most part.

Somewhere around the time in the script that Graham finds his brother, Paul said to me, "When are we going to end this thing?" I think I said, "When the characters stop talking." We didn't know where we were going. If you look at the movie — this was either organic or it was accidental, but certainly we didn't know we were doing it — all the long speeches are at the top of the movie. Little by little, as the movie goes along it changes. Near the end there's almost no talking.

Did the Characters Transform? Were They Redeemed?

PAUL: It didn't really interest me what happened in the end. I didn't really care whether a character was redeemed, or what character wasn't. I think that's just nonsense. I didn't redeem any of these characters. I wanted to give the characters a chance to glimpse themselves in someone else's eyes. That's all I wanted. This is much like the character Ryan. He's in this burning car and looks into this woman's eyes; she would rather be burned to death than be saved by him. And so the question would be, "What would that do to a man?" Here's a man who believes himself to be a hero in spite of everything. Most police officers do. Most firemen do. They're supposed to be the good guy. And this character actually did believe himself to be that despite all the evidence. And then he has to see this woman who he's stooping to save, refuse to be saved. And that's got to change him. I don't know how it changed him. I don't know if it changed him for good or for ill. And I don't know how long it changed him for. It could just be thirty seconds. So you'd want to see what happens next to all these characters. You didn't want Jean to wake up in the morning and go downstairs and suddenly be a changed person with her maid. It's nothing that happens. She's going to try her best, and then the maid is going to do something that annoys her, and she would go to Maria and say, "I love you, but the dishes, please." But for that moment the wonderful thing about life is that we get to glimpse ourselves occasionally, and that's what I wanted to look at. Those are the moments I wanted to investigate, the moments where we glimpse ourselves and there's a chance for us to change.

BOBBY: Do I see this as redemptive? Absolutely. I see this movie with much of it about redemption or the loss of redemption. We were hoping to drive these characters to places where their only redemption was to recognize what was in their souls, regardless of whether it was hatred, whether it was fear, whether it was anger. Then, in facing that, some of them would say, "Okay, this is what I've done. And this is what I need to do." Most notably, I think of Hansen, when he sees these kids around the fire and realizes that he's walked away from everything he was as a human being. If that's not redemption, I don't know what is!

Of course, I'm not so sure that the character, Ryan, doesn't go back to exactly who he was the day before the movie takes place. That's a loss of redemption. I can go through each and every character and talk about whether I think there's a chance of redemption there or the loss of a chance at redemption. I mean, if you're not examining the human condition and saying we all have a chance at changing, then what the hell are you writing about? I think each and every character in this movie had the chance to be redeemed. Some of them take that chance. Some of them don't.

Selling the Script

PAUL: I started writing it in 2000, and I finished in 2001 with Bobby. And then we just started slugging it around. But it was tough to sell. I gave it to my agent, Larry Becsey, and my producing partner, Mark Harris, and they just started knocking on doors. We were turned down by every single studio — quickly. I knew that would happen because it was not a studio picture. And then we were turned down by all the independent financiers. They just didn't really like the style of this film. There were too many story lines. Then we found a couple of people who liked it but wouldn't put up any money for us to make offers. And so that didn't really help. And then another liked it and wanted to buy it, but said I couldn't direct. And I said I think I can. And they didn't trust me and said, "You can't." So I moved on from that until we found Bob Yari and Cathy Schulman. And they agreed to put up a little bit of money if we were able to package the film. And we were. We skipped out to agents and begged. And we got Don Cheadle, who was the first person we went for. That really made a big difference because people started thinking there must be something behind this because Cheadle is such a trusted actor. They figured they didn't know who I was, but if Cheadle trusts him, then we will, too. It started very slowly. We started to get actors interested. We had eleven actors. We had all the eleven major roles before we got a green light. And we got six and a half million dollars to make the picture.

The Editing Process

PAUL: In editing, besides trying to make the performances shine and trying to find the best moments for the actor, we tried to keep the story moving. And also in Act Two we just juggled around a couple of scenes. But the biggest problem we faced was, as we prepared to shoot, we got word that one of the actors was sick — was so sick that she had to turn around and go home. She couldn't get there. So I shot the scene with Cathy Schulman, the producer, standing in. And then it's a two-day scene we're shooting. I'm half way through the first day and another person gets deathly ill. It's flu felling people. And she's the fourth person in the scene. And she's got a huge speech to deliver. And then I know we're going to lose this location. So, I just keep shooting. I shoot the close-ups of the people who are still standing. I get to the end of the two days, and I'm just in tears because it's just in jagged pieces. Well, we had a huge Christmas tree in that scene. In a normal film you'd go in and you'd buy that tree and you'd stick it up and you'd put the lights up and it'd cost you a hundred thousand dollars and that would be part of the expense. Well, now we're shooting before Christmas because we need the Christmas tree there, and we can't afford it. So, it's already there and we're shooting. So, if we go back after Christmas to re-shoot, that tree will be gone, and we'll have to re-shoot even more. And then we can't get the location back and then Don has to leave to do *Hotel Rwanda*, and Brendan Fraser has another picture. And so we just can't go back to finish the scene. So I was scratching my head, and Bobby and I were sitting there trying to figure out what to do, so we wrote the character Flannagan who came in to say all the things that poor Gaye had to say in the other scene, and to put this choice to Don Cheadle. It really actually worked out so much better than what we'd written before. The actors were doing a great job, but the writing was a little wonky. I think it worked much better this way.

The Music

PAUL: I worked very closely with the composer, Mark Isham. Early on I said I wanted this to be the tower of Babel. I wanted this sort of cacophony of voices from around the world. But we couldn't afford to do that, of course, because our budget for music was about seven cents. So Mark reached out to these libraries of music, of traditional music. And he found Welsh, and he found Persian, and he found various languages. And then he sampled them. I knew I wanted that feel that had a sense of fate to it.

Right before the Welsh song, there was a Persian piece. And then he pulled them together so it almost sounded like the same piece. The music changes as Matt Dillon gets out of the car.

On one level the music pulls you in and on another level it seems to distance. I wanted to suck you in. And I wanted you to say,

"You know what? Sit back and relax and something bad is going to happen and you can't do anything about it."

Winning the Award

PAUL: I don't want to sound pretentious about this, but it wasn't a film I was trying to write. It was an experience. I wanted you to experience these little moments in people's lives. And I wanted you to get inside them somehow. So, that's why I didn't know whether it was a movie or not. When I got to the end I was pretty happy with some of the experiences. I thought I was going to twist people around in their chair. I thought that we would start the audience out judging people very quickly and easily. And then make them really uncomfortable with some of those choices they've made. I wanted people to have this visceral reaction because it was how it affected me. And, I wanted to keep twisting these things around. I got to the end and I wasn't sure if it added up to anything. And I still don't know.

BOBBY: I was surprised when we won the Academy Award. We had done well the year before with *Million Dollar Baby,* but you write because you love what you do and you hope that people get it. You don't think about awards. Some people do, but I wouldn't know how to do that.

PAUL: People had been telling me in the weeks leading up to the awards, "You know, you've got a good chance of winning." Hollywood always has some sort of game going on. And in fact, several weeks before the voting closed, they take you around to these Q&As and interviews and lunches, and I felt I was becoming a whore and promoting myself, and I was uncomfortable with it. So I called the studio and publicists, and I said, "I'm sorry. I'm leaving for France." And they freaked out. I said, "I'm going to go write some things. Cancel everything." They started yelling. They were saying,

"This is really unwise." And I said, "They're going to vote for the picture, or they're not going to vote for the picture." So I packed up and went to Paris and wrote for three weeks. And it was great. I loved it. For that reason I think I escaped some of the stories that were circulating that made it into a horse race.

I thought we probably had a good chance of getting the Academy Award for writing because we'd won everything else that year. And everything else that evening was going just like everything else had gone. *Brokeback* had won best adaptation and we'd won best original. But we didn't think we could win Best Picture. I knew that *Brokeback* had it just hands down.

In fact I had my best loser face on. That good smile you try and paste on there. Ang Lee was sitting across from me, that's one of the producers of *Brokeback*, and I was getting ready to applaud for them. I heard Jack say *Crash* and I didn't quite understand what that meant. And I looked to my right and looked at my wife who was standing. And I thought, "What the hell is she standing for? Does she love Ang Lee that much?" And then I said, "Oh, my God." All in a millisecond. I was thunderstruck. Shell shocked.

It was a great year for films. *Brokeback Mountain, Capote, Good Night and Good Luck, Munich...* These were wonderful, wonderful pictures. They are all pictures I truly, truly loved. They all deserved the award!

STORY BEATS FOR CRASH

Opening credits/Resolution (Graham and Ria Story)

1 min.   Tire skid marks on snow-covered blacktop; abstract auto headlights and taillights; credits.

2 min.   Abstract flashing red lights; credits; Graham's voiceover re "the sense of touch."

3 min.   Graham is in the passenger seat, telling Ria that in L.A., we're all behind metal and glass; the only way we touch is to crash into one another. A Motorcycle Cop asks if they are okay; Ria says Graham may have hit his head. Ria explains collision details to Graham, says she'll go seek Graham's lost frame of reference.

1st Turning Point (Kim Story)

    Graham approaches the Motorcycle Cop and Kim Lee, who blames the accident on an incredulous Ria.

4 min.   Ria mocks Kim's mispronunciations, throws in anti-Asian insults, tells the Motorcycle Cop that she's a detective. Graham passes the trio, a coroner's van and police tape to a road-side crime scene. He's greeted by a Detective who calls him "detective" and notes that it might snow tonight.

5 min.   The Detective tells Graham they've got a "dead kid." Graham examines a sneaker in the bushes marked as evidence, sees something further ahead that makes him stare. Cut to establishing shot of Hollywood, with title "Yesterday."

Set-Up (Farhad Story)

6 min.   A Gunshop Owner presents a handgun to Farhad, asks which ammunition is desired. Farhad and Dorri speak subtitled Farsi about the question, Farhad's ignorance of ammunition, Dorri's reservations about him buying a gun. The Owner interrupts with Arab-slanted insults to hurry up. Farhad mangles a question about being insulted; the Owner mocks him. It escalates and the Owner calls for Security, pulls back the gun. Farhad is shown out, lamenting that the Owner has cheated him.

7 min.   Dorri hopes to abort the sale but the Owner pushes forward. On her question about ammunition, he overwhelms her with

options and lascivious remarks. She randomly chooses the red box and cuts off the Owner as he asks if she knows what they are. She departs with the gun and ammo.

Set-Up (Anthony and Peter Story)

Anthony grouses about being discriminated against as he and Peter exit a restaurant, and Peter's responses calmly reject Anthony's "victim" point of view.

8 min.   Anthony continues to grouse, twisting each of Peter's rejoinders into evidence that they are, indeed, discriminated against for being black. Peter cracks up at Anthony's endless schtick.

Set-Up (Jean and Rick Story)

Jean and Rick walk down the street, arguing over whether Rick can go an evening without a call from Karen. Jean sees the guys and slips her arm into Rick's; Anthony notices and points it out to Peter.

9 min.   Anthony insists that she's afraid of them because they are black, and Peter discounts the notion. Anthony points out that, as the only blacks on a street in Brentwood, it's the two of them who should be afraid.

Catalyst (Anthony and Peter/Jean and Rick Story)

When Peter points out that they are armed, they pull their guns and carjack Rick and Jean's Navigator.

10 min.   Anthony drives; Peter puts a St. Christopher on the dash. Anthony harasses him; Peter says Anthony's driving warrants the protection.

Set-Up (Conklin-Lewis Story)

Graham and Ria are on-scene where Conklin, an off-duty narc cop, was in a fatal shootout with a Mercedes driver who cut him off and shot at him. Graham thinks that Conklin looks mighty relaxed.

1st Turning Point (Conklin-Lewis Story)

11 min.   With no witnesses as to which driver actually shot first, Graham asks to talk to a witness. At the Mercedes, he and Ria find the driver's handgun, car registration for a woman, and the wallet of

the driver William Lewis — another detective. Graham comments that Conklin "shot himself the wrong nigger."

Set-Up (Daniel Story)

Jean passes Daniel as he changes the locks on a door at her house.

12 min.   Jean pulls Rick from a meeting with his aides, insists on having the locks changed again. Rick tries to calm her; she rails that he not patronize her. Maria interrupts them as she leaves for the night.

1st Turning Point (Jean Story)

13 min.   Jean repeats that she wants the locks changed, by someone who's not a gangbanger. Rick argues that Daniel is not a gangbanger; Jean is convinced he is and that he'll send burglars to their house. She says she failed to act on her fear of Anthony and Peter to avoid being called a racist, and they got carjacked. She insists that Daniel is a gangbanger and demands that Rick give a shit.

14 min.   Daniel, having heard it all, leaves Jean her keys and walks out. Rick returns to his aides, including Karen. They discuss that a DA's car theft will make the news, and Rick worries that if he's tough about the incident he'll lose the black vote.

1st Turning Point (Rick Story)

He wants an antidote — a black man to proclaim a hero.

15 min.   Rick posits a firefighter, but Bruce says that the man is Iraqi — dark-skinned but not black. When Bruce reveals the man's name, Rick blasts him for suggesting that he proclaim an Iraqi named Saddam a hero.

Set-Up (Ryan-Shaniqua Story/Immigration/Choi Story)

At a diner, Park hands a check to Choi who says he's on the way to pick them up. He passes Officer Ryan, on the phone with Shaniqua over his father's medical woes. Shaniqua fails to satisfy with her HMO spiel, says he can make an appointment to talk further.

16 min.   Ryan hears Shaniqua's name, makes an insulting remark, and she hangs up on him. Choi drives past in his van;

Set-Up (Ryan-Hansen Story)

Ryan returns to his patrol car and partner Hansen. The police radio announces a carjacked Navigator; Ryan pulls out after a similar vehicle. Hansen says that's neither the vehicle nor the driver in question. Ryan aims the spotlight, sees a woman sit up in the passenger seat, says they were doing something.

Set-Up (Cameron-Christine Story)

17 min.   Ryan pulls the vehicle over, he and Hansen approach warily. Christine applies lipstick as Ryan asks for registration. She smirks as Cameron obediently gets the registration.

18 min.   Christine and Ryan exchange guarded pleasantries. Christine cracks up as Ryan leaves with the registration. Ryan hands off to Hansen, returns and has Cameron exit the vehicle. Christine has smart remarks; Cameron is compliant.

19 min.   Ryan administers a sobriety test. Christine opens her door, makes smart remarks and gets out despite Ryan telling her to stay put. Cameron warns her back, but she argues and Ryan tells them both to turn and lock hands on heads. The more they argue or try to explain, the more Ryan gets physical, and the more Christine gets belligerent. Ryan makes a lascivious comment as he shoves Christine.

20 min.   Christine becomes insultingly belligerent as Cameron implores her to be quiet. As Hansen professionally pats down Cameron, Ryan lingers over frisking Christine, feeling her up and taunting Cameron. Cameron watches as Ryan slides his hand up Christine's crotch and trumps up a public sex-related charge to scare the couple.

21 min.   As Christine squirms in anguish, Ryan glares at Cameron for his input. Cameron apologizes and asks for lenience while Christine stares daggers at him. Ryan gloats, flaunts his power, and lets them go as Hansen stands by, shocked. Ryan leaves with a flippant remark.

22 min.   Back in their vehicle, Christine cries and shrinks from Cameron's touch. Hansen stands, dazed. Shereen struggles with a door that won't close at the market as Dorri loads the handgun for Farhad. Farhad wants protection.

23 min.   Shereen says the door won't close; Farhad sends Dorri off to work, goes to tend to the door.

1st Turning Point (Christine and Cameron Story)

At her home, Christine rails about Ryan's treatment and blasts Cameron for just standing there. They argue over his passivity, whether he's protecting his image.

24 min.   She blasts him for trying to hide/ignore that he's black; he defends his restraint with the police. They trade insults about each other's elite or sheltered background, about not being black or knowing what it means. Christine mocks him viciously; he is very hurt and angry.

25 min.   Daniel arrives home, checks on his daughter, finds her hiding beneath her bed.

26 min.   Daniel draws Lara out about her fears. She heard a bang, maybe a gun. He reminds her that they moved to a safer neighborhood. She is still worried about a stray bullet.

27 min.   Daniel tells Lara about the fairy who gave him an invisible magic cloak that is impenetrable.

28 min.   Daniel says that the cloak always protected him, and that he forgot to give it to Lara. He offers it to Lara, takes it off.

29 min.   Daniel ties the cloak around Lara's shoulders, puts her to bed. She's comforted.

30 min.   Daniel gets a page on his beeper, leaves home again. Anthony and Peter drive in their stolen vehicle, argue about hip-hop.

31 min.   Peter switches to country music, makes up lyrics about lynching blacks as Anthony educates him about intelligent black songwriters and how the FBI replaced them with mindless hip-hop writers.

1st Turning Point (Choi Story/Illegal Immigrant Story)

Mid-argument, they unwittingly hit Choi as he stands next to his van, pull over and find they have a "Chinaman" under the vehicle.

32 min.   Anthony wants to drive away; Peter insists that man is stuck.

Peter argues to help him; Anthony argues that it will only lead to trouble, somehow.

33 min. When Peter brings up the specter of murder charges, Anthony helps him extract Choi.

1st Turning Point (Hansen Story)

At the station, Hansen asks to be assigned to a new partner. His Lieutenant harasses him over raising a "racial prejudice" claim, urges Hansen to find an excuse that will not reflect poorly. Hansen struggles to dream up another excuse.

34 min. The Lieutenant prompts Hansen to claim that his own flatulence is the reason he wants to be reassigned to work solo. Hansen balks but the Lieutenant alludes to his own struggle to reach his position in the racist LAPD and pushes Hansen to drop the racist argument.

35 min. Anthony and Peter dump Choi at an emergency room. At Farhad's market, Daniel can't make a new lock work on a ruined door.

1st Turning Point (Farhad Story)

He tells Farhad he needs a new door; Farhad can't understand, is sure Daniel is trying to cheat him.

36 min. Farhad will not listen or cooperate, gets irate, calls names, insists that Daniel fix the lock. Daniel offers to drop the labor charge but Farhad won't even pay for anything. Daniel wads up the invoice, drops it in the trash, walks out as Farhad screams to return and fix the lock. Anthony and Peter arrive at a chop shop.

1st Turning Point (Anthony and Peter Story)

37 min. Lucien, chop shop owner, refuses to clean up and sell the vehicle, citing that advanced forensic technology will surely bite him in the ass with the Chinaman's blood all over and inside the vehicle.

38 min. Peter snags the St. Christopher and the pair leave.

2nd Turning Point (Graham-Ria Story)

At his place, Graham ignores Ria's insistence that he not answer the ringing phone, and he interrupts their sex to answer and tell his mother that he's not seen his brother. Ria dresses to leave, confronting Graham over avoiding intimacy.

39 min. Ria busts Graham on having referred to her as Mexican, informing him that she's Salvadoran and Puerto Rican.

Climax (Graham–Ria Story)

He responds with an all-encompassing insult, and she walks out. In his home, Ryan awakes and rises from bed.

Set-Up (Ryan's Father Story)

40 min. Ryan finds his father in agony in the bathroom, patiently and gently helps him.

41 min. Ryan's Pop sends him away and Ryan suffers silently. Dawn breaks over the L.A. streets. Farhad finds his market broken into, burglarized and vandalized.

42 min. The market is a disaster. Rick and Karen discuss the Conklin-Lewis crime. Rick wants Graham to keep it quiet, come to him with his report. Peter and Anthony walk their neighborhood; Anthony rails at Peter for being friendly with a brother who steals from blacks.

43 min. Anthony's car won't start. Jean gives Maria needless grief over clean dishes being left in the dishwasher. Anthony and Peter walk, arguing whether it's ethical to steal from blacks.

44 min. Anthony is floored when Peter suggests they ride the bus; Anthony says buses are another way for whites to humiliate blacks. At the studio, Cameron finishes shooting a scene, heads out.

45 min. Fred talks to Cameron, suggesting that Cameron do another take because he feels their black actor has lost the black edge to his speech. Cameron tries to laugh it off, but acquiesces.

46 min. Cameron agrees to do another take.

1st Turning Point (Ryan's Father Story)

Shaniqua arrives at work to find Ryan waiting for her. Ryan apologizes, describes his father's condition.

47 min. Ryan insults his father's HMO doctor; Shaniqua says they are welcome to go out-of-network, an unacceptable option

to Ryan. Ryan insults Shaniqua, noting the whites who are out of work since she got this job. She tells him to leave. He challenges her to show compassion like others have shown compassion to her people.

She calls for security.

48 min.   Ryan explains his father worked alongside blacks, then got shut out of his job when minorities got preferential treatment. He asks for Shaniqua to make up for this by helping Pop. She tells him that he blew it for his father, and has him escorted out.

Climax (Ryan's Father Story)

49 min.   Ryan storms out. Daniel's manager talks via phone with Farhad about his failure to replace the door when Daniel recommended it. Shereen and Dorri lament that the vandals scrawled anti-Arab graffiti — incorrectly labeling them. Farhad demands Daniel's name but the manager refuses.

50 min.   Graham, at his mother's, sees evidence of her drug use, finds her in an addled daze, brings her in out of the cold.

51 min.   Graham's Mother asks about his missing brother, laments her backslide into drugs.

52 min.   Mother asks again if Graham's found his brother, urges Graham to find him. Graham sees her empty refrigerator, throws out rancid milk, returns to Ria in their car.

53 min.   Ria tells Graham that Internal Affairs found something in the Mercedes. Cameron breaks for lunch; Christine has come to see him. He reluctantly greets her; she tries to make amends, to explain herself, and apologizes.

54 min.   Christine reiterates her humility, her disbelief that Cameron didn't stand up for her, her humiliation for him, too, and recasts her behavior during the incident to be about her trying to protect Cameron. He can't hear it and walks away, leaving her in tears.

55 min.   Farhad cleans up, hears from the Asian insurance agent that failing to fix the door voids his policy for the claim. Farhad is crushed; he's ruined.

56 min.   Dorri tries to comfort Farhad; he sends her away.

57 min.   At the station, Ryan wishes Hansen well on his reassignment, then clamps his hand and alludes that Hansen has no idea what years on the police force will turn him into.

58 min.   Hansen drives off, gets razzed by the radio dispatcher about his flatulence. The Internal Affairs officer shows Graham and Ria a stash of cash in the Mercedes' trunk.

59 min.   Cameron sits, thinking.

2nd Turning Point (Farhad Story)

Farhad retrieves Daniel's invoice from the dumpster.

60 min.   Ryan and his new partner Gomez reach the site of an auto accident. Ryan goes to an overturned auto, tries in vain to open it.

61 min.   Ryan finds the woman driver, moves in to help her as he sees the threat of fire.

62 min.   Ryan sees the woman is Christine; she screams for him to get away, not touch her. He says he's trying to help; she becomes hysterical with fear. He shouts that he won't hurt her, then gently explains that she must cooperate.

63 min.   Ryan gently, compassionately helps Christine, nose-to-nose and conscious of the damage he's done to her psyche. He's all professional, keeping her calm.

64 min.   Ryan cuts Christine's seatbelt, as gasoline flows and flames ignite. The vehicle is engulfed; he is pulled out, she is left behind. He crawls back in to save her.

65 min.   Both just having reached safety, the auto explodes. Christine breaks down, is taken way with a long look back at Ryan.

66 min.   Karen and Flanagan see Graham. Flanagan explains that Conklin has a record of shooting black men and should hang; Graham reveals that $300K was found in the Mercedes. Flanagan recoils, goes into spin mode.

67 min.   Flanagan hears the facts from Graham, effortlessly spins stories that will suit his purposes. Flanagan excuses Karen, asks who knows about money.

2nd Turning Point (Lewis-Conklin Story)

68 min.   Flanagan spins the story so that Lewis is clean, Conklin can still be hung. When Graham notes that Lewis was likely on cocaine, Flanagan does a 180, says that Lewis, then, is just another black who couldn't resist drugs, shoving this in Graham's face.

69 min.   Flanagan switches gears again, encouraging Graham to agree to making Lewis a hero in return to getting Graham a promotion. Graham refuses, so Flanagan brings up Graham's brother's car theft record.

70 min.   Flanagan notes that the brother has an outstanding warrant, and urges Graham to let Conklin hang, even if it's not the moral thing to do.

Climax (Lewis-Conklin Story)

71 min.   Flanagan pushes Graham for a decision. When Rick arrives, Graham implies that Conklin is the culprit to crucify.

72 min.   Graham stands alone. Rick holds a press conference, glossing over his carjacking and moving swiftly onto the Lewis-Conklin case. Farhad arrives in Daniel's neighborhood.

73 min.   Lara arrives home. Farhad takes his gun. Cameron sits in his vehicle, and is carjacked by Anthony and Peter. He fights back and attacks Anthony.

74 min.   Peter struggles to get Cameron off Anthony. As the thieves leap into the vehicle, Cameron attacks again and a police car drives nearby.

2nd Turning Point (Peter Story/Anthony Story)

Peter runs, Cameron drives off with Anthony in the vehicle. The police chase, and Hansen joins the chase, recognizing the vehicle's license.

75 min.   The police chase Cameron into a cul-de-sac, draw guns and order Cameron out. Anthony crouches to hide.

2nd Turning Point (Cameron Story)

Cameron makes a decision, secures Anthony's gun and gets out of the vehicle, yelling anti-police epithets.

76 min.	Cameron challenges the police, shouting insults. Hansen rushes forward, says he knows Cameron, calls the other cops off. Cameron challenges him too while Hansen tries to talk him down. Hansen implores the other cops to stand down and give him time.
77 min.	Hansen talks to Cameron in blunt language to warn him of the danger he is in; Cameron continues to argue and refuses to comply. Hansen compromises, and Cameron cooperates. Hansen asks the other officers for a favor, to let Cameron go with a warning.
78 min.	Hansen warns Cameron, but Cameron is still ready to fight. Hansen sends Cameron home, and Cameron gets in the vehicle and drives off.
79 min.	Hansen stands, in thought, then drives away. Cameron stops, gives Anthony his gun, tells Anthony that he is an embarrassment. Anthony gets out.
80 min.	Cameron drives away. Anthony walks. Farhad sees Daniel's van arrive. Lara is at the window. Farhad approaches, gun drawn, demands money from Daniel.
81 min.	Daniel warns Lara to stay inside, calls for Elizabeth, fends off Farhad. Lara runs out to protect Daniel, leaps into his arms as Farhad fires. Anguish all around, and then —

Climax (Daniel Story)

82 min.	Lara is fine, and says she'll protect Daniel. Happy tears, and Farhad stands, dazed. Daniel carries Lara away.

Climax (Farhad Story)

	Farhad pockets the gun.
83 min.	Farhad walks away. Graham finds his mother asleep, puts bags of food into her refrigerator. Jean complains on phone to a friend about her rage at everyone.
84 min.	Jean laments that she's still mad, realizes she's like this all the time. Her friend begs off.

2nd Turning Point (Jean Story)

85 min.	Jean slips on the stairs, her cell phone goes flying, she lays injured. Peter tries to thumb a ride, walks the dark streets.

86 min.   Ryan drives.

2nd Turning Point (Hansen Story/Peter Story)

Peter hitches, Hansen stops to give him a ride.

87 min.   Hansen and Peter make awkward small talk. Peter compliments country music, Hansen is skeptical. Hansen becomes suspicious; Peter's smart replies only make Hansen more wary.

88 min.   Peter cracks up at seeing a St. Christopher on Hansen's dash. Hansen perceives an insult, pulls over to make Peter get out.

89 min.   Peter moves for his own St. Christopher, Hansen perceives a threat, shoots Peter.

Climax (Peter Story)

Peter agonizes, dies, reveals his St. Christopher. Hansen checks him, pushes him from the car.

90 min.   Hansen exits the car, stoops to look at Peter's body. Fade out and back in to Graham arriving at the fatality scene, noting the sneaker as evidence.

91 min.   Graham sees Peter's body, goes into stunned shock. Anthony rides a bus, surveys the passengers around him.

92 min.   Anthony gets off the bus, drives off in Choi's van. Kim Lee runs in a hospital, calling out, insults the white nurse, finds Choi, cries in relief.

Climax (Kim Story)

93 min.   Choi directs Kim to get the check he received, cash it right away.

Anthony takes the van to Lucien, who finds the back filled with illegal aliens.

2nd Turning Point (Illegal Immigrant Story)

94 min.   Lucien offers to take the van and the immigrants. Lucien clarifies they are Thai, and offers Anthony the van back plus $500 per alien. Graham accompanies his mother to the morgue where she freaks out at seeing her son's body. Ria stands by, helpless, along with Dorri, the pathologist.

95 min.   Graham's mother grieves, and puts the blame on Graham for his brother's death. Graham absorbs the venom.

96 min.   Graham's mother sends him away, says that the brother delivered groceries to her as his last act. Graham walks out, in agony. Dorri returns to the market.

97 min.   Farhad tells Dorri that he shot a little girl, but she's okay. He's stunned, says that his angel protected him.

98 min.   Farhad gives the gun to Dorri, comforts her.

Resolution (Farhad Story)

99 min.   Dorri finds the box of bullets — blanks. Jean calls Rick at his office, relates her situation and how no one would help her. Rick leaves Karen, wordlessly, to go to Jean.

Climax (Jean Story)

100 min. Maria helps Jean and Jean tells her that Maria is her best friend, hugs her tight. Hansen douses his car with gasoline, lights it.

Resolution (Hansen Story/Ryan's Father's Story)

101 min. Hansen walks from the burning car, pensive. Ryan helps his Pop in the bathroom as Pop cries. Rick checks the locks on his door at home and gazes into space.

102 min. Elizabeth and Lara sleep while Daniel gazes out the window into the night. Cameron drives, sees snow? He stops, recognizes the snow for what is really is —

103 min. Hansen's car burns, sending up ash into the sky. Kids throw items onto the bonfire and Cameron joins in. His cell phone rings — Christine.

Climax (Cameron and Christine Story)

104 min. Christine and Cameron reconcile, trade "I love you's."

Resolution (Peter Story)

Graham gazes at the city lights, finds Peter's St. Christopher in the dirt.

Climax (Illegal Immigrant Story)

105 min. Anthony stops Choi's van in Chinatown, lets the aliens go free. They are confused; he urges them out and they start to disappear into the sea of humanity, awed at America.

106 min.   Anthony gives the aliens cash for food while simultaneously insulting them. Anthony drives off in Choi's van as Shaniqua is rear-ended by some brand of foreigners whom she proceeds to insult and shout at.

107 min.   As we pull out to survey the scene, it starts to snow. And it snows and snows.

EPILOGUE

As a result of reading this book, hopefully you will be able to apply these ideas to the analysis of any great script. Hopefully you will have a whole new set of tools to use in your own writing, as you confront the challenges and issues of each script you write.

You can begin by asking: "What is unique and special about the script? What is unique and special about my own script?" Is it set in a unique context, like *Sideways*? Does it find connections between a historical period and our contemporary way of thinking, such as *Shakespeare in Love*? Does it layer the theme, with the deep explorations of *Crash*? What can I learn by studying these scripts that can help my own writing?

You may find it helpful to break down the structure of a number of great scripts in the same genre as your own, to see how they work and why they work. Are there any unusual structural principles applied to the storylines which you might find useful for your own work?

You might brainstorm the associations you have with the themes of great films, and use the same analysis for your own work. You might do more research, to find specifics in dialogue and characterizations, as all of these writers had to do with these Academy Award–winning scripts.

You might look at the functions of the characters, or how the characters show different facets of the theme, or how the characters use action and dialogue to achieve dimensionality, and then apply the same techniques to your own work.

You may have noticed that none of these scripts were first scripts for the writers. All the writers had already found their artistic voice through years of writing. All the writers show considerable technique and ability with the craft of writing. Technique is learned through a long process of studying, experimenting, and finding the subtleties that are part of every great work. The pianist spends hours learning scales and experiments with different fingerings for difficult passages and learns how to shade a note to create crescendos and play staccato and legato; the basketball player, who might already be gifted, still spends hours watching game films to learn about the competition, practicing the fundamentals and practicing new strategies until it's second nature. So does a writer learn all the basic principles of screenwriting, but then goes further with nuances and shadings, and learns to work with images and metaphors to create award-winning films.

In my conversations with these writers, it was clear they had learned from the discipline of writing and rewriting, reading books, watching many films, and then figuring out what to do with the particular challenges of these scripts. They didn't start by being great. They became great. Like all great work, their writing went through a long process before it achieved brilliance!

I hope this book serves you well as you move forward to creating splendid, award-winning scripts!

Linda Seger

www.lindaseger.com

ABOUT THE AUTHOR

Dr. Linda Seger began her script consulting business in 1981, based on a method she developed as part of her doctoral dissertation. Since then, she has consulted on over 2,000 scripts, and given seminars on screenwriting in thirty countries around the world. She is the author of ten books — eight on screenwriting — and lives in the Rocky Mountains of Colorado with her husband, Peter, and her cat, Sally; her horse, Shane, lives down the road. Her website is *www.lindaseger.com*.

THE WRITER'S JOURNEY
3RD EDITION

MYTHIC STRUCTURE FOR WRITERS

CHRISTOPHER VOGLER

BEST SELLER
OVER 170,000 COPIES SOLD!

See why this book has become an international best seller and a true classic. *The Writer's Journey* explores the powerful relationship between mythology and storytelling in a clear, concise style that's made it required reading for movie executives, screenwriters, playwrights, scholars, and fans of pop culture all over the world.

Both fiction and nonfiction writers will discover a set of useful myth-inspired storytelling paradigms (i.e., "The Hero's Journey") and step-by-step guidelines to plot and character development. Based on the work of Joseph Campbell, *The Writer's Journey* is a must for all writers interested in further developing their craft.

The updated and revised third edition provides new insights and observations from Vogler's ongoing work on mythology's influence on stories, movies, and man himself.

"This book is like having the smartest person in the story meeting come home with you and whisper what to do in your ear as you write a screenplay. Insight for insight, step for step, Chris Vogler takes us through the process of connecting theme to story and making a script come alive."
> – Lynda Obst, Producer, *Sleepless in Seattle, How to Lose a Guy in 10 Days*;
> Author, *Hello, He Lied*

"This is a book about the stories we write, and perhaps more importantly, the stories we live. It is the most influential work I have yet encountered on the art, nature, and the very purpose of storytelling."
> – Bruce Joel Rubin, Screenwriter, *Stuart Little 2, Deep Impact,*
> *Ghost, Jacob's Ladder*

CHRISTOPHER VOGLER is a veteran story consultant for major Hollywood film companies and a respected teacher of filmmakers and writers around the globe. He has influenced the stories of movies from *The Lion King* to *Fight Club* to *The Thin Red Line* and most recently wrote the first installment of *Ravenskull*, a Japanese-style manga or graphic novel. He is the executive producer of the feature film *P.S. Your Cat is Dead* and writer of the animated feature *Jester Till*.

$26.95 · 300 PAGES · ORDER NUMBER 76RLS · ISBN: 193290736x

SAVE THE CAT! GOES TO THE MOVIES

THE SCREENWRITER'S GUIDE TO
EVERY STORY EVER TOLD

BLAKE SNYDER

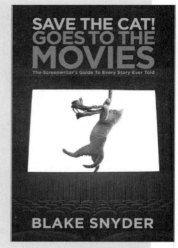

In the long-awaited sequel to his surprise bestseller, *Save the Cat!*, author and screenwriter Blake Snyder returns to form in a fast-paced follow-up that proves why his is the most talked-about approach to screenwriting in years. In the perfect companion piece to his first book, Snyder delivers even more insider's information gleaned from a 20-year track record as "one of Hollywood's most successful spec screenwriters," giving you the clues to write *your* movie.

Designed for screenwriters, novelists, and movie fans, this book gives readers the key breakdowns of the 50 most instructional movies from the past 30 years. From *M*A*S*H* to *Crash*, from *Alien* to *Saw*, from *10* to *Eternal Sunshine of the Spotless Mind*, Snyder reveals how screenwriters who came before you tackled the same challenges you are facing with the film you want to write — or the one you are currently working on.

Writing a "rom-com"? Check out the "Buddy Love" chapter for a "beat for beat" dissection of *When Harry Met Sally*... plus references to 10 other great romantic comedies that will make your story sing.

Want to execute a great mystery? Go to the "Whydunit" section and learn about the "dark turn" that's essential to the heroes of *All the President's Men*, *Blade Runner*, *Fargo* and hip noir *Brick* — and see why ALL good stories, whether a Hollywood blockbuster or a Sundance award winner, follow the same rules of structure outlined in Snyder's breakthrough method.

If you want to sell your script and create a movie that pleases most audiences most of the time, the odds increase if you reference Snyder's checklists and see what makes 50 films tick. After all, both executives and audiences respond to the same elements good writers seek to master. They want to know the type of story they signed on for, and whether it's structured in a way that satisfies everyone. It's what they're looking for. And now, it's what you can deliver.

BLAKE SNYDER, besides selling million-dollar scripts to both Disney and Spielberg, is still "one of Hollywood's most successful spec screenwriters," having made another spec sale in 2006. An in-demand scriptcoach and seminar and workshop leader, Snyder provides information for writers through his website, *www.blakesnyder.com*.

$22.95 · 270 PAGES · ORDER NUMBER 75RLS · ISBN: 1932907351

SAVE THE CAT!

THE LAST BOOK ON SCREENWRITING YOU'LL EVER NEED

BLAKE SNYDER

BEST SELLER

He's made millions of dollars selling screenplays to Hollywood and now screenwriter Blake Snyder tells all. "Save the Cat" is just one of Snyder's many ironclad rules for making your ideas more marketable and your script more satisfying — and saleable, including:

- The four elements of every winning logline.
- The seven immutable laws of screenplay physics.
- The 10 genres and why they're important to your movie.
- Why your Hero must serve your Idea.
- Mastering the Beats.
- Mastering the Board to create the Perfect Beast.
- How to get back on track with ironclad and proven rules for script repair.

This ultimate insider's guide reveals the secrets that none dare admit, told by a show biz veteran who's proven that you can sell your script if you can save the cat.

"Imagine what would happen in a town where more writers approached screenwriting the way Blake suggests? My weekend read would dramatically improve, both in sellable/producible content and in discovering new writers who understand the craft of storytelling and can be hired on assignment for ideas we already have in house."
> – From the Foreword by Sheila Hanahan Taylor, Vice President,
> Development at Zide/Perry Entertainment, whose films
> include *American Pie, Cats and Dogs* and *Final Destination*

"Want to know how to be a successful writer in Hollywood? The answers are here. Blake Snyder has written an insider's book that's informative — and funny, too."
> – David Hoberman, Producer, *Raising Helen, Walking Tall,*
> *Bringing Down the House*

"Blake Snyder's Save the Cat! *could also be called* Save the Screenwriter!, *because that's exactly what it will do:* Save the Screenwriter *time,* Save the Screenwriter *frustration, and* Save the Screenwriter's *sanity... by demystifying the Hollywood process."*
> – Andy Cohen, Literary Manager/Producer; President, Grade A Entertainment

BLAKE SNYDER has sold dozens of scripts, including co-writing the Disney hit, *Blank Check*, and *Nuclear Family* for Steven Spielberg — both million-dollar sales.

$19.95 · 216 PAGES · ORDER NUMBER 34RLS · ISBN: 1932907009

CINEMATIC STORYTELLING

THE 100 MOST POWERFUL FILM CONVENTIONS EVERY FILMMAKER MUST KNOW

THE 100 MOST POWERFUL FILM CONVENTIONS EVERY FILMMAKER MUST KNOW JENNIFER VAN SIJLL

CINEMATIC STORYTELLING

THE 100 MOST POWERFUL FILM CONVENTIONS EVERY FILMMAKER MUST KNOW

JENNIFER VAN SIJLL

BEST SELLER

How do directors use screen direction to suggest conflict? How do screenwriters exploit film space to show change? How does editing style determine emotional response?

Many first-time writers and directors do not ask these questions. They forego the huge creative resource of the film medium, defaulting to dialog to tell their screen story. Yet most movies are carried by sound and picture. The industry's most successful writers and directors have mastered the cinematic conventions specific to the medium. They have harnessed non-dialog techniques to create some of the most cinematic moments in movie history.

This book is intended to help writers and directors more fully exploit the medium's inherent storytelling devices. It contains 100 non-dialog techniques that have been used by the industry's top writers and directors. From *Metropolis* and *Citizen Kane* to *Dead Man* and *Kill Bill*, the book illustrates — through 500 frame grabs and 75 script excerpts — how the inherent storytelling devices specific to film were exploited.

You will learn:
- How non-dialog film techniques can advance story.
- How master screenwriters exploit cinematic conventions to create powerful scenarios.

"Cinematic Storytelling *scores a direct hit in terms of concise information and perfectly chosen visuals, and it also searches out... and finds... an emotional core that many books of this nature either miss or are afraid of.*"
— Kirsten Sheridan, Director, *Disco Pigs*; Co-writer, *In America*

"*Here is a uniquely fresh, accessible, and truly original contribution to the field. Jennifer van Sijll takes her readers in a wholly new direction, integrating aspects of screenwriting with all the film crafts in a way I've never before seen. It is essential reading not only for screenwriters but also for filmmakers of every stripe.*"
— Prof. Richard Walter, UCLA Screenwriting Chairman

JENNIFER VAN SIJLL has taught film production, film history, and screenwriting. She is currently on the faculty at San Francisco State's Department of Cinema.

$24.95 · 230 PAGES · ORDER # 35RLS · ISBN: 193290705X

THE SCRIPT-SELLING GAME
A HOLLYWOOD INSIDER'S LOOK AT GETTING YOUR SCRIPT SOLD AND PRODUCED

KATHIE FONG YONEDA

There are really only two types of people in Hollywood: those who sit around wearing black clothes in smoky coffee shops, complaining they can't get their scripts past the studio gates... and then there are the players. The ones with the hot scripts. The ones crackling with energy. The ones with knowledge.

Players understand that their success in Hollywood is not based on luck or nepotism; it's the result of understanding how Hollywood really works.

The Script-Selling Game brings together over 25 years of experience from an entertainment professional who shows you how to prepare your script, pitch it, meet the moguls, talk the talk, and make the deal. It's a must for both novice and veteran screenwriters.

"Super-concise, systematic, real-world advice on the practical aspects of screenwriting and mastering Hollywood from a professional. This book will save you time, embarrassment, and frustration and will give you an extra edge in taking on the studio system."
> — Christopher Vogler, Author, *The Writer's Journey: Mythic Structure for Writers*, Seminar Leader, former Story Consultant with Fox 2000

"I've been extremely fortunate to have Kathie's insightful advice and constructive criticism on my screenplays. She has been a valued mentor to me. Now, through this wonderful book, she can be your mentor, as well."
> — Pamela Wallace, Academy Award® Co-Winner, Best Writing, Screenplay Written Directly for the Screen, *Witness*

"This book is essential, invaluable, and necessary for any screenwriter wanting to make it in the competitive buyer's world. Yoneda gives the screenwriter the insider's view in a kind, encouraging, insightful way, and makes the impossible seem possible."
> — Dr. Linda S. Seger, Script Consultant and Author, *And the Best Screenplay Goes to...* , *Making A Good Script Great*, *Creating Unforgettable Characters*, *Making A Good Writer Great*

KATHIE FONG YONEDA is an industry veteran, currently under contract to Paramount TV in their Longform Division, and an independent script consultant whose clientele includes several award-winning writers. Kathie also conducts workshops based on *The Script-Selling Game* in the U.S. and Europe.

$16.95 · 196 PAGES · ORDER NUMBER 100RLS · ISBN: 0941188442

FILM & VIDEO BOOKS

Cinematic Storytelling: *The 100 Most Powerful Film Conventions Every Filmmaker Must Know* / Jennifer Van Sijll / $24.95

Complete DVD Book, The: *Designing, Producing, and Marketing Your Independent Film on DVD* / Chris Gore and Paul J. Salamoff / $26.95

Complete Independent Movie Marketing Handbook, The: *Promote, Distribute & Sell Your Film or Video* / Mark Steven Bosko / $39.95

Could It Be a Movie?: *How to Get Your Ideas Out of Your Head and Up on the Screen* / Christina Hamlett / $26.95

Creating Characters: *Let Them Whisper Their Secrets* Marisa D'Vari / $26.95

Crime Writer's Reference Guide, The: *1001 Tips for Writing the Perfect Crime* Martin Roth / $20.95

Cut by Cut: *Editing Your Film or Video* Gael Chandler / $35.95

Digital Filmmaking 101, 2nd Edition: *An Essential Guide to Producing Low-Budget Movies* / Dale Newton and John Gaspard / $26.95

Digital Moviemaking, 2nd Edition: *All the Skills, Techniques, and Moxie You'll Need to Turn Your Passion into a Career* / Scott Billups / $26.95

Directing Actors: *Creating Memorable Performances for Film and Television* Judith Weston / $26.95

Directing Feature Films: *The Creative Collaboration Between Directors, Writers, and Actors* / Mark Travis / $26.95

Eye is Quicker, The: *Film Editing; Making a Good Film Better* Richard D. Pepperman / $27.95

Fast, Cheap & Under Control: *Lessons Learned from the Greatest Low-Budget Movies of All Time* / John Gaspard / $26.95

Film & Video Budgets, 4th Updated Edition Deke Simon and Michael Wiese / $26.95

Film Directing: Cinematic Motion, 2nd Edition Steven D. Katz / $27.95

Film Directing: Shot by Shot, *Visualizing from Concept to Screen* Steven D. Katz / $27.95

Film Director's Intuition, The: *Script Analysis and Rehearsal Techniques* Judith Weston / $26.95

Film Production Management 101: *The Ultimate Guide for Film and Television Production Management and Coordination* / Deborah S. Patz / $39.95

Filmmaking for Teens: *Pulling Off Your Shorts* Troy Lanier and Clay Nichols / $18.95

First Time Director: *How to Make Your Breakthrough Movie* Gil Bettman / $27.95

From Word to Image: *Storyboarding and the Filmmaking Process* Marcie Begleiter / $26.95

Hitting Your Mark, 2nd Edition: *Making a Life - and a Living - as a Film Director* Steve Carlson / $22.95

Hollywood Standard, The: *The Complete and Authoritative Guide to Script Format and Style* / Christopher Riley / $18.95

I Could've Written a Better Movie Than That!: *How to Make Six Figures as a Script Consultant even if You're not a Screenwriter* / Derek Rydall / $26.95

Independent Film Distribution : *How to Make a Successful End Run Around the Big Guys* / Phil Hall / $24.95

Independent Film and Videomakers Guide - 2nd Edition, The: *Expanded and Updated* / Michael Wiese / $29.95

Inner Drives: *How to Write and Create Characters Using the Eight Classic Centers of Motivation* / Pamela Jaye Smith / $26.95

I'll Be in My Trailer!: *The Creative Wars Between Directors & Actors* John Badham and Craig Modderno / $26.95

Moral Premise, The: *Harnessing Virtue & Vice for Box Office Success* Stanley D. Williams, Ph.D. / $24.95

Myth and the Movies : *Discovering the Mythic Structure of 50 Unforgettable Films* / Stuart Voytilla / $26.95

On the Edge of a Dream: *Magic and Madness in Bali* Michael Wiese / $16.95

Perfect Pitch, The: *How to Sell Yourself and Your Movie Idea to Hollywood* Ken Rotcop / $16.95

Power of Film, The Howard Suber / $27.95

Psychology for Screenwriters: *Building Conflict in your Script* William Indick, Ph.D. / $26.95

Save the Cat!: *The Last Book on Screenwriting You'll Ever Need* Blake Snyder / $19.95

Screenwriting 101: *The Essential Craft of Feature Film Writing* Neill D. Hicks / $16.95

Screenwriting for Teens : *The 100 Principles of Screenwriting Every Budding Writer Must Know* / Christina Hamlett / $18.95

Script-Selling Game, The: *A Hollywood Insider's Look at Getting Your Script Sold and Produced* / Kathie Fong Yoneda / $16.95

Selling Your Story in 60 Seconds: *The Guaranteed Way to get Your Screenplay or Novel Read* / Michael Hauge / $12.95

Setting Up Your Scenes : *The Inner Workings of Great Films* Richard D. Pepperman / $24.95

Setting Up Your Shots : *Great Camera Moves Every Filmmaker Should Know* Jeremy Vineyard / $19.95

Shaking the Money Tree, 2nd Edition: *The Art of Getting Grants and Donations for Film and Video Projects* / Morrie Warshawski / $26.95

Sound Design: *The Expressive Power of Music, Voice, and Sound Effects in Cinema* / David Sonnenschein / $19.95

Stealing Fire From the Gods, 2nd Edition : *The Complete Guide to Story for Writers & Filmmakers* / James Bonnet / $26.95

Storyboarding 101: *A Crash Course in Professional Storyboarding* James Fraioli / $19.95

Ultimate Filmmaker's Guide to Short Films, The: *Making It Big in Shorts* Kim Adelman / $16.95

Working Director, The: *How to Arrive, Thrive & Survive in the Director's Chair* Charles Wilkinson / $22.95

Writer's Journey, - 2nd Edition, The: *Mythic Structure for Writers* Christopher Vogler / $24.95

Writer's Partner, The: *1001 Breakthrough Ideas to Stimulate Your Imagination* Martin Roth / $24.95

Writing the Action Adventure: *The Moment of Truth* Neill D. Hicks / $14.95

Writing the Comedy Film: *Make 'Em Laugh* Stuart Voytilla and Scott Petri / $14.95

Writing the Killer Treatment: *Selling Your Story Without a Script* Michael Halperin / $14.95

Writing the Second Act: *Building Conflict and Tension in Your Film Script* Michael Halperin / $19.95

Writing the Thriller Film: *The Terror Within* Neill D. Hicks / $14.95

Writing the TV Drama Series: *How to Succeed as a Professional Writer in TV* Pamela Douglas / $24.95

DVD & VIDEOS

Field of Fish: *VHS Video* Directed by Steve Tanner and Michael Wiese, Written by Annamaria Murphy / $9.95

Hardware Wars: *DVD* / Written and Directed by Ernie Fosselius / $14.95

Sacred Sites of the Dalai Lamas– DVD, The : *A Pilgrimage to Oracle Lake* A Documentary by Michael Wiese / $22.95